HIKING THE
Pacific Crest Trail
MEXICO TO CANADA

Bruce "Buck" Nelson

Hiking the
Pacific Crest Trail
Mexico to Canada

Bruce "Buck" Nelson
Copyright © 2018

For a gear list, a free video of my PCT thru-hike, or to order
this or my other books, DVDs and more visit:
www.bucktrack.com

ISBN-10: 1727567927
ISBN-13: 978-1727567922

First printing October 2018
Second printing June 2019

Dedication

This book is dedicated to the trail volunteers. Your time, sweat, and generosity make the Pacific Crest Trail a reality, and our world a better place.

Hiking the Pacific Crest Trail
Mexico to Canada

Table of Contents

ACKNOWLEDGMENTS...1

INTRODUCTION 3

THE TRAIL TO CAMPO 5

NORTH FROM MEXICO 9

SOUTHBOUND 81

OREGON.. 159

WASHINGTON...227

CANADA BOUND 259

EPILOGUE 285

ADDITIONAL INFORMATION...........................287

Acknowledgments

Thank you to everyone that supported my hike and the writing of this book: my mother, Marlys Nelson, for her always efficient support from Minnesota, including mailing homemade treats to the trail; to Jim Griffin, for all-around help and being my fishing "guide" after the hike; to Rod Dow, author of *Just a Few Jumper Stories*, for his editing, for twice meeting me on the trail and generously giving me some of the best trail food I've eaten; to Murry Taylor, author of *More or Less Crazy*, for editing and Trail Angeling for me; to John McColgan, for food and lodging at his beautiful home; to "Stephanie" for her assistance on this trail and others; to Casey Freise, for storing some of my belongings and shipping my GPS to the trail; to Tabatha and Marty in Fairbanks, who shared and cared for our little dachshund Duke; to my cousin Pam for the food, place to stay, and conversation; to Ken Coe, for keeping an eye on my cabin and for countless airport shuttles; to John Lyons and James Newlon for their manuscript suggestions; to Trail Angels Scout and Frodo, the Saufleys, the Andersons, Pooh, Firefly, Piper's Mom, the Dinsmores; and to the many people I've forgotten to list or whose names are unknown to me, thank you for the rides, the food, the kindness and support.

And finally, a sincere thank you to all those who made the Pacific Crest Trail possible, and to those who maintain and defend the trail today.

INTRODUCTION

The creek rushes past, swollen by snowmelt. Wyoming, my hiking partner, anxious to put the crossing behind her, wades out into the current. The fast, frigid water swirls around her calves and then her thighs. Halfway across the torrent surges against her waist, her body creating a churning eddy below her. I hold my breath as she begins to lose her footing. She stumbles and gasps as she falls, the icy water sweeping her away in the merciless current, around the corner, out of sight. I sprint frantically up the bank to the trail, running downstream to the main crossing, hoping to grab her as she passes. I look upstream and down, desperately trying to see her.

"Wyoming!" I yell, sick with dread, my face white. If she got past here she went over the waterfall...

"Wyoming!"

THE TRAIL TO CAMPO

The **Pacific Crest Trail**: the name evokes images of a wilderness trail through wildflower meadows, of switchbacks climbing mountain passes, of sunsets at remote campsites. All were important reasons for me to hike the PCT, but equally as important was the epic physical and mental challenge, and the opportunity to live life fully for five months. Experiences like that give my life meaning. I wanted to look back at a summer on the Trail and think, *That was freakin' hard. That was beautiful. That was a true adventure.*

I had planned my thru-hike of the Pacific Crest Trail for months. Two weeks ago, I locked up my cabin near Fairbanks, Alaska and flew to the Lower 48 to visit my friend Stephanie in Buffalo, Wyoming. Yesterday Stephanie dropped me off at the little airport in Sheridan, bound for San Diego and the PCT trailhead near Campo. My first flight ran late and I missed my connection in Denver. I called Scout and Frodo, my Trail Angels, to let them know the new flight would arrive just before midnight. They were unfazed.

In San Diego at last, I retrieved the box holding my pack from the luggage carousel and stepped outside. An SUV approached with a yellow pom-pom sticking out the passenger window. That was the signal for my ride. I waved them down and hopped in.

The couple in front were friends of Scout and Frodo, helping them out, Trail Angels for the Trail Angels. Palm trees were visible along the roads, an exotic sight for an Alaskan. In the darkness, we pulled up to a nice house and they quietly ushered me inside to show me my room. My roommate had kindly chosen to sleep on his sleeping pad on the floor, leaving me the bed where I quickly fell asleep.

Somewhere in my subconscious, I realized my wristwatch alarm was going off. I opened my eyes and knew immediately where I was and where I was going, to the southern terminus of the Pacific Crest Trail.

Surprisingly, perhaps, I'd slept rather well in the brief five hours since my arrival. I headed to the garage to sort out my gear. I topped off my water bottles, then filled my stove bottle with fuel Scout and Frodo had donated for the hikers. Most of the food from my pack I put in a box labeled with my name. They will bring the box to the Kick-Off for me. A dark-haired girl walked in to fetch something. When we exchanged quiet good mornings I knew she was one of the Israeli girls they had mentioned.

In the kitchen, Scout and Frodo hustled around. When they turned on the lights people sat up in their sleeping bags in various corners.

"Good morning. I'm Scout and this is Frodo."

"Hi, I'm Colter," I replied. We were using our "trail names." Some hikers choose their own trail name, many accept a name bestowed on them by other hikers, while a few thru-hikers take no trail name at all.

As an admirer of John Colter of the Lewis and Clark expedition, I chose my trail name just before hiking the Appalachian Trail.

"We'll have coffee and breakfast here in a bit. There's the computer over there if you want to go online before we leave."

Hikers crawled out of their sleeping bags and stretched sleepily. One by one they came in to get coffee.

Soon breakfast was ready and several of us filled our plates and sat down.

"I'm Plod," said one fit-looking fellow as we shook hands.

"I'm Chris," said another. They were both about my age. Plod was English and a veteran of the Appalachian Trail. Chris was a Kiwi. This would be his first long hike.

Twenty minutes later we gathered outside with our packs, sorting ourselves out into two cars. I rode with Squatch, an experienced PCT hiker like Scout and Frodo. We drove through beautiful residential neighborhoods before getting on the highway that led east out of town.

Alex, another Englishman, sat in the back. I asked him about his pack. He said he sewed both his pack and his tent himself! Somehow, I happened to mention Namie Bacile's name. Alex looked surprised.

"Where do you know Namie from?"

"I stayed at his place in Pagosa Springs when I was hiking the Continental Divide Trail. Do you know Namie?"

"He stayed at my place in London." A small world indeed!

I looked out the window. "Is that SNOW???"

"I think so!" said Squatch. The flurry grew into a snowstorm, coming down hard enough so it started to build up. The car thumped into some slushy snow and fishtailed slightly. "Holy shit!" Squatch yelled, but maintained control. Ahead, a car bounced off a guard rail. Inexplicably the driver continued to drive slowly and unsteadily along the shoulder of the road with his airbag out but only partially deflated. Couldn't he see? Was he knocked loony? Happily for us, the rest of the drive passed without incident.

NORTH FROM MEXICO

"I find I'm so excited, I can barely sit still or hold a thought in my head. I think it's the excitement only a free man can feel, a free man at the start of a long journey whose conclusion is uncertain."

—Red, *Shawshank Redemption*

Day 1, April 21, Mile 0

It's a gray dawn on the Mexico border. A hard, cool breeze buffets me as I walk up to four staggered and weathered wooden posts. Upon them is inscribed:

SOUTHERN TERMINUS
PACIFIC CREST NATIONAL SCENIC TRAIL
MEXICO TO CANADA
2627 MILES
ELEVATION 2915 FT

A car door slams. Another car has pulled up. A dozen hikers gather, chattering excitedly in the chill. We hand the Trail Angels our cameras and gather around the monument to pose for photos, smiling and hopeful. On some faces there are confident smiles, the Israeli Girls appear especially jubilant, but in other faces there is a hint of apprehension.

Thru-hikers at the border of Mexico. Front: the "Israeli Girls."
Others, left to right: Plod, Dave, Alex, unknown, Chris (later Turbo)
unknown, Gray Fox (on post) unknown, me, and unknown

I am the first to leave.

"Thanks!" I wave to the Trail Angels. "See you down the trail!" I say to my fellow hikers, then turn to take my first steps north, towards Canada. Before the trail disappears into the chaparral I glance back and see that someone has clambered up to the top of the monument. Other hikers are shouldering their packs.

Now, I'm actually hiking down the Pacific Crest Trail, with my fate in my own hands. It has truly begun. The promise of all the adventures ahead is thrilling. Yakky catches up and walks with me. Dave soon joins us. We lose the trail where it crosses a road and scout until we find it. Yakky is giddy with excitement to be on the trail. The trail skirts some yuccas with their wicked, stiffly-pointed leaves.

"Watch those yucca plants!" I say to Yakky. He promptly punctures his leg as he leans over to check one out. He pulls up his pant leg and blood trickles down.

"Sonofabitch!" he yells happily. Some of the yuccas have six-foot-tall stalks topped with a cluster of purple-tinged white blossoms.

Yakky stops to get water at a normally dry stream. Dave and I push on ahead through the rocky desert. There is a small faded pack next to the trail. Next to it is a full can of tuna, a Colorado Rockies cap, a shirt and a pair of pants. On the pack is written: "Lost 30 days, heading west. Don't eat my tuna." This is a crossing point for people illegally crossing the border. We've already seen numerous pieces of abandoned gear, which some joker has taken advantage of here.

It begins sprinkling, then raining. We walk steadily to ward off the chill. Dave has put his pack cover on. I've already lined my pack with a trash bag. The rain turns to snow and back to rain then more snow. I take a photo of Dave on the trail, snow on his pack, ice-cold water running down the trail.

Braving the snow is a large clump of wild lilacs, heavy with pale blue blossoms. The air is thick with their sweet, dry fragrance. The ground is now white with snow. We stop to take a closeup photo of the base of a manzanita tree, its shiny wet red-brown bark contrasts beautifully with the snow.

At a road crossing, we once again have trouble picking up the trail on the other side. Dave consults his guidebook and we follow the road downhill. There is a sign next to the trail:

CUIDADO!
– NO EXPONGA SU VIDA A LOS ELEMENTOS! –
NO VALE LA PENA!

... along with *"Hay agua potable!"* with a slash mark through it. Pictured is a blazing sun, cactus, a rattlesnake and mountains. My Spanish is less than fluent, but it probably means something like, "Don't let the elements kill you, and you better have your own drinking water." It's obviously for people sneaking across the border.

Rain and snow! First day in the famously hot and dry Sonoran Desert

Around 2 PM we reach Hauser Creek, our destination for the day. Plod is here, cheerfully squaring away his tent near the trail. Dave and I look for campsites. A sign identifies a patch of poison oak. This is the first poison oak that hundreds of hikers will encounter. The sign is a valuable reminder even for those familiar with it. I find a nice flat opening under some (non-poisonous) oak trees. From the stream, I collect two quarts of water. While I set up my tent I snack. I am exhausted from the excitement, the flying, the short night's sleep and the long walk in the cold rain and snow. I crawl into my tent and remove wet shoes, wet socks, and wet pants, then pull on dry long underwear bottoms, dry socks, and balaclava. With my down jacket for a pillow, I quickly fall asleep.

April 22, Day 2. Mile 16; 2,640 Miles to Canada

What a glorious night's sleep. Fourteen solid hours! When I crawl out there's a tent set up nearby.

"Good morning, Colter."

"Alex, is that you?"

"Yes. I wanted to talk to you last night but you were already sleeping."

"Sorry about that. I was tired."

He's had a good day yesterday and his self-made tent had worked well.

I pack up and soon pass several other thru-hikers camped on the other side of the creek. It's a 1,200-foot climb between my camp and Lake Morena, only five miles away. It is raining off and on again today. I stop to photograph rain dripping off beautiful white and purple yucca flowers. From a boulder-strewn ridge, Lake Morena appears below, clouds drifting low over the water.

When I walk into the Lake Morena campground there are already people gathered under an awning.

"Good morning. I'm Meadow Ed," says one. "Do you want a cup of coffee?"

"That would be great."

"How about a piece of cold pizza?"

"Sure, thanks!"

Next stop is registration. A dozen hikers wait in line to sign in. Volunteers are checking off registered names, issuing name tags, and handing out this year's class bandana. Several veteran hikers have again generously donated these bandanas to the current year's class. They feature an outline map of the path of the PCT crossing California, Oregon and

Washington. To the right of the map is a list of trail towns with their distance from Mexico. On the left edge is printed *HIKER TO TRAIL*, on the right edge *HIKER TO TOWN*. Hitching has a big role in thru-hiking. This bandana is a multi-use item. Genius!

Each year has its own color bandana. This year it is pink. I'm cringing slightly thinking about holding up a pink sign each time I want to hitch along the trail, so when I see a blue version from 2007 for sale, I buy one.

I head over to the camp area I will be sharing with this year's thru-hikers and set up my shelter in case it starts raining again. That's a habit of mine. If there is any possibility of rain, I set up my shelter first.

Over at the Pavilion, many hikers gather. Plod comes in, as does Dave, Alex, Chris and other hikers I've already met. I ask Plod how the Israeli girls fared. They had apparently arrived in the U.S. and gone to REI to be completely outfitted.

"They had a great time. They were laughing about all the cold rain," Plod says. That's the attitude!

The pavilion is a perfect place to hang out. It's raining, sleeting and even hailing from time to time. In past years some hikers have attempted to hike the "desert section" shelter-less. An exceedingly imprudent idea it seems to me, and it surely is under these conditions. It rains so hard that a sizable brook is running through the park, something Annual Day Zero Pacific Crest Trail Kick-Off (ADZPCTKO) veterans say they have never witnessed before. This is not the dry, sun-baked desert I had envisioned.

This evening is the first official gathering, featuring "Trail Jeopardy." As an introvert I have no interest in being a contestant, but agree to be a scorekeeper. The questions are about trail towns, Trail Angels, and other trivia. One contestant, Psycho, hiked a sizable chunk of the trail a few years ago, and is a Trail Jeopardy whiz. Another contestant, not so much. He is drunk. Whether he's trying to win or to be funny he's not doing particularly well at either. His final score is minus 4,400 points. Freebird dubs him "Sub-Zero." And thus, trail names are born.

April 23, Day 3. Kick-Off

It's a beautiful morning. What a difference! Most hikers are still sleeping in shelters that have weathered the storm in fine shape. But other hikers have yet to learn the finer points of site selection and setting up; several shelters are partially or totally collapsed. There will be some wet, sad campers this morning. Yesterday, it turns out, set the record for the coldest April 22nd in Campo history, at 49 degrees for a high, shattering the old record of 51 degrees.

Dave and I walk over to the store for some coffee and maybe some breakfast. A vulture perches on an electric pole, drying its spread wings in the sun. A wiry hiker with a long gray beard walks towards us. I recognize him as Billy Goat. He tells us he's lost his bamboo hiking poles behind a vending machine in front of the store. On the way, I find a stick and Dave uses it to poke the poles far enough so I can grab them.

There are numerous vendors at the kick-off. Most are serious hikers themselves. I know several from the internet as a gear customer or from backpacking forums. I say hello to Yogi, a veteran of several PCT thru-hikes and the author of the PCT Handbook which I am using. I feel like I know her from her book, but naturally she doesn't know me at all. I talk to Ron Moak and his son, of Six Moon Designs. I'm using one of their ultralight shelters, the Wild Oasis. Ron and Henry Shires are joking around. Henry is another manufacturer of ultralight shelters that are very popular with thru-hikers. They are competitors and good friends. The vendors know exactly what hikers are looking for on the PCT. I'm like a kid in a candy store, except I already have the gear I need.

I attend the Desert Hiking Techniques class. Squatch is one of the presenters. They give us some simple but important advice: take care of your feet, wear a hat that provides shade, avoid sunburn, make sure you stay hydrated.

Back at my campsite I find tents springing up all around, mostly state-of-the-art ultralight tents and tarp-tents. Gray silnylon dominates the color scheme. At the nearest picnic table, I join another thru-hiker.

"Where are you from?" I ask.

"Alaska."

"Really? Me too! Have you done other long hikes?"

"I did about half of the AT. I hurt my knee."

"It happens a lot. Are you excited about the PCT?"

"Yes. But I'm a little nervous, too."

"That's natural, I think. If you had to guess, what do you think your chances are of making it to Canada?"

"I don't know. Maybe forty percent. How about you?"

"Maybe ninety percent. You never know for sure, though. I'm going to do my best, one way or another." To be truthful, I'm surprised that she has admitted up front that she probably wouldn't make it. It's often true that *"If you think you can, or you think you can't, you're probably right."*

Just before lunch, Ceanothus presents a class, "Flora and Fauna of the PCT." After lunch, there is a snow and water report presentation. We are given a handout with current information on snow levels and water sources along the southern part of the PCT. It will be invaluable. The Lagunas, just north of us, were hammered by snow in the last days, but it's predicted to melt rapidly and have little impact on us. Farther north is a different story. Many hikers have started early and returned for the kick-off. One reports falling on the steep snow slope near Idyllwild, 150 miles ahead, saving himself by a "self-arrest" with a pair of Leatherman pliers! The Sierras are buried in snow, with more falling. It's a long time until we get to the Sierras, though. Things can change dramatically by the time we arrive.

There is an epic burrito-based meal at 5 PM. A crew of people has been working enthusiastically to prepare it and by all appearances had a good time in the process. With limited cooking skills I have signed up to help in setting up the dining area, and later with serving. The food is wonderful.

April 24, Day 4

Another beautiful day with a few wispy clouds. A bagpiper begins to play in the morning sun, standing on a huge boulder by the lake. My neighbor, Anne, joins me for the walk down to the store for coffee. She's a runner and fit. Anne says her sleeping bag wasn't warm enough, though, and plans to order a warmer one.

Back at the kick-off, there is a class on mountain lions. There is virtually no chance of being attacked by a mountain lion this summer so it's an easy choice to give the class a pass. I listen to the Mountaineering Skills class with interest, however. It covers both snow travel and stream crossings. It is interesting listening to the reaction from the hikers. Some of them are a little spooked. Some think the class bordered on fearmongering. I think it was quite sensible. Steep snow and swift stream crossings ARE potentially quite dangerous, and it's important to be smart about them. Hundreds of people have completed the PCT safely. But some haven't. In recent years at least one hiker has fallen to his death. In 2005 a thru-hiker disappeared near Mount San Jacinto. His body wasn't found until the next year, a likely victim of hypothermia. At least two hikers have been hit and killed by cars while walking into town. Section hikers have drowned.

In late afternoon hundreds of people gather down by the lake. Each "class year" takes a group photo. Our class, 2010, gathers around a huge boulder. With several others I climb up on a ledge of the boulder, balanced precariously, hoping I don't end my hike early with a fall to the ground. Many more hikers clamber atop the boulder with the rest around the base, perhaps 200 fellow thru-hikers in all. Most are still strangers, but already we are building friendships. A veteran hiker says, "Some of these people will become your friends that will share an adventure that you will never forget."

Last year's class replaces us. They have had a good turn-out and it's fun to see and hear them fall back into their thru-hiker personas, teasing each other as old comrades do.

"The Onion" walks by and I stop him for a chat. He is one of the first two people to complete a "Yo-Yo" of the Continental Divide Trail. He hiked from Mexico to Canada along the Rocky Mountains, an enormous task in itself, then turned around and walked back to Mexico. Incredible! Despite this accomplishment he is humble and witty, and keeps bringing the conversation back to my hikes.

At 5:00 is "Burgerama," a wonderful feed. The planning involved with feeding 700 people must be enormous. It's a huge success.

After eating, I head back to my campsite and pack up. I want to start walking this evening as there will undoubtedly be a giant herd leaving in the morning. Some hikers avoid the kick-off entirely for this reason. In twenty minutes, I'm packed up. Grabbing my hiking poles, I head for the trail. The murmur of the gathering quickly recedes behind me. Just before the trail leaves the lake I turn back for one last look at the hive of activity, then turn and walk steadily down the trail.

This feels like the true beginning of the hike. It's warm enough that I am a little sweaty. The back of my wide-brimmed hat is hitting the top of my pack. Taking it off I bend the back brim up, but it's still hitting. My neck gets a little stiff, probably from trying to hold my head so my hat doesn't touch. The trail is fairly flat though, and I'm cruising.

The second time the trail reaches a creek crossing there is a small group of teenage Boy Scouts on the other side. "Let's see what this guy does," I overhear one of them saying. On the bank I take off my shoes and socks and wade across on a sandy bottom, through warm, knee-deep water.

"How was it?" one asks.

"A piece of cake," I say. "What are you guys trying to figure out?"

"We don't have a towel," one says. They stand there discussing what to do. I am appalled that a group of older Boy Scouts would be stymied by the crossing of a shallow, warm, creek. I don't have a towel, either. It doesn't need to be labeled "towel" to be used as a towel. Bandanas or spare clothing will work fine. Or the sun. I rub my feet with warm dry sand, then brush it off. The leader, one of the Scouts, finally makes a command decision. They'll trespass the mile and a half on this side of the creek so they can reach the road without getting their feet wet.

At Boulder Oaks campground I fill my water bottles. I find a pretty camp spot near a boulder beneath a large oak tree. I roll out my sleeping pad then shake out my sleeping bag and lay it on the pad. Camp is set up. Sitting down I take off my shoes and sweaty socks, then plot my camp on my guidebook map. It's good to be on the trail. I absorb the experience: the beautiful evening light on the gargantuan oaks and boulders, a gentle breeze wafting the dry sweet smell of sage. In the quiet, I fall asleep quickly. I awaken briefly during the night, the sage, oaks, and boulders aglow beneath a bright moon.

I wake up very early and take a photo of my camp before packing up. The profile map shows I'm starting at 3,150 feet today and that there is considerable climbing ahead. As I walk I think about my general game plan for the PCT. This is April 25. Standard advice is to wait until about June 15 to enter the Sierra. That usually allows enough time for the summer snowmelt to be well underway. Kennedy Meadows (the southern one — there are actually two Kennedy Meadows!) is at mile 703. This morning I'm at Mile 27. 703-27 = 676 miles. Let's see, there are six days left in April including today, 31 days in May, plus 14 days in June. So there are 51 days before June 15. That's only 13 1/4 miles a day including days off. If I don't set a leisurely pace, I'll reach Kennedy Meadows way too early. But it's good to have plenty of time. It's important not to push too hard early in the hike. Even strong hikers often have feet that need to toughen up to trail conditions. It's way better to slowly adapt to the trail than to push too hard early on and chew up your feet or injure yourself in some other way.

Today's the day when I will establish my routine. The water report we were given at the kick-off shows water about five miles ahead. After packing up I fill a quart of water from the campground spigot, swing by the outhouse, then hit the trail. Looking at the map there are a lot of places labeled "CYN," like *Fred CYN* and *Long CYN*. Must be a local term? I laugh next time I check my map. CYN is *canyon*.

At Fred Canyon Creek there is a good flow of water. Another hiker is there.

"Hi, I'm Colter."

"I'm Caveman. Are you doing the PCT?"

"Yeah, how about you?"

"Yup."

With this handy water, I decide to cook a brunch. I set up my stove, scoop some water, and while it heats I lay out my sleeping bag and socks to dry in the bright sun. Several hikers stop for a break, with most of them being thru-hikers.

By mid-afternoon, I've climbed from 3,150 feet at Boulder Oaks to about 6,000 feet. There are patches of snow several inches deep. Plod comes motoring down the trail, looking strong and fresh. We swap cameras to take photos of ourselves standing in the snow among the towering

Coulter Pines. The trail reaches a fountain and we stop for a break. Plod swings his pack off and sets it next to a tree. Soon another hiker shows up.

"Chance," he says when I ask his name.

"Are you heading into Mount Laguna?" he asks.

"No, I don't think so."

He says he's going to check it out. It's hard to pass up a handy town on the trail.

More hikers pass. One with a bushy brown beard sits nearby. He leans against a tree and digs into his pack. It's Guthook. Drift comes striding up, his kilt swinging. Both are veterans of the Appalachian Trail, as are many of us. From the back of his pack, Drift pulls a short paddle. A sticker on it says, "Yes, I walked here from Maine." At the kick-off, he'd given a presentation, "50 Uses for a Paddle," or something to that effect. One use was for a stove stand. He sets his stove on the paddle blade, but it wobbles. He tries to prop it level with stones. After several tries, he gives up and sets the stove on the ground.

"Are you going to camp here?" Plod asks me.

"I think so. It's a nice spot. This fountain is handy."

"I think I will, too."

As we lounge, talking, a guy in a Forest Service uniform shows up. He's going to fix the leaky fountain. He talks as he works. "This oughta be the good part," he says. "I'm gonna get wet." A couple of us ready our cameras to capture the hilarity. The water jets high into the air but for the most part, he avoids it. To be frank, we are a little disappointed he doesn't get wetter.

Later I set up my shelter well off the trail, on a flat spot beneath a mighty pine tree. At dusk, I hear a wild turkey gobble somewhere in the forest.

Early in the morning, I pass the fallen remains of a large snowman. I set him back up and stick my poles in for arms and put my hat on his head. That looks better. I take a photo then retrieve my gear.

It's getting warm and I'm getting low on water. Near a road, there's a pickup parked with several camo-clad men leaning over a map and talking. One of them turns to me and the others look up.

"Have you seen any turkeys?" he says.

"I haven't seen any, but I heard a gobbler last evening."

"Where was that?"

I point out the general area on the map, then ask, "Is there any water here?"

"No, I don't think so," one says. The thought occurs to me that they could have offered me one of the bottles of water visible in the bed of their pickup, especially after I gave them a good lead on turkeys. We wish each other good luck and I head down the trail. In a few steps, I see a cache of water in plastic jugs. I pour a little into my water bottle, but it has such a strong plastic taste that I don't take any more.

It's hot. The trail is crossing desert country under a blazing sun. There are huge boulders off the trail a stone's throw away. I walk over and relax in a perfect little cove of cool shade amongst them. Another hiker passes by but doesn't see me. He's carrying an umbrella for mobile shade. Some hikers love them but I'm not an umbrella guy. I use my rain jacket for rain, wind, warmth and to wear while doing laundry. I use my hat for shade. Gear is subjective.

When I start walking again I catch up with another hiker, Will. He doesn't have a trail name yet. There's an AK patch on his pack. Alaska.

"Where are you from?" I ask.

"Fairbanks."

"Yeah, me too!" It's a small world. He's the third hiker from Fairbanks that I've met on the trail. Soon we reach a small brook of clear water, a brook that wouldn't exist right now without all the recent rain. We stop to fetch water and to take a break. For water treatment I usually use Aquamira. It's light, works well for me, and there are no working parts to fail or filters to plug. There are two small bottles and you mix a few drops of each, Part A and Part B, to activate it. I put seven drops from the first bottle in the mixing cap, and when I reach for the cap of the second bottle I see a "B" on it. I pick up the other bottle and look at the label. "B." Crap. I can't believe it. That's exactly what I did when I started the Continental Divide Trail! I can see how it happened, though. The two bottles are from two different batches where the color scheme is different. I'd grabbed two different bottles without realizing they were two "B"s that just looked different. I think about asking Will to use his filter but I'm too humiliated by my error. I decide to chance it and fill my bottle and take a swig. It tastes OK. I'm uncomfortable not treating water in this country, though.

In the early evening, the trail is passing through gentle brush-covered hills. Fingers of meadow follow the drainages. A patch of green grass beneath an oak tree catches my eye. In the shade I unsling my pack and sit down, leaning against it, and take off my shoes and peel off my socks, which I invert and hang in the sun to dry. A gentle breeze cools and dries my sweaty feet. What a beautiful little oasis in the desert. Well, an oasis without water. I'll camp right here, under the stars.

Once again I sleep great and wake up well before dawn, fully refreshed. I feel for my glasses and lie on my back, hands behind my head, looking at the bright desert stars in the clear black sky, a cool, gentle breeze on my face. The stars are so bright I decide to start hiking. I turn my drying socks right side out, then grab my shoes and clap the bottoms together to dislodge stones, dirt and any scorpions.

I have to watch carefully to avoid cactus as I head toward the trail, barely visible when I step on it. I use the feel of the tread beneath my feet as much as sight to follow the flow of the trail. It's only 4 AM. A meteor streaks across the sky, and moments later, another. It reminds me of the most spectacular meteor shower I've ever witnessed. I was deer hunting in a remote area of northern Wisconsin, walking in the dark to be far from any road by the time dawn broke. It was the peak of the 33-year Leonid meteor shower cycle. Meteors streaked across the sky, blue or green tinted, many with lingering, glowing trains of dust behind them. Sometimes two were visible in the sky at once. I saw hundreds that morning. Yup, hundreds. It was magical.

A gray smudge appears in the east, slowly seeping up into the sky until a warmer red glow appears beneath it. When the sun breaches the horizon I watch as it rises, partially screened by the spikes of a yucca plant. The sunlight quickly flows across the desert.

Hiking into the dawn

The trail descends a hillside with an abundance of yellow and pink flowers. Yucca plants are in full bloom, their white blossoms delicately fringed with pink. The wash at the bottom is still shadowed and cool. I see a hiker packing up. It's Anne. She tells me she hasn't been able to switch to a warmer bag yet, so she walked for hours last night to stay warm.

Ahead there are several small tents and shelters as well as a larger tent. A local outfitter has set up a tiny remote store out in the desert. I am welcomed warmly and say hello to the other hikers. There are some tubs to wash out socks. The idea is to go from tub to tub so the water in each is progressively cleaner, but they are all pretty dirty. Nevertheless, I "wash" two pair of socks. Anne arrives. The outfitter briefs me on how to use the shower. I take a quick, warm shower and use my bandana as a towel. It feels great to be clean. I check out the supply tent: serendipity! Water treatment tablets. What are the odds of being able to buy them out in the desert? I buy the tablets and a soda.

One hiker reaches into a Ziploc and hands me a small cube of homemade energy bar. Knowing that he probably hasn't washed his hands in two days or more I try to politely avoid eating it. It's one of my rules on the trail. Hygiene is often terrible. I don't eat food touched by anyone else's dirty hands.

Back on the trail, two enormous trumpet-shaped blossoms emerge from the granular soil. The petals rise from a green tube then flare out into a white and violet bell. The flowers have a strong, sweet smell. It is Jimson weed. It's poisonous.

A particularly beautiful clump of plants catches my eye. I am framing a photo when Conductor comes striding down the trail. Together we admire the natural garden. In the foreground is a clump of cacti crowned with shocking pink flowers. Behind them is a spray of delicate yellow flowers I don't recognize. Next are twelve-foot tall agave. Their green flowering stalks rise from rosettes of stiff, wide-bladed, dagger-tipped leaves.

Some say agave stalks can grow over twelve inches in a single day! They are often called the century plant because it has been thought they take a century to bloom. I've read they actually bloom a single time, in about 30 years or less, after which they die.

The sun is baking down now. There is an overhanging ledge of rock a few feet off the trail. I pull out my sleeping pad and roll it out to rest in the cool shade. When I lean back something stabs my hand and I see several cactus needles poking out of my skin. I stand up and pull them out, then pick up my pad from which I remove a couple dozen more needles. A significant advantage to closed cell foam in this country: no need to worry about puncturing an inflatable. Finding a sticker-free spot I relax again, shoes off and a cool breeze on my damp feet. Three hikers walk by a few feet away without spotting me in the shade.

Anne comes walking down the trail. Just as she's about to pass, I say, "Good thing I'm not a mountain lion."

She jumps and laughs. "You startled me!"

"Sorry about that. Do you want to sit down?"

She glances at the rock slab above my head. "You're not worried about that rock falling on your head?"

"Well, maybe I should be. But I figure if it's stood here thousands of years it's probably not going to fall right now."

"Any idea how far it is to Scissors Crossing?"

"I'm not sure, maybe about five miles?"

"OK, I'm not ready for a break yet, maybe I'll see you there."

It is a hot, but easy walk to Scissors Crossing. It is the first major water cache on the trail, in a long, usually waterless stretch. There are dozens of gallon water jugs there. Full ones line the shelves of a cabinet, across the top of which is the PCT emblem with the words: "Relax-Enjoy.

Trail Ratz-Dave-Dave-John." A couple of dozen empty jugs are strung on a cord to prevent the strong desert winds from scattering them. I sit on a chair of homemade 2×4 construction and dig out my copy of the water report. The next dependable water is Third Gate Cache. Fourteen more miles. It's about 1:30. I've come, what, 17 miles already today? I'll be camping before the next cache. So I'll eat lunch here, and get fully hydrated. I'll bring three quarts with me: a quart for the afternoon's walk, a quart for cooking and eating tonight, and a quart to last until the cache in the morning.

After leaving the paved road the trail passes through a virtual botanical garden of cacti. I find myself stopping frequently to admire and photograph them. One shot shows hedgehog cactus with their bright purple blossoms, Parish goldeneye flowers, orange California poppies, agave, yucca, and cholla cactus, fuzzy with their evil-looking spines, all in a cluster of bone-white boulders. Beyond them are lush green cottonwoods lining San Felipe Creek. Farther still is the smoky blue of the Volcan Mountains Wilderness.

A fierce wind rises. I'm buffeted as I climb. At least it makes the heat more bearable. The botanical garden continues. I've never enjoyed plants more while hiking. There are tall, stick-like ocotillo swaying in the gusts, barrel cactus with yellow flowers, beavertail cactus, and prickly pears. Something moves next to the trail just ahead: it's a rattlesnake. Staying well beyond its striking range I approach and take a photo as it slithers across the trail and retreats into the brush.

It's still fairly early when I start looking for a camp spot. It's steep and options are limited. Protection from the wind is going to be important. There are some nice, flat sandy spots in places where the trail crosses drainages. There are marks from sleeping pads where people have slept recently, but it looks like it could rain tonight. I don't care to sleep wondering if I'm going to be flooded out. When the trail reaches the main ridge I drop over the back side and find a decent spot, but it's early in the day and the spot is rocky so I explore a bit farther. Two mule deer jump up and go bounding away. After a short search I find a beautiful spot, well protected by junipers but with a good view up the opposite hillside.

I roll out my sleeping pad onto soft, coarse sand, then shake out my sleeping bag and lay it on top. After taking off my shoes and socks I lie back in the luxury of the cool shade, and admire the fascinating plants and breathtaking desert scenery. The wind roars up on the ridgetop but here it is only a gentle breeze. A distinctive lenticular cloud forms to the north-east, looking like dollops of vanilla pudding inverted in the sky. I watch in awe as sunset approaches. The cloud is illuminated in layers, purple on the bottom, then orange, next a band of purple and more bands of colors in alternating circles. Agave stalks rise into the sky as if trying to puncture this giant glowing bubble.

During the night I feel some patters of rain, so I quickly set up my shelter and fall asleep again. When the sun hits I crawl out of my shelter and see a rainbow in a dark stormy western sky with the desert below in bright sunlight.

Just as I approach the trail I see two people ahead of me, a young guy following a young lady. The guy is chatting steadily. I've seen them both before and know they aren't a couple and it's clear to me that he would like to be.

At about 10 AM I'm getting low on water and looking for Third Gate Cache. Ahead is a gate and just beyond are water jugs in the shade of juniper trees. It must be an enormous amount of work, and a considerable expense, to buy and haul all this water to the top of this ridge from the nearest road.

Some hikers are lounging there.

"I'm Croatian Sensation," one says when I introduce myself.

"Not-A-Chance," says his lady friend.

"Wolf Taffy," says a young guy.

"I'm Neon," says a young gal.

Presumably, Croatian Sensation is of Croatian descent. I'm not sure how Not-A-Chance or Neon got their names. Wolf Taffy says he has worked with timber wolves.

Not far past the water cache is a green metal box on the trail. "Lead Cache," says the label. "Take only what you need and leave the rest for others." Lead Cache? Leading where? I open it. It is full of weights, lead weights. I laugh out loud. The register inside has many notes thanking the prankster.

The windy trail contours high on the San Felipe Hills. I am repeatedly staggered by strong blasts of wind that continue for hours. The roar and the buffeting are exhausting both physically and mentally. As the trail begins descending on the lee side the wind finally relents. My relief turns to delight when I see "100" spelled out in stones on the trail. One hundred miles of the PCT completed! Although there are many miles and several months of trail ahead, it's a real sense of accomplishment.

The trail nears the road, which means Barrel Springs is just ahead. There is a series of handwritten signs on the trees: "PCT Hikers! Beer! Hot Dogs! Chili!" A hiker feed. Awesome! Hopefully they are still there. And they are. There are two RVs and a gaggle of people. They welcome me warmly, offering me a bonanza of goodies of my choice. I gratefully accept hot chocolate and a brownie for starters. Apparently they have been Trail Angels many times before, driving up from San Diego annually. Later they serve up chili dogs, chips and more which we share with other hikers as they trickle in. The Trail Angels suggest I camp here and grab breakfast in the morning. I am happy to oblige.

Breakfast is equally bountiful and I thank them profusely before shouldering my pack and heading across the road. I walk for a while with Kerry, a short, cheerful college student from Bozeman, Montana. The trail crosses gentle, wildflower-strewn meadows with clumps of live oak, all drenched in the rich, low sunlight of early morning. We spot a perfectly round hole in the rock, an ancient Indian grinding stone, or mortar. When were those people here? What were they grinding? Acorns?

On a low ridge, there are clusters of boulders. I know one formation is Eagle Rock, one of the more famous landmarks on the PCT. Climbing up to one clump, Eagle Rock is instantly recognizable. Another hiker is passing below from an angle where it isn't visible.

"Hey!" I shout. "This is Eagle Rock!"

"OK," he says, and keeps walking without a second glance.

You know how some rock formations take some real imagination to turn into the objects they are supposed to resemble? Eagle Rock is not one of those. It is remarkable: an eagle with upraised wings, with an obvious body, wings, head, and beak. Earlier this month my San Diego Trail Angels Scout and Frodo officiated a wedding here. The couple was two PCT thru-hikers, Three Gallon (who started out carrying 3 gallons of water) and Cucumber Boy (a girl). I frame a photo to show the eagle in the sunlight against a dark sky with purplish-blue lupines in the foreground. Wolf Taffy walks up. I hold up a glove I picked up an hour before.

"Hey," he says. "You found my glove, thanks!"

A few miles out of Warner Springs a middle-aged hiker sits next to the trail studying his knee.

"How's the knee?" I ask. He glowers at me and doesn't say a word, so I keep on walking. What was up with that? He must have thought I was making fun of him or something. Soon another daypack-wearing hiker approaches.

"Would you like something to drink?" he says.

"Sure!" He opens the pack and allows me to select a drink and insists I accept some cookies as well. As we talk the grumpy guy with the sore knee approaches, all cheerful now.

Eagle Rock and lupines, with stormy skies beyond

I walk into the small town of Warner Springs just before noon. My first stop is the small post office. "You should have a general delivery package for Bruce Nelson," I tell the clerk. He finds it easily and I head over to the Warner Springs Ranch to get a room. Wolf Taffy is at the desk, getting a room for several people. I ponder. It would be easy to wait for a bit and find some other hikers to share a room, but they are giving thru-hikers a discount. I decide to splurge and rent my own room.

My room is half of a white, adobe brick building shaded by trees and surrounded by colorful shrubbery. Rugged dark beams hold up the ceiling of a white room that is clean and cool. I peel off my clothes and jump in the shower. Dirty suds run down my lower legs and swirl down the drain.

I gather up my dirty clothes, which consist of everything I've been wearing plus another pair of socks and underwear.

I walk over to the laundry, wearing my rain jacket and a pair of black silk shorts. There are at least two loads of laundry ahead of me. A hiker in her early 20s walks in behind me and looks a little crestfallen to see the line for the single washer.

"This could take a while," I say.

"Looks like it."

"I'm Colter."

"I'm Thru-Cry."

"Thru-Cry?"

"Yeah. I've been crying quite a bit," she laughs. I immediately like her.

"Tell you what. If you want to combine loads, I'll pay for it if you'll run the load for us. That will save both of us time."

"Sounds great."

I head back to my room wondering what the tourists think of me wearing a rain jacket in the baking sun.

The contents of my package are strewn across the bed. There's the usual hiker food plus guidebook pages for the next section, batteries, a razor, and a few other small items. I have a little food left from the first stretch. My spreadsheet shows 69.6 miles to Idyllwild, the next resupply point. I've got five and a half days of food in the box. I'll have more than enough so I rip open a packet of Pop-Tarts to eat while I sort through things.

Over at the library, I wait for a computer. A young couple at the computer next to me is talking about her infected foot blister and trying to figure out how to obtain medical advice. Infected blisters can knock people off the trail and may lead to blood poisoning. Chewed up feet, in general, are plaguing hikers already. Many are limping noticeably. People are doing too many miles before they are in shape.

A hiker has gone way over his allotted computer time and appears to be purposely oblivious to those of us waiting. Thankfully, a librarian asks him to wrap it up and waits to make sure he does. I quickly scan through my emails and respond to the most important ones. Then I go to my blog and do a quick update. That's the most efficient way for me to let friends and family know what's going on.

At the washers, my clean laundry is waiting. At my room, I change and notice one pair of underwear is missing. I buy a burrito, some ice cream and an apple at the small store. Thru-Cry comes walking by.

"Hey, Thru-Cry, is my underwear in your room?" I call out.

She laughs. "Yeah. When we sorted out the laundry there was an extra set and I figured it was yours but I didn't know what room you were in."

The hot springs pool is a treat. Numerous thru-hikers have gathered here, floating around on foam "noodles." It's pure luxury. Most of the guys are whiskery, everyone is partially sunburned. All are freshly clean and well-fed, discussing the trail and enjoying the break. These are my people. This is my tribe.

In the morning I head over to the golf course grill. An obvious thru-hiker is sitting at a table. He introduces himself as Pat and invites me to join him. I have a giant breakfast burrito and a couple cups of coffee. Pat's hiking partner Shawn joins us. They are a cheerful duo.

Back at my room I carefully sort through all my gear and supplies. I then put together a small package of unneeded items to mail home. I check out of my room, swing past the post office to mail my package, then head off down the road. I nearly miss the turn-off. The trail crosses a sunlit meadow carpeted with a dense patch of yellow wildflowers, then passes under some shady oaks.

Something moves on the edge of the trail; a well-camouflaged horned lizard freezes in place. Much of his body is covered with wicked looking scales that resemble shark's teeth. Horns surround the back of his head. He looks like a miniature fugitive from the Cretaceous.

In the afternoon the trail enters a huge wildfire burn from a few years ago. Stones have cracked in the intense heat, flakes of rock sliding off huge boulders. Yet life remains. I smell the sweet, dry scent of wild lilac flowers before I spot them along the trail ahead. In late afternoon I pause on a ridge to admire the evening shadows on the desolate, beautiful landscape.

Camp tonight is on soft dry sand along a creek bed. I lay in my sleeping bag looking at the stars as a cool breeze rustles the willows, frogs croaking in a tiny trickle of water a few feet away.

It's the first of May! I sling my pack at 6 AM. Two tiny figures hustle down the trail far above me. Somebody has gotten an early start. As they get closer I recognize their clothing, it's Whitebeard and 3rd Monty. Veterans of a 2005 thru-hike, they are not the youngest on the trail. Whitebeard is 70, I believe, but they know how to pace themselves and can crank out the miles. One way to do that is to start hiking early and hike late.

The trail enters Anza-Borrego Desert State Park and then crosses Chihuahua Valley Road, with no tiny dogs in sight. I pass an enthusiastic trail crew and stop just long enough to thank them for their hard work.

Chihuahua. That reminds me of my little dachshund Duke, back home in Alaska with his other family. He adopted me when he got abandoned by a neighbor. That chance event was one of the happiest things that ever happened to either of us. Oh, how he makes me laugh! On the trail I often think of him, trotting down the driveway at forty below in his parka and boots. Bravely standing his ground, he'll bark at a moose nearly 100 times bigger than him: *"This is our yard, go away!"* He'll plow through fluffy snow on a hopeless chase after a snowshoe hare, briefly disappearing in the powder, wild with enthusiasm. Sometimes Duke runs right out of his coat at top speed. How is that possible? Oh, Lil' Duke.

At Combs Saddle there are snowy mountains ahead, the San Jacinto, where I'll encounter the first challenging snows of the trip. I pull out my tiny MP3/radio and immediately hear some startling news. A few days ago there was a catastrophic explosion on an offshore drilling platform. Oil is pouring into the Gulf of Mexico. They estimate that it might take until August to stop it. August?! It might leak for three months? How can that be?

Many hours and many sweaty, wearying miles later, the looked-for water cache appears ahead, perfectly timed in the heat of the day. My jubilation wanes considerably when I spot the hiker I've dubbed "Mr. T." Mr. T is the grumpy fellow with the sore knee. In a subsequent encounter, he had been grouchy with me again. Nonetheless, I fake it and say, "Alright, plenty of water!"

"You sound disappointed," he says flatly. He's ticked me off yet again.

"Now why would I be disappointed? You and I don't get along very well, do we?"

He looks away, into the desert. "I annoy people."

Pretty soon Holly and Stitch arrive. Stitch and I have the same pack. We've made a similar modification to the lift webbing to hold the top of the pack closer to our shoulders, closer to our center of gravity where it's more comfortable. His sewing prowess earned him his name. Pat and Shawn come marching up. With all the new arrivals the mood is much improved.

I camped last night in an open area in the brush just above the trail. Once again I start very early and soon spot Mr. T just ahead, packing up near the trail. "Crap," I say under my breath and walk past quietly. Miraculously, he doesn't see or hear me.

It's mid-morning when the trail reaches the Pines to Palms Highway. There are people gathered around a camp. Trail Angels! Doc, the Trail Angel, has some goodies for hikers. He is also working on people's brutalized feet. He washes Elderly Ellen's feet then doctors her blisters. Elderly Ellen (Double E) is silver-haired but otherwise looks and acts more like a cheerful 35-year-old. Her husband Yeah-But is also here along with Pat and Shawn and... drat, Mr. T is walking up. We all lounge in yard chairs and sip drinks. Bojangles has lost his hat somewhere and looks sunburned and a little frazzled. Some of these hikers are going to hitch into Idyllwild from here. I elect to press on for another 27 miles and then hike down the Devil's Slide Trail into town. That will give me a shorter food carry after Idyllwild and a lighter pack for the climb from this highway.

The profile map shows a climb from 4,900 feet to 7,100 ahead. It's hot but bearable. Penrod Canyon feels like the setting for an Apache ambush in a Hollywood western, with giant jumbled boulders and pines. A black lizard scurries out onto the trail, where he pauses, cocking his head up towards me with a disgusted look on his face. I stop for lunch in the shade of Coulter pines near a tiny brook. It's a perfect place to cook a hot lunch.

I pick up my cooking gear. The cooking pot is an empty 25 oz. Foster's beer can. The stove itself is made out of an empty pop can. The windscreen/pot stand is sized perfectly for the pot. It all nests together nicely in a plastic cylinder which screws together in the middle. Each end of the cylinder then becomes a bowl or cup. The whole package including the "cozy" (pot insulation) and measuring cup weighs a touch over six ounces.

I unscrew the plastic cylinder and pull out the Foster's can. From inside the can I remove the rolled-up windscreen, a mini BIC lighter, a measuring cup, the stove and the cozy. The cozy slides over the top of the can. I assemble the windscreen by sliding the dovetailed sides together. I flip it over so it looks like a metal cone with the large end down and the top of the small end cut off. I nestle the Foster's can halfway down into the windscreen and pour in two cups of water and put on the lid. The pull tab serves as a handle. I pour 20 ml of alcohol into the stove. I set the stove down on a flat rock, light it, and set the windscreen/pot over the flame.

I sit on my sleeping pad, leaning back against a big boulder. Baby-blue-eye flowers and orange Indian paintbrush decorate the setting. Enormous pinecones are scattered all about. I hear voices and two couples approach. They don't notice me until I say hi.

"Yikes, you surprised us!"

"Sorry about that."

"Are you a thru-hiker?" one guy asks.

"Yup. Where are you guys headed?"

"This guy is hiking the whole Pacific Crest Trail," the guy says to the others, then turns back to me. "We're just doing an out and back from our car." We chat for a bit before they move on.

The trail leaves the canyon and climbs steadily. There's no water near the trail according to the water report. One option is Live Oak Spring, a mile off the trail and hundreds of feet downhill. Another is Tunnel Spring, which Reaper has described thusly in the Water Report: "Flowing out of pipe into scummy trough. Stinky like sulfur and tasted funny." When I reach the trail to Cedar Spring, Mr. T is sitting there.

"Are you going to Cedar Spring?" he says.

"Ah, I don't think so. How about you?"

"Maybe. Where are you going to camp?"

"I think I'll just keep walking and see where I end up. How about you?"

"I was thinking about Cedar Spring."

An hour later, I'm checking out a possible camp spot when Mr. T comes up the trail.

"We are almost to Fobes Saddle. We can be there in less than an hour if we hustle," he says.

"Looks like it's about a mile," I say noncommittally. When he's gone I cowboy camp right here, under the mature trees on a bed of pine needles, down to my last quart of water.

Mr. T is still asleep in his tent when I hit Fobes Saddle. There are some water jugs, all empty, leaving me no option but to hike a half mile downhill to procure water from a creek. There, I fill and treat two quarts. I retrace my steps and quietly pass Mr. T's tent again and begin a long climb past beautiful cedars.

There are patches of hard snow on the trail which follows near the top of this very steep ridgeline. The Water Report says: "very icy and steep exposed snow crossings... 3–4 feet of snow... journals from 4/6/10 tell several stories of NEAR DEATH EXPERIENCES." Yikes. It's always hard to tell how much of a story is hyperbole but reports of several close calls means something. Of course, it's nearly a month later now. I reach a wide patch of hard snow on a particularly steep spot, a place where a fall could be really dangerous. This is where the "near-death experiences" took place. Here the hiker saved himself by jamming his Leatherman into the snow as an emergency self-arrest! For the first time on this hike, I pull out my ice axe. I carefully place each foot before jamming the handle of the ice axe into the snow ahead of me as an anchor should I slip. When I make it across I look back. Not a big deal now that I'm across, but one bad slip in a place like that could be the end of a hike.

The trail is now a "goat path" on the mountainside, but snow-free in most areas. I enjoy looking back to see the trail traversing the steep rocky slope. But then I hit a flat area where the trail disappears. I find some tracks but they turn back. So does another set. I circle around trying to spot the PCT. Where the heck is it? Eventually, I figure out that the trail has done a 270 and is heading the other way. What a dope! I follow hiker tracks through nearly-continuous snow.

Presently the tracks fan out and I don't know which set to follow. I search for traces of the trail and occasionally pick up a clue but then lose it again. Finally, I just guess, and follow the freshest set of tracks which are headed down and across the hillside. In a few minutes, I see someone heading up the hill towards me.

"Don't follow me, I lost the trail," he says.

"Me too. That's why I was following you," I laugh.

"I was following other tracks but they started scattering. I finally lost the set that seemed to be going in the right direction."

"Well it's not a big deal. We'll just figure it out. I'm Colter, by the way."

"I'm Danny." We each dig out our maps and ponder them. It seems likely we are just past the big kink where I first lost the trail.

"So where do you think we are?"

Danny points at his map. "Right about here, somewhere."

"That's what I think. How about we backtrack to the last known trail and then we'll go from there?" He agrees so we start backtracking. Pretty soon we run into Mr. T, sitting on a rock looking at his GPS.

"What's your GPS say?" I ask reluctantly. My question pleases him.

"It says we are right here," he says, pointing to his map at a spot very close to what Danny and I were thinking. He continues, pointing, "That peak there is this one on the map, and that bigger one over there is this one. Man, I love orienteering."

The three of us begin looking for the trail. It soon becomes clear that it is going to be easier to just head for Saddle Junction where the PCT eventually goes. Plus I am already wearied from Mr. T's pontificating on navigation.

"You know what, I'm just going to wing it to Saddle Junction."

"That sounds good. I'll go with you," Danny says. I am honored by his faith in my navigation (even if I had lost the trail when he met me!). We head down and across the slope which is covered with gigantic pines, the snow steep and slippery and icy in places. Eventually we find our way to where it flattens out and we sit down to take a break. While sitting there I spot a trail. The maps shows it must be a side trail that leads to Saddle Junction.

"Pizza is on me!" Danny says.

"I accept."

After the break, we meet a hiker heading towards us through the snow. "Are you guys thru-hiking?" he says as he nears.

"Yes. Did you just come from Saddle Junction?"

"Yup, it's only about fifteen minutes that way. How the heck do you guys know where you are going, anyway?"

"Well, we didn't, for a while."

We hit Saddle Junction without incident and head down the Devil's Slide Trail and shortly we are out of the snow. After a long steep descent, we see the parking lot. I have been bragging about my hitchhiking skills. Danny heads into the outhouse while I start hitching. The very first car stops and offers a ride which is waiting when Danny arrives. In a few minutes we are sitting in a booth, ordering a pizza, chatting with our fellow hikers, many of whom have similar stories of losing the trail.

Danny and I camp at the park in Idyllwild along with other thru-hikers, many of whom I haven't seen before. I call my friend Stephanie who is moving from Wyoming back to Alaska. She answers her cell phone and tells me she is just driving into Anchorage with her brother and the trip has gone marvelously. Like most moves it's been stressful, but she seems so relaxed and joyful now that she's there that it really lifts my spirits.

I'm taking my first "Zero" today, as in zero miles walked. It will be nice to relax. Over at the cafe I have a leisurely breakfast with Conductor, Bojangles, Mole Man, Bob, and others. I have a big omelet, hash browns, and toast, along with coffee. It's a real treat after all that trail food. The talk is all about the snow ahead and whether or not Fuller Ridge is safely passable.

At the Pacific Crest Trail Association (PCTA) office they tell me that some thru-hikers headed over Fuller Ridge yesterday. They plan to call with a report. Until then the PCTA is suggesting that hikers find a car ride eight miles to the Black Mountain Road, then hike up the road to tie back into the PCT.

I walk to the outfitter store, considering getting better shoes for the snow, but decide to buy a set of MICROspikes instead. They should give me the traction I need. The shoes I'm wearing are lighter and it will be snow free most of the way to Kennedy Meadows. Additionally, I buy a detailed topographic map of the next stretch of trail.

I walk the aisles of the grocery store looking for new varieties of food for my resupply. I run into Danny on the way out. He says Mr. T has new scratches on his arm and face, apparently from sliding down an icy slope. Danny razzes me for my unsympathetic reaction.

Back out on the street I see the bouncing gait of a short hiker, a pinwheel spinning merrily on top of her pack. "I'm the Chocolate Bandito," she says. I like her attitude.

I check into the Idyllwild Inn and take a nice hot shower, then sort through my stuff and relax. Danny has lent me his smartphone which I use to check my email and update my website. Late in the afternoon, I head over to the PCTA office. On the way, I see Anne on the other side of a quiet street. When she sees me she heads over with a smile on her face, but when she gets close she begins to cry.

"Colter, can I talk to you?"

"Of course."

"I needed to tell someone. I just found out my mother died." Tears fill her eyes.

"Oh, Anne, I'm so sorry." Tears well up in my own eyes and I hug her. She will need to leave the trail soon to fly home for the funeral. She'll be coming back to the trail again later.

I walk over to the PCTA office in a subdued mood. They have heard from those hikers who went ahead and have posted this report:

> On 05/04/10 PCTA received a trail condition report from thru-hikers; it took 9 hrs to travel about 12 miles. Fuller Ridge is still dangerous and under ice/snow with lots of exposure. They had a good topographic map and compass and had to do quite a bit of route finding and still ended up off track a few times but made it to Black Mt. Rd. late last night.

Tonight I treat Danny to dinner, and tell him I'm going to tackle Fuller Ridge tomorrow. His feet are beat-up and he decides to take one more day to heal up.

It's a steep climb to Saddle Junction where I find the trail soon buried with snow again. It's only mid-afternoon but I choose to camp at one of the last patches of bare ground so I'll have a full day to tackle Fuller Ridge tomorrow. There's no liquid water here. I use my ice axe to chop chunks of hard snow to melt. Suddenly the handle breaks completely off the pick head! I'm stunned. Un-freaking-believable. It's a good thing I didn't have to use it for a self-arrest. For the next couple of hours, I work on my repair. I use a hiking pole as a splint, with tent stakes inside the shaft for additional reinforcement, all held together with duct tape and parachute cord. On testing, it seems stronger than new, which says more about the pathetic initial construction than it does about my repair.

Tonight I'm cowboy camping, which is sleeping under the stars, without setting up my shelter. I have a grand view of the sunset from my sleeping bag, high up in the mountains, overlooking cold, snowy ridges.

It doesn't take long before I abandon the trail which is buried somewhere beneath the snow. I navigate by map and compass. The snow is dense and hard, good for my MICROspikes. When I reach an overlook there is no sign of the trail ahead, but after studying the map the approximate route of the trail seems obvious.

A set of tracks leads me across a saddle and up a slope. Hmm, the trail has to be somewhere below me. I ponder the map and consider ignoring the route of the trail for the time being. I could stay high, and cut off a big loop of trail. It would mean more climbing but less contouring in deep snow. But there are some snow-free patches below. I hesitate, then head down-slope hoping to find some clear trail. Wicked brush claws at my legs as I descend, but in ten minutes I find snow-free trail and follow it as it contours the hillside. I am making good time now. Maybe it's not going to be so bad. There's a sign:

SAN JACINTO

WILDERNESS

SAN BERNARDINO National Forest

There are more snow patches and finally, it's all snow again. I follow the route by a combination of meandering footprints and map and compass. It's slow going. The snow is deep, but luckily it's dense enough to stay on top. Most of the time. It's tough to keep track of where I am in the trees because the "big picture" views are hidden. A mapping GPS would be extremely handy right now. Contouring for miles in the snow is hard work.

I'm crossing another steep slope. My foot suddenly punches into a deep hollow. I lose my balance and fall backwards, down-slope. Luckily I slide to a stop even before

I need my repaired ice axe/pole. My heart is pounding from a burst of adrenaline. Good thing it wasn't steeper, and good thing I didn't wrench my leg. The hollow was caused by snow melting around a rock. Subsequent snows had concealed the top of the hole. There are very real hazards and luck plays a significant role.

Almost exactly five years ago this was the area where a thru-hiker disappeared in the snow. The next year two day-hikers got lost for three days and stumbled upon his abandoned camp. The items they found, including dry socks, matches, and a sweater, likely saved their lives. A few weeks later the thru-hiker's body was found.

When the trail reaches openings in the trees I try to reorient to the map. Finally, I angle across and up slope to intersect what I believe is Fuller Ridge. After walking a short distance along the ridge, I see fresh tracks and then a short segment of clear trail. Excellent! It's nice to know exactly where I am and where I'm going. The trail is now following this obvious ridgeline so navigation is a no-brainer. When the tracks start leaving the crest I pull out the map and look above me. That must be Castle Rocks up there. The map shows the trail contours on a fairly steep slope (bad news) until it hits Black Mountain Road maybe two miles ahead (good news).

Tracks from previous hikers soon disperse and I'm back to winging it. There are slide marks in the snow where people have slid short distances down the steep hillside. The snow has softened enough for me that I can stomp steps, so it's not particularly frightening but it is slow going and the hours grind by.

I stand, soaked to the thighs by the wet snow, puffing and trying to pick the best route ahead of me. Clink, snap, clink. What is that noise? I walk steadily towards the sound and see two familiar people.

"How's it going?" I call out as I climb up to meet them.

"Not too bad. How far do you think we are from the road?"

"I don't know. Less than a mile maybe? I hope so anyway. I'm Colter, by the way."

"I'm Assface, and this is Hatchet."

"So you've got a trail name now, Hatchet. Good for you."

There are some fairly common trail names. Turtle. Or Rabbit. Or Stryder. A young Swiss lady is likely to be Swiss Miss. But there's only one Assface.

"What's the story behind the Assface trail name?" I ask.

"When I hiked the AT, I thought it was funny people were giving themselves all these cool names. So I decided to go the opposite direction. I picked Assface."

"What year did you do the AT?"

"2001."

"Yeah, me too."

We take a compass bearing and head off together. Pretty soon we see stumps which we take as a sign we are out of the wilderness and near the road. Sure enough, pretty soon we hit a snow-covered logging road. The ease of walking down a road covered with a few inches of snow is delightful. We stop for a quick break. Assface tells Hatchet to please stop whizzing in the creek from which following people will surely be drinking.

Later we halt to study the map, then turn to follow the road uphill to where the actual trail must cross. Assface leads, followed by Hatchet, then me. I stop to pick up a fallen hatchet and hand it to its owner at the next stop. Hatchet is new to backpacking, having just gotten on the trail at Idyllwild. His belt hatchet, something experienced thru-hikers don't carry, became an instant moniker. Assface and Hatchet decide to follow a spur road uphill to hit the trail faster. I elect to keep going because it will be shorter overall.

What a relief to spot the PCT emblem on a post! The trail has suddenly become nearly snow free. Two hikers are hiking down from a bend in the road to intersect the trail.

"I'm Captain Bivy. And this is Slow-Joe."

"Actually, it's So-Jo," his partner adds, sounding slightly annoyed.

They've taken the suggested alternate up the Black Mountain Rd. and are interested to hear how Fuller Ridge was. At the next break spot, I decide to camp while there's still enough snow to melt for drinking water. It's been a tough day. I roll out my sleeping pad and bag in a dry spot next to the flat, sunny face of an enormous boulder. As the snow melts in my cooking pot I look up at the snow on Fuller Ridge, thankful to be here, out of the snow.

May 7, Day 15. Mile 191; 2,465 Miles to Canada

I'm cruising along the trail, the snow and pines supplanted by wildflowers and desert. The guidebook shows about fourteen miles from my camp to the next dependable water. The water report says this year there's seasonal stream in about 11 miles. I've got enough melted snow to make it there. I stop to take a photo of a shiny black lizard warming itself on a rock in the morning sun, amid blue and yellow flowers. The trail is descending, thousands of feet. On a mountain bike it would be a delightful coast, but when you're backpacking it takes muscle power to brake every step. It's a pounding to the knees and feet. Still, it's much preferable to plowing through deep snow on Fuller Ridge.

Hatchet is sitting next to the trail with a piece of beavertail cactus in his hand.

"Do you think this cactus is poisonous?"

"I don't know. I doubt it. Why?"

"I took a bite. I shouldn't have, but I read about it. My mouth is full of stickers. It didn't look like it had any. Do you have any tweezers?" He is gingerly trying to pull tiny spines out with his fingernails. I hand him the tweezers from my tiny Swiss army knife. The beavertail cactus looks like a standard prickly pear cactus without the long spines. I've already found that they are covered with tiny, hair-like spines that can be very difficult to remove. He doesn't seem to be in any serious trouble so after getting my tweezers back I keep walking.

Lizard and wildflowers

Ahead I see a puff of smoke. Is that a wildfire? Over a little rise I see the fire on a sparse blackened slope of brush and grass, mostly burned out but with smoke puffing up along the perimeter. One person is working on a hotspot near the top of the fire. The trail skirts the fire and there are some yellow fire shirts ahead. Below is a gaggle of firefighters clad in orange. They are a "con crew" from a prison. The trail cuts through the fire. Ash puffs up with each step. There's the smell of smoke and the chatter of radios and the clink of firefighting tools. I hear a plane orbiting and search the sky and recognize an OV-10 air-attack plane. There's a good chance it's someone I know. It's all eerily familiar and a collision of two usually distinct worlds that have played a major role in my life. Two years ago I retired from a career in wildland firefighting.

One guy is giving instructions on the radio and I divert over to him and wait until he's finished talking.

"How's it going?" I ask.

"Pretty good."

"There's still some smoke on the perimeter up on top." I can't help it. There's a bunch of people working in the middle of the fire down here where it isn't doing much good. Nobody is working up there where the fire still has a real chance of escaping.

"OK, thanks."

"Any idea how it started?"

"Hikers, I think," he says.

"Thru-hikers? Pacific Crest Trail hikers?"

"I don't know. Is this the PCT?" Of course, I realize firefighters often come from far away and can't be expected to know the local area.

"Yeah. Well, good luck."

"Thanks. Good luck to you."

I pass the con crew. It's a good program. They are carefully screened and receive a small wage. Seems like a sensible way for them to get outside and do useful work as well.

As I continue down the trail I pass another con crew walking up the steep, hot trail. Several ask how much farther it is and are encouraged when I can tell them they are almost there. It's nearly noon when I reach a narrow, paved road. I have descended well over 5,000 vertical feet today so far!

Two people are lounging near the road. They introduce themselves as Sunshine and Grateful. They are a father-daughter team. He is late 40s, her, perhaps 19. When I ask them the source of their names the father explains:

"Well, I named her Sunshine because she likes to sleep in until the sun hits her tent." Sunshine laughs. "I call myself Grateful because I'm just happy to be out here on the trail."

"Those are good names. How do you like hiking with your dad, Sunshine?"

"It's fun."

Man, it's hot. Really hot. I fill up my canteens and rest in the shade of a fire vehicle, some of the only shade around. A Forest Service K-9 vehicle arrives. He says a PCT hiker started the fire by mistake with his stove. I'm bummed to hear it was a thru-hiker.

After a gentle road walk, the trail leads me across a stretch of baking desert to Interstate 10. Under the shady bridge, a pickup is parked. Next to the pickup is a trash can with a keg of beer nestled in ice. A fellow in a Chinese hat, Chai Man, a 2006 thru-hiker, is there with trail magic. Normally not a beer enthusiast, I'm happy for a cold beer on this hot day, but I drink it very slowly so it doesn't knock me out cold. Hikers arrive by ones and twos.

An SUV shows up and the driver leans out. "I'm Dave. Anybody want a ride to the Cabazon A&W?" Several of us pile in. Soon we are washed up and chowing down on burgers, fries and icy root beer in air-conditioned comfort. Dave tells us to watch for Steve-O out on the trail, a buddy of his, who is making another attempt at completing the PCT.

Back on the trail again I think about all the extremes: deep snow to desert, freezing to extreme heat, trail food to rich restaurant food. Ahead dozens of white wind turbines spin. Three hikers sit next to the trail and I plop down next to them for a break. It's Girl Friday, Zero/Zero, and Fire Marshal. We walk together to the wind farm where we get water for the next stretch.

I head out and soon find a pleasant camp spot, flat and out of the wind. Down the shadowed drainage the blades of sunlit windmills spin against the snowy backdrop of the San Jacintos. I fall asleep to the gentle creaking of the turbines.

May 8

I start walking before sunrise to take advantage of the cool of the morning. Twenty minutes later I pass Hatchet packing up his camp. It's a steep climb to the top of a saddle where I pause to admire the desert view. A hiker catches up to me as the trail contours around a drainage. It's Worldwide. His cruising pace is much faster than mine but we walk together for an hour or so on easy trail. Eventually, I let him go ahead so I can resume my more natural pace. It's still early morning when the PCT reaches an overlook of the Whitewater River. I sit down on a rock among yellow wildflowers and look over the desert hills. It's all about the light. This same scene at noon would simply be washed out looking hills. Now it's all rich light and shadow, every fold standing out in stark contrast. There is the crunch of footsteps and two couples come up a side trail. They have driven up from Palm Springs this morning for an early hike.

They peg me as a thru-hiker and I field the usual string of questions. When did you start? Where did you start from? How long do you think it will take? What do you eat? Are you hiking by yourself? Isn't that scary? How much does your pack weigh? I hand them my pack and they are amazed at how light it is. The same with my carbon fiber hiking poles. One of them hands me a Sacagawea coin to carry for good luck and there are good wishes all around when we part company.

On the descent to the river a small group warns me of a rattlesnake just off the trail below, but I don't see it. The trail follows an old jeep road near the river and it's a flat cruise. The river crossing is a wide, rocky riverbed with a clear stream about twenty feet wide. After walking upstream for a little way I see where other hikers have laid logs across narrow gaps between boulders. Using my poles for balance I walk across the logs then step from stone to stone and make the crossing dry-shod. Captain Bivy, Hatchet, and Assface are taking a break here. Hatchet is wearing a tank top. The sun is blazing down on his white arms and shoulders. I want to warn him about sunburn, which can be a serious issue, but I don't want to offend him. Maybe he's using sunscreen.

The guidebook shows the next water is at Mission Creek, 6 miles away. Halfway there I run across Zero/Zero, Fire Marshall and Girl Friday taking a break. I join them for a while in the shade of some bushes, then push on to Mission Creek. On a long climb I run into Steve-O, looking like he's doing pretty good on his 6th thru-hike attempt. After a final steep descent, the trail nears the creek. Man, it is ridiculously hot and I'm getting low on water. At the creek crossing I throw my pack down next to Captain Bivy in the shade of a tree, then fill up my water bottles and mix some Aquamira to treat the water. As I relax I glance over at Captain Bivy's pack.

"Hey, Bivy, you've got ants swarming your pack." I look around and there are ants everywhere. Damn, it's a nice spot, too. I grab my pack and walk upstream and find another good shady spot. This is the hottest day of the hike by far. For the first time, I do what I'd expected to be doing almost daily on this stretch — I hole up for a few hours until the heat of the day has passed.

Down the trail, I find a fire has burned through here a few years ago. What would have been beautiful shady cottonwood trees have been killed and denuded of leaves, making this hot day feel even hotter. Luckily there are numerous creek crossings. Unluckily it is tough to follow the trail at times, it's as if the trail is repeatedly crossing the creek to throw me off track.

As I stop to cook a dinner of couscous, an athletic hiker approaches. "I don't think we've met. I'm Pika."

She's a nurse, from Colorado. She's waiting on her hiking partner, appropriately called Catch Up. When he arrives I'm done eating and we head up the trail together, and soon start looking for good campsites. They'd had one in mind which they didn't find, likely due to the wildfire. Finally they find a spot they like, but not wanting to be a third wheel I push on for another 20 minutes, finally camping in a sandy spot near the creek.

May 9

It's a climb today, with many more creek crossings. The trail leaves the desert and returns to big timber where Worldwide naps next to a stream. He likes to walk at night to avoid the heat of day. The trail reaches a dirt road. I have rather complicated instructions on how to find a local spring. Instead, there is a trickle of water in the creek bed which I use to cook a meal and fill my water bottles. A snapped-off ultralight hiking pole lies next to a log.

There are deep patches of snow on the trail in places but it's not a serious problem. At one point I go well off the trail to relieve myself. Just as I drop my pants I see a hiker who either doesn't see me through the thin screen of brush, or politely pretends not to. There must be a big switchback in the trail.

Ahead there is some fencing just off the trail. Presently I'm surprised to see large cages containing two grizzly bears. One is pacing back and forth and the other is focused on licking some food out of a colossal bowl. It is both interesting and depressing. A photo doesn't seem appropriate. It's not a memory I care to capture.

A cold wind begins to blow. It's time to call it a day so I look for a campsite protected from the wind. Near the trail, there is a site that looks serviceable. When I crawl into my shelter, it's getting buffeted hard enough that I decide to suck it up and find a better place. I take down my shelter and pack up. This is the windward side of the ridge. I climb all the way up and over the ridge. I find a spot on the leeward side in a nice opening in a dense stand of oak brush. The wind still roars overhead but there's just a breeze here. Moving was a good call. It's hard to sleep soundly in a flapping tent. Looking at the maps there must have been at least 3,600 feet of climbing today and a similar amount yesterday. I think it's easy to greatly underestimate the climbing or descending during the course of a day. It's rarely a steady incline or decline, but a series of climbs and descents. Plus there are countless little ups and downs that aren't reflected at all in the contour lines.

May 10

It was cold last night and it froze hard. I wore my balaclava, long underwear bottoms, wool socks, and down jacket in my 30-degree sleeping bag and put the foot of my bag in my pack. I slept toasty that way. I make it to Highway 18 in mid-afternoon and put out my thumb to hitch into Big Bear. In just a few minutes a small car pulls over and the passenger door swings open. It's a young woman who works in a nearby town and lives in Big Bear. She's familiar with the PCT and hikers hitching into town which is why she is comfortable with giving me a ride.

She drops me off at the Nature's Inn where a banner reads: *WELCOME PCT HIKERS*. I thank her and double-check to make sure I've got all my stuff. She gives me a friendly wave as she drives off. Inside, the owner is super friendly and helpful. He briefs me on Big Bear and the amenities of the hotel. I decide to share a room with other hikers. When he opens the door to show me the room Danny is there with his pack and a big grin on his face.

"Do you have another room?" I ask the owner. Danny laughs.

Danny has been hiking off and on with Old Scout, who is our roommate. After I take a good hot shower we head down to the restaurant for dinner and I have a huge burger, fries, and a piece of pie.

Zero days are a wonderful break from the trail, but there are always chores. The laundromat manager gives me a free scoop of detergent. Danny and I walk to the post office to mail out some gear. Danny sends his "bounce box" ahead. A bounce box contains items that you don't want to carry but want available at town stops. They often contain chargers, spare batteries, razors, shampoo, spare clothing, flip-flops. Things like that. I send my MICROspikes to Kennedy Meadows, my broken ice axe back to the manufacturer, and used guidebook pages home. The ladies at the post office arc awesome, extremely friendly and helpful. They insist on taking pictures of each of us, which they immediately post on their board — "PCT 2010: Mexico to Canada." Along with each photo is the hiker's name, usually their trail name, their age if they've chosen to share it, and their home state or country. I'm amazed at how many people I know, and equally amazed at how many people are on the trail just ahead or behind that I don't recognize at all.

"Good luck! Send us a postcard when you get to Canada!" one of the ladies calls out as I leave.

"Thanks, I will," I say with a wave. It's all about attitude, isn't it? Those ladies have a post office job just like thousands of other post office jobs. They could act sour and angry about all the smelly hikers who vastly add to their workload. They don't. They turn lemons into lemonade. They make thru-hiker season an enjoyable, exciting event. Here are more hikers! Another face for the photo board! They share our adventure.

With fellow hikers I enjoy an enormous meal at Thelma's, shooting for big calories. At the grocery store I buy food for the next stretch of trail, then stop by the bookstore and eventually select *Lord of the Flies*. I read and answer emails and call my parents. There is a hiker gathering at the hostel in the other part of town. I grow tired of waiting for the bus (where is it?) and head over to Thelma's again for a double quarter-pounder. Back at the room and I read most of *Slaughterhouse Five*, which Danny has lent me. It's one of my favorite books.

Later at the motel lounge, I update my website:

Big Bear City, California: 265 Miles/10% of the PCT Done! ... The hike is continuing to go very well. My knees and feet are doing great. I really like my shoes, they are a perfect fit for me... I'm still ahead of schedule. There's big snow ahead in the Sierras so I don't want to go any faster, but want to give it plenty of time to melt.

May 12

One more trip to Thelma's for Danny and me. I order their biggest omelet. We've arranged a ride, $10 each, back up to the pass in some old military surplus vehicle. It's cold and crazy windy and we are bundled up to the max and laughing.

The trail is an easy cruise and I walk with Danny for miles. We are having lunch in the shade next to a brook a when Turtle, a Japanese hiker, walks up and hands Danny his umbrella that he'd dropped. I've been razzing Danny about his umbrella and I find this amusing. As usual, he's a good sport.

Later in the day, I catch up with Slowpoke. He's got a heavy looking pack and looks unbalanced and uncomfortable. He's wearing blue jeans and a cotton shirt. The blue jeans especially make me wince. He's carrying at least double the water I'm carrying, plus more days' worth of food PLUS about three days of spare food. I don't carry spare food on a trip like this. If I'm running low the last day or two of a section I can stretch it out if need be. His pack must easily weigh double my pack. But we each do what works for us and perhaps there will come a time when he can chow down or chug an extra quart of water when I'm running low. The question is whether carrying it all those miles will be worth it.

On a downhill stretch my pace is faster than his so I go on ahead, making really good time. Suddenly it dawns on me that the trail has really been dropping. A lot. It just doesn't seem right. A quick check of my guidebook tells the story: we missed a turn and we're heading down the Cougar Crest Trail. Son-of-a-B%**!!! I quickly shoulder my pack and climb back up the trail as fast as I can manage until I meet Slowpoke.

"This isn't the PCT. We missed a turn." Slowpoke groans in disappointment and frustration. Not only were we not making progress but we were going the wrong way AND have to make a steep climb to return to where we goofed up. Triple drat! It's my biggest navigational screw-up of the trip so far.

When we get back to the missed turn, sweating, I see how it happened. It's a hairpin turn and the PCT sign is only visible if you turn around and look back the way you've come. Really lousy trail marking. On the other hand, if I'd been paying attention to the map there's no way I would have made that mistake. I notice that someone has scratched "Not PCT" on the sign we passed. Slowpoke and I take a couple of minutes to mark the turn with arrows made of small stones. We lay small sticks across the other trail, the standard indication of "wrong way."

Slowpoke takes a break and I continue on and after a while discover a stash of trail magic next to the trail with sodas, juice, fruit, and cookies. I enjoy a treat then sign the logbook thanking them for their largesse. The trail passes through a large burn then descends to Holcomb Creek. Turtle is camped there. I cross the river and camp on a bed of needles under mature pines.

I'm walking by 5:45 AM. There are stretches of burned country again, but there are also many wildflowers, and about three knee-deep creek crossings. I see Captain Bivy who reports having trouble with shin splints, a common hiker ailment. At Deep Creek Bridge we find Girl Friday there with trail magic. She's nice. I eat an orange as she tells of her hike. She injured her knee and has decided she doesn't want to hold the rest of the team back. She has bumped ahead with Zero/Zero and Fire Marshall's packs so they can "slack pack" (hike without a pack) this section.

"Looks like I'm a section hiker now," she says with evident disappointment. She says they have done quite a lot of night hiking. They are Team Far Sight, and Zero/Zero is blind! Night hiking, naturally, makes sense for him, especially when it's hot. Girl Friday describes how one of them will hike ahead with a headlamp and tap rocks and other obstructions to alert Zero/Zero to the hazard. Despite that, he's already fallen dozens of times. I am amazed that I've taken two long breaks with them and hadn't a clue he was blind.

"He's really completely blind?" I ask, incredulous. She assures me he is. And he's already hiked the Appalachian Trail!

The trail continues over the bridge and along the very steep slopes above Deep Creek. "I wouldn't want to fall over here," I think. "Man, how about Zero/Zero? One misstep in the wrong place and that's it!" The danger isn't purely theoretical. No Way Ray was a well-liked and respected PCT hiker, with many ties to the trail. Just four years ago he was thru-hiking this area, walking just twenty yards ahead of his wife. When she came around the corner, he was gone, having fallen about 200 feet to his death. It was a terrible tragedy and a shock to the hiking community.

It's nine miles from the bridge to Deep Creek Hot Springs. I'm not going to pass this spot up without a good soak. Two locals have spotted an immense rattlesnake and are foolishly chasing it around, poking at it and trying to lift it up with a stick. There are three nice hot pools above the river. I stand under a two-inch pipe cascading hot water down upon me. Luxury! I climb back up and sink into the upper hot springs pool and relax in the shade of the overhanging tree. Pretty soon a twenty-something couple climbs up from the middle pool. They look like thru-hikers, but they are trail crew members just passing through on their way to a new job. They have been working on the Continental Divide Trail. When I tell them I hiked the CDT two years ago we enjoy comparing notes.

At dark, most of the locals have left to hike back to the road. The tub begins to fill with a mixed gaggle of thru-hikers. People seem to have the impish delight of three-year-olds to be running around naked. We talk about the trail and look up at the stars and soak until we can't stand the heat anymore, then head back to our campsites.

In the morning the trail has a different feel as it approaches Mojave Dam. There are many rocks with spray-painted graffiti. Where there are enough people around there are always a few knuckleheads.

Near the dam the trail is confusing. Slowpoke is walking up the trail as I head down. Together we take another look at the map and head down together, spotting a trail marker at the bottom.

At an easy river crossing, we meet three young thru-hikers packing up. They introduce themselves, Roo, then Happy Feet, who are guys. The gal says, "And I guess I'm Kara-bou."

"Caribou? How did you happen to get that name?"

"They gave it to me. My first name is Kara."

It's hot, but easy walking today. I'm getting low on water so I'm looking for a piped spring described in the water report. I notice a large flock of pelicans circling overhead. I hear a crunch and turn to see two hikers walking up.

"I was just watching the pelicans. Did you guys happen to see the piped spring?"

"We are already past it."

"Did you see it?"

"No, but I remember it from last year. There's a stream just up ahead, though." It's Joker, who is hiking with Motor. They were at the hot springs yesterday. We stop at the creek for water. Motor manages to lose her balance and get her shoes and socks wet. She giggles at herself. Giggle is actually part of her full trail name, which is Motor Giggle Bootie Butt. Joker's name is well deserved, as he's got an exceptionally quick wit.

"So did you thru-hike last year?"

"Yup, and in 2008, too."

"Wow! You must like the PCT."

"I do. But this year I'm only going as far as Kearsarge Pass."

We walk and talk for miles. As usual, my pace is faster when walking with other people. Part of the reason, I'm guessing, is that people don't want to be the slow one. At least I don't.

"There should be trail magic just up ahead," Joker says. I am amazed at his memory of the trail.

"Now you've got our hopes up."

When we arrive Joker flips open the cooler. We stand looking sadly at empty bottles and wrappers. There is a register there and we laugh as we compose Haiku to express our disappointment.

Somewhere along Silverwood Lake, two more thru-hikers join us. Around 4 PM we walk into the Cleghorn Picnic Area where there is water and bathrooms.

"Anybody want a soda?" Cloudbuster asks.

"Sure!" we say.

"I'm going to Yogi something."

To "Yogi," in thru-hiker parlance, is essentially to hint about getting something from a non-hiker without actually asking. For example, instead of saying, "Would you give me a ride into Wrightwood?" you might simply say, "Do you know how long of a walk it is into town?"

Cloudbuster has wild hair and orange gaiters and a hiker kilt. He and Joker head over to nearby picnickers, a large group of people, probably a family reunion by the looks of it. Quite a contrast between them and us.

Soon they are back with several sodas. "Here you go," Cloudbuster says.

"What did you say?" I ask.

"I asked if we could buy some and they said they didn't have any to sell. So I just stood and stared at a case of sodas sitting there. They finally gave me these and wouldn't take any money for them when I offered."

"I was really uncomfortable," Joker adds.

"Wow. I couldn't do that," I say.

"Doesn't bother me a bit," says Cloudbuster. Regardless, we all enjoy the drinks. Soon a Trail Angel shows up and gives us a bunch of goodies, including a bag of oranges. Nice!

After an hour or so I head back to the trail and put in about seven more miles. I cowboy camp on a flat spot just above the trail, watching from my sleeping bag as the last evening shadows move across the desert hills. I tally up how far I walked today: 30 miles. I believe I can count the number of 30+ mile days I have backpacked on one hand.

The sun rises while I hike. There are several hikers packing up along a creek bed. It looks like a camp of homeless people, the guys all whiskery and gear scattered about in the morning sun. As I climb I'm listening to "No Surrender" by Bruce Springsteen on my MP3 player. I am struck by the appropriateness of the words:

Now we could sleep in the twilight
By the river bed
With a wide open country in our hearts
And these romantic dreams in our heads
'Cause we made a promise we swore we'd always remember
No retreat, baby, no surrender

Happy Feet says hello as he passes me while I look down from an especially good viewpoint of desert with more snowy mountains just ahead. I talk to Kara-bou for a bit during the long descent to Interstate 15. A road grader sits right next to the trail, with an electric tower in the background. The PCT isn't all wilderness.

This morning we likely all have the same destination and it's a highlight of the PCT for many people: the McDonald's at Cajon Pass. That might sound silly, being excited about a McDonald's, but it's a different world on long trails. Appetites are often ravenous and people tend to crave food and fats and lots of both.

At long last, I'm standing in line studying the breakfast menu. "Let me see your foot," someone says. I turn around. It's Kara-bou.

"What?"

"Let me see the tread of your shoe." I show her. "I've been following that track a lot," she says.

I have a goal. I'm going to order every single item off the dollar menu.

"Let's see, I'll have one small coffee, one sausage biscuit, one hash browns, one hot fudge sundae, one sausage burrito, and one sausage McMuffin." I return to my seat, triumphant. However, Roo claims victory in the value department with 1,100 calories for less than $4. SoJo joins us now, as does Boat.

After watering up I return to the trail. It passes under the interstate, out across the desert, then through a giant culvert. I spot a perfect photo. Snowy blue mountains rise in the background. In the middle distance, brown and green desert hills bake in the sun. Yellow and blue flowers provide color in the foreground. I love the contrast in colors and angles and temperatures.

I know there is a trail closure due to damage from last year's Sheep Fire. When I arrive at the detour I think hard about ducking under the ribbon and heading on down the trail. But I decide to follow the rules and take the road detour.

It's a long pull up a hot road. When a pickup passes the dust is choking. Luckily there's almost no traffic. I've got a little extra water that I don't want to carry all the way to the top of the ridge, so I find a shady spot and sacrifice a little water to wash up. Hopefully, a car won't come around the corner and see my fish-white butt. I do a quick scrub and hang my sweaty socks to dry in the sun.

It's cooler in the late afternoon. It's a pleasant, scenic downhill walk to Applewhite Campground, past horses and green fields irrigated by circling plumes of water. The campground is expecting PCT hikers and I am directed where they want us, a nice grassy spot under the trees. I call Stephanie. She has lost her cat at her new home in Anchorage and is distraught. He is a great cat, sleek and confident and personable, and I feel bad for Stephanie and her cat, lost and alone in a strange city. I rarely feel lonely, but I feel lonely in empathy for them both.

In the morning I have a long climb, thousands of feet, back up over the mountains to reach Wrightwood. There are long views up top, tall trees with plenty of snow in sight. I find parts of the trail deeply buried. I reach the highway at the same time as Happy Feet. I'm concerned that two of us will make the hitching more difficult than if I was hitching alone, but we are offered a ride into Wrightwood in short order.

In town, I find a list of Trail Angels. I give one a call and am surprised when they have a mandatory $25 donation. I always try to donate to Trail Angels who put hikers up, but a mandatory donation seems more like a fee than a donation. They come to pick me up. My room is beautiful and immense. It has a cathedral ceiling with sun streaming in the large windows and skylights onto hardwood floors. There are pine trees just outside. Near the fireplace is a grand piano. The mandatory donation now seems insignificant!

Clouds in the mountains. Yucca in foreground

In the evening I head into town for the famous taco special at the local bar. I eat with Cloudbuster and Chance and we discuss the Trail and greet other hikers while chowing down.

I eat a huge breakfast with Pat and a gaggle of other hikers, my rolling trail family. I wander the aisles of the grocery store looking for food ideas. In an hour, I'm standing on the outskirts of town with a *PCT HIKER TO TRAIL* cardboard sign. I'm confident I'll get a ride in minutes, but I've been standing here a while. A pickup heading the other way pulls over and rolls down the window.

"Are you heading to the PCT?" the driver asks.

"Yeah."

"I'll give you a ride when I get back if you don't have one already."

"Thanks!" Before he gets, back another car pulls over and I'm soon back at the trail.

There is another major trail reroute ahead due to last year's big wildfires. On the reroute map there is a notation for Mt. Baden-Powell: "Bad Ice and Snow, Need Ice Capons." Presumably they meant crampons, not capons, which would be a type of domestic fowl. I have neither capons nor crampons. Nor an ice axe.

There are many standards of "trail purity" when it pertains to following the route. On the Appalachian Trail, there are purists who make a point of walking past each of the thousands of white blazes marking the trail. Most AT shelters have shortcut paths leading in each direction back to the trail. The true purists will backtrack each time to hit the same point of the main trail so as to not miss a blaze. Most hikers don't worry about that detail. Most hikers don't worry about taking alternate routes when they deem it to be necessary. Some hikers don't mind skipping significant stretches of trail, sometimes hundreds of miles.

Jackie McDonnell ("Yogi"), the author of *Yogi's Pacific Crest Trail Handbook*, talks about "connecting your steps" all the way from Mexico to Canada. By that she means to walk the whole way, and to follow the official PCT where possible, while hiking an alternate route in places where it makes sense. The Western trails, like the Continental Divide Trail and the Pacific Crest Trail, are significantly different from the AT in some respects. For one, the trails aren't blazed, at least not continuously. The CDT isn't even completed. There are often fire closures which may or may not be official. There are semi-official snow reroutes, such as the suggested reroute bypassing Fuller Ridge this year. Many people take unintentional reroutes when they lose the trail in deep snow.

People often take low routes to miss especially deep snow or to miss dangerously steep icy/snowy sections.

My personal standard will be Yogi's, to "connect my steps" all the way from Mexico to Canada. Looking at the map, I decide to start the reroute a few miles early. That way I can avoid the reportedly treacherous Baden-Powell.

Late in the day, I reach South Fork Campground. There are picnic tables, a little creek, fire rings, outhouses, the whole shebang. Another hiker has just arrived as well. I think I recognize her.

"Hi, I'm Colter. Wyoming, I presume?"

"Yeah. How did you know I was Wyoming?" she asks in a very soft, quiet voice.

"Motor pointed you out at Deep Creek Hot Springs."

We talk about the Trail while setting up camp. She has worked in country very familiar to me, like Denali National Park, and near Buffalo, Wyoming. Stephanie lived in Buffalo, where I spent many happy months in recent years.

In the morning we are both up early and hike out together. We reach a very confusing trail junction. My photocopied reroute map is pretty poor. Wyoming has a better map but we are still unsure which fork to take. We each scout a few hundred yards ahead, have a pow-wow, and make our best guess. We guess right and stop for a break and water at Devil's Punchbowl Park. Beyond that, there's lots of road-walking. Road-walking tends to be hard on your feet, especially on pavement. I theorize that on hard, level surfaces your feet tend to hit the same way time after time. On backcountry trail, each step is a little different.

We spot a Burger King a mile or more off the route. Like good thru-hikers, we take the time to detour to chow down. It's awesome. We take a cross-country shortcut on the way back and stop to soak our feet in a pleasant little creek. Back on the road, we run into Anne and we all walk together. A

Trail Angel stops and gives us some oranges. He is also very concerned that we have enough toilet paper.

In the evening, we camp together in a nice flat area off the road. Jaybird sees us from the road and asks to join us. We have a nice conversation as each person sets up for the evening and has dinner.

May 21

Anne, Wyoming and I set out for a day of road walking. Wyoming's feet are hurting but she's a trooper and doesn't complain. It's fun to have people to talk to on this long road walk. Turns out Anne knows "Meat Loaf" the musician! Her grandmother would inadvertently call him Meatball. As we are blabbing away Wyoming notices we have just missed a turn-off. We thank her for paying attention. However, heavy mining trucks are passing us on this dirt road and we are getting dusted out big-time. We talk it over and decide to hike cross-country to escape the road. It's an awesome plan until we hit an orchard. I'm really uncomfortable with walking through what must be private land. But at this point, we are committed to the plan by the miles we've already covered since leaving the road. A pickup comes hustling down the dirt road and the driver rolls down the window and says.

"Hey, you can't walk through here! This is private land. You're going to have to go back."

We apologize and explain the situation and tell him we will beeline off the land in the direction we are going and we won't be any problem. He doesn't have the authority to let us through but we tell him he's done his job and we will be gone before he knows it. He lets us continue.

In late afternoon we come to our destination, a KOA campground, and thru-hikers trickle in. There are tents everywhere. It's fun to have a hiker community around. I wake up during the night. Is that lions roaring!?

Wyoming and Anne on our cross-country fire reroute

May 22

It turns out I *did* hear lions roaring. There is a "big cat" sanctuary nearby! Anne is still sleeping so Wyoming and I hit the trail. And I mean trail because we are back on the PCT! After many miles we walk through a shady, cool tunnel and beyond that through Vasquez Rocks. With its canyons and rugged rock formations, it feels like some kind of cowboy movie setting. In fact, it has been, many times! This area has been a location for television shows like *Daniel Boone*, *The Rifleman*, and *Star Trek*, as well as movies like *Blazing Saddles* and *Austin Powers*.

In Agua Dulce, we stop for root beer floats. Mr. T approaches and sits down at our table, uninvited. He reaches across the table and grabs my guidebook without asking and begins thumbing through it. I yank it out of his hands and knock over a glass of water, which spills largely onto Wyoming.

"How about you sit somewhere else?" I say, steaming.

"Seriously?" he says.

"Yeah, seriously." He gets up and sits at another table.

I apologize to Wyoming for getting her wet. I am still angry and embarrassed for losing my cool, but Mr. T has been obnoxious every single time and doesn't seem to take a hint.

The vibe turns positive when we get to the Saufley's, aka Hiker Heaven. And hiker heaven it is. Donna Saufley greets us and we are given a quick tour. Dozens of packages are organized on shelves, waiting for hikers to retrieve them. There are showers, Wi-Fi, tents, an information board, washers, and wall tents for the hikers. "Hiker boxes" hold excess food and gear other hikers have donated. It's an incredibly well thought out operation with just the kind of things hikers are looking for. Soon Anne arrives and the three of us share a wall tent, complete with cots. There must be two dozen thru-hikers there at Hiker Heaven. The price for all this? Nothing, it's free. Like most hiker's though, I leave a donation in the hiker jar. This costs them many thousands of dollars every year. Imagine the many needs for rides, medical attention, counseling, you name it. And think of all the set-up and take-down and clean-up. What kind, generous, patient people!

May 21, Day 29. Mile 455; 2,201 Miles to Canada

Wyoming, Anne and I take a "zero" in Agua Dulce. I sign up for a ride to the nearest REI. A friend of the Saufley's drives us into town. It's a significant drive, and quite a favor for complete strangers. As we load up my heart sinks when Mr. T climbs in. Luckily there are a couple of other hikers and the driver I can talk to.

I'm looking for a new pair of shoes. Mine are nearly shot with a couple hundred trail miles on them before this hike and well over 400 so far on this one. We stand out from the crowd at REI, sunburned and with clothes and shoes battered by weeks on the trail. We are the subject of some disapproving looks, like we are homeless people who've wandered into a fancy party.

"Ignore these people," Cloudbuster tells us. "They're buying all this fancy hiker clothing so they can *look* like they're doing what *we are* doing." We laugh. I buy a new pair of running shoes. Most thru-hikers don't wear hiking boots these days.

Wyoming makes a horse friend at Agua Dulce

In the evening Anne, Wyoming and I ride loaner bikes down the road for some Mexican food. We are living large!

The three of us hike out early in the morning. Wyoming stops to pet a gigantic, friendly horse on the nose. We turn down the wrong road for a few hundred yards. When we head cross-country back to our route our shoes and socks are driven full of thousands of cheatgrass seeds which poke into our feet. We have to stop to pull them out.

Everyone has fears. For Anne, it's snakes. To help her deal with her fear she has taken to naming each snake she sees, alphabetically. Today she's looking for Fred.

We make very good time, motoring through the miles as we talk. In some shady chaparral, we find several comfy chairs and a cooler full of drinks. An inflatable palm tree, a plastic skeleton, a large "2010" banner, a pink flamingo and more hang from the branches. This is a goodie cache left by the Casa de Luna, our next stop! It's only mid-afternoon when we reach the road, where we give Casa de Luna a call and start hiking in their direction. A passing van starts veering off the road heading straight for us at full speed. I jump off the road and the van comes skidding to a stop. My heart is pounding. It is our ride. I am not particularly amused. In fact, I'm pissed. My anger quickly ebbs, though.

Yogi says: *24 miles ago you experienced corporate efficiency at the Saufley's. Get ready for Hippy Day Care at Casa de Luna!* That's an apt description. Things are very relaxed here. There is a rack of Hawaiian shirts. We are each told to select one to wear. A volunteer gives us a tour of the place. He is mellow yet animated and appears to have a significant buzz going. The manzanitas around the camping area look like a hobbit forest. The Andersons make a huge taco salad in the evening, and there are bushels of beer. A white sheet hangs on the wall which all the hikers sign with markers. Many use considerable imagination. Psycho transforms the "P" in *Psycho* into a knife dripping with blood. Caveman's name appears on a caveman club.

In the morning they make us all-we-can eat pancakes and when our first shuttle group gets ready to go we are told to line up to have our picture taken. As the shutter snaps, Mrs. Anderson moons us. Now I get it, Casa de Luna, House of the Moon. I say a sad goodbye to Anne who will be leaving for her mother's funeral. Mr. T hops into the van just before we leave. There is no escaping him.

May 25

Today we reach a PCT trail marker with "500" on it. 500 miles! Nearly 1/5 of the whole trail. It is Wyoming's birthday. I present her with a Little Debbie snack cake with a candle in it. She is surprised and moved. In the afternoon we are walking with Jaybird on the long downhill to Hikertown. Wyoming's feet hurt so she's walking in her sandals.

Jaybird is a sharp guy. I ask for his opinion on my theory that free will is largely an illusion, that we do make choices, but we make those choices based on our genetic wiring, how we were raised, our environment and our life experiences. Jaybird disagrees. To illustrate his point, he picks up a tuft of grass and throws it into the breeze.

"That's *free will*. I *chose* to do that," he says.

"But you were reacting to your environment, to what I just said." I go on to explain that if we don't do something for certain reasons, that implies randomness. Is randomness Free Will? If we could go down the same timeline of our lives again, would we really make different decisions at the same crossroads, would we not be here on the PCT next time? Regardless, we agree that choices matter.

Hikertown looks like a town set for a Western film, which was likely its original purpose. There are various false front buildings with *SHERIFF, POST OFFICE, HOTEL*, etc. For

71

a while each year it serves as a stop for hikers. Wyoming and I are shown a room with a single large bed, but we explain that we are not a couple and are soon set up with appropriate accommodations.

The owner loans us his car for a trip to a small store nearby. That's mighty nice! Surprise, Mr. T manages to make the trip with us. Why does he, of all people, seem to appear everywhere?

The low, rich early morning light of the desert is especially beautiful. Wyoming and I hike along the Los Angeles Aqueduct. Pink and white wildflowers grow next to the cool, blue water of the canal. The trail turns and heads straight north. Across the desert toward distant hills we hike for miles, following the giant, partially buried steel pipe in which the aqueduct now runs. A hundred years ago 52-mule teams hauled these 30-ton sections of pipe across the desert. It's still delivering vast amounts of water today. What an incredible feat of engineering!

Under a bridge two sleeping thru-hikers wake up at our approach. It's Green Mile and Redhead. Redhead has taught Wyoming one of her favorite recipes: unwrap all your candy bars, Cliff Bars, Power Bars, etc., and put them into a large plastic bag and seal it well. Put that in the top of your pack where the sun can heat it and let it all melt together. Put it in a cool place. Eat. I am not a fan of the idea, but she loves it.

We are walking past large, beautiful Joshua trees, looking like a cross between a cactus and a tree but actually a type of yucca. Some have bunches of sage-green three-inch fruit.

"We should flip a coin to see who has to eat one of those," I say, nodding towards a particularly inviting pod.

"I'll try one," Wyoming says. She plucks one off the tree and takes a bite, pretending to enjoy it until she spits it out.

"What if it's poisonous?" I say, laughing.

"I guess we'll find out!"

Wyoming takes a break in the shade of a Joshua Tree

There are some buildings ahead and kennels with dozens of dogs. "Those sure look like wolves," I say as we walk past. A lady is working outside and Wyoming walks over to the fence.

"Can we see your dogs?" she asks. The lady is very friendly and gives us a tour. She explains that they are 97% wolf. She takes us into a pen to see a giant white male, well over 100 pounds. I am glad he is friendly. Outside, the lady hands Wyoming a tiny wolf puppy. Wyoming coos as she holds the soft, innocent-looking little puppy against her face.

At about 3:00 we reach tiny Cottonwood Creek. There is a spigot for water, the first water in 16 miles. Although we've come only 17 miles today we are well ahead of schedule for getting to the snowy Sierra. There is water here and nice campsites amongst the Joshua Trees. We decide to camp early. Every passing hiker stops and it's a mini-reunion. Assface, Jaybird, Green Mile, Redhead. And Mr. T. We joke around and cook dinner together. It's typical hiker fare and includes instant potatoes, Knorr's Sides (primarily pasta or rice or a combination thereof), cheese, tortillas, peanut butter, ramen. The fanciest cooking involves boiling water. Most of us are using tiny alcohol stoves.

It's cool and cloudy in the morning. Ahead, the trail winds far across the desert flats towards the distant Tehachapi Mountains. In the midst of a long 3,000-foot climb, the temperature drops even more, a breeze rises, and a cold mist begins to fall. During a brief, chilled break Wyoming consults her guidebook.

"What's it say?" I ask.

She pretends to read... "At the top, right next to the trail, is a McDonald's!" I laugh. Climbing again, she talks about what she's going to order at this mythical oasis, starting off with a large cup of hot coffee.

We are near the road. Wyoming has a package in Tehachapi, I have a package in Mojave. I decide to go into Mojave this evening. Wyoming elects to camp here. Out at the road, I make a *MOJAVE* sign and pick a strategic spot. It takes a while, but a pickup finally pulls over. The driver works in security for the wind farms in the area. I ask him some questions, like why are so many turbines not working, how much electricity do they produce, things like that. Surprisingly, he has no answers. Chief Daddy and Cloudbuster are hiking along the road and put their thumbs out, but my driver isn't interested in giving them a ride. It's his choice, but those two look crestfallen as we zoom past.

I thank the driver and walk over to Motel 6. Thru-hikers usually split a room to save on costs, and Assface said he'd be staying here if I wanted to split a room. I walk up to the desk.

"Did you have a hiker with a white hat check in here today?"

"I think so. What's his name?"

Hmmm. He probably didn't register as "Assface," and I am clueless on his real name.

"Sorry, I don't know."

The clerk calls the room of the hiker who she thinks must be him.

"What's your name?" I hear her ask, then she turns to me. "He says his name is 'Face'."

I get his room number and he gives me a beer and we talk about our day. He didn't know if I was going to make it to town so he just paid for a single, so I rent my own room. At the library, I'm given limited time on the computer and rush through my most important emails and update my blog online. We have a fine dinner at the restaurant. Before bed, I call Stephanie. She is feeling down again which makes my spirits sag.

In the morning I resupply at the grocery store then walk to the post office where I pick up a package. It has my new guidebook for the next section and a few other miscellaneous supplies for the next section. I sort through my pack, throw away trash, and mail my used guidebook home.

Back on the trail, the wind is howling! The trail passes rows of wind turbines, hundreds and hundreds of them. It's very scenic in its own way, like a garden of whirling flowers. The wind staggers me repeatedly and my rain jacket hood and bits of loose material on my clothing and pack flaps wildly. When a piece of hood drawcord gets loose it rapidly whips my face so hard it hurts. I am alternately laughing and cursing. I hold my camera at arms-length to record myself describing the madness. When I play it back the wind is so loud I can't hear a single word I've said.

The wind slackens when the trail leaves the ridgetop. I haven't seen Wyoming's tracks so I know she's behind me. I take my time. Late in the day I look behind me and see her hustling down a series of switchbacks. Even from a distance, I can see her smiling. She had a quick hitch into town this morning and a Trail Angel gave her a ride back to the trail. Total strangers bought her breakfast. We'd been teasing each other about which would be the best town for our mail drops. I begin making up wild stories about Mojave's scenic splendor and the astounding generosity bestowed upon me there.

May 30, Day 40

Today we passed the 600-mile mark. The miles and days are passing swiftly. Like most hiking partners one or the other of us is often hiking a few hundred yards ahead or behind the other. Wyoming often listens to her little radio and passes the news on to me. I often listen to my MP3 player. I try to carry key items in consistent locations. My MP3 player/radio goes in my shirt pocket but I notice it's missing. I search everywhere and try to think where I might have left it. I can picture the spot. Although I always check before leaving a break spot I must have missed it. Before heading back I go through everything one last time. Two other hikers show up and I tell them to let Wyoming know I went back to find it. I know she will stop at the spring just ahead. Thru-hikers hate to backtrack. I am definitely no exception, but I have an audio journal and all my music on it. I suck it up and walk back three miles, until I find the spot. I search around and am relieved to find it, a small black device, partially hidden beneath pine needles. If it had been some bright color

I likely wouldn't have overlooked it before. Regardless, an hour later I rejoin Wyoming at the spring. My error costs me over two hours and six miles of extra walking.

We are cruising along the trail together when a loud buzzing startles us. A rattlesnake stands up high on its coils, rattling furiously, its tongue flickering out. I've never seen one act so aggressive. We snap a few photos from a safe distance and circle cautiously around him.

A coiled rattlesnake rattles angrily at us

There have been long stretches without water so we are keeping careful track of how much we have and how far it is to the next source. Caches placed by Trail Angels are wonderful, but not dependable, so there's always a risk-benefit analysis. How much more effort will it be to carry the extra water "just in case," versus the consequences of running out and having to push to the next source? Wyoming is more conservative. I carry a little less water. Tonight we are pushing for Bird Springs Pass where we hope to find a water cache. If it's empty, it's seven more miles to the next source which would make it a 31-mile day. Cliffhanger and Milk Sheik, a couple from Brooklyn, catch up to us with the same goal in mind. I watch as Milk Sheik reaches Bird Springs first. He raises his arms in triumph. Water! We take a break together then search out campsites to escape the strong wind. I find a fine, flat spot with pinyons providing a safe harbor from the gale.

The days are flowing by. We hike through desert and trees, across flats and up and down steep mountains. Occasionally we can see the snow-covered Sierra in the distance. At one pass we hitch into Onyx with a maniac driver. At the little store, I buy a half-gallon of ice cream while Wyoming chooses Captain Crunch and a cold beer. Sunshine and Grateful left just minutes ago. Drat. They are from Oregon and had given me the idea to do a "flip" to Ashland, Oregon and hike south, giving the highest Sierra more time to melt. I'd been hoping they had some recent intel on the snow levels in northern Cal. (In recent years social media has made information like snow levels much easier to find.)

Hitching a ride back is tough. A pickup heading the wrong direction pulls over. It is Just Tom, a Trail Angel from Kennedy Meadows. He turns around and drives us all the way back to the pass! He tells us that he has left a cooler with Subway sandwiches and other Trail Magic. I am already hungry again. Wyoming thinks we should leave the sandwiches because we've just been in town. I think that other hikers can hitch into town, too, if they like, and we are hikers and we are hungry. We compromise and split a sandwich.

Heading back to the trail in the morning we see scattered trash. A bear has gotten into the cooler and eaten virtually everything. There are going to be many sad hikers when they see this. We gather the trash and leave a note suggesting no more food be left here since there is a problem bear.

We hike through the Owens Peak Wilderness and the Chimney Rock Wilderness. For a whole day, we don't see another soul except for one other. On another day we hike for miles with Milk Sheik and Cliffhanger. I am walking ahead of everyone in a remote area on a baking hot day. I take a stick and write, *ICE CREAM, 1/4 MILE.* Cliffhanger later says that although she knew it couldn't be true she was still disappointed to find out it wasn't.

June 6, Day 47. Mile 706; 1,950 Miles to Canada

It's exciting to be walking through the pines and sage along the South Fork of the Kern River. Kennedy Meadows is a major landmark along the trail and a big decision point. Ahead is the snowy Sierra. There are three options I'm mulling over:

1) Wait here for a few days giving the snow a little more time to melt.
2) Head straight into the Sierra tomorrow.
3) "Flip" up to Ashland, hike SOBO (south) back here, then head back to Ashland to complete the hike.

Veteran hikers usually try to leave Kennedy Meadows after June 15. We are early, and this is one of the biggest snow years ever. It will be really tough for me to sit around and wait for snow to melt, but hundreds of miles of deep snow do not appeal to me. Barring some new information, I'll probably flip to Ashland.

There must be twenty hikers here, if not more. We set our packs down at the picnic tables and take a seat, angering the grill cook. She orders us to remove our packs from the porch.

Inside they are welcoming and quickly locate our packages for us. I have a replacement ice axe waiting. And a bear canister, which is a strong bear-proof plastic cylinder required on the trail ahead. We pay for hot showers and laundry. After we are all cleaned up I order a burger from the grumpy cook. It's awesome!

I call Stephanie from the pay phone. She has been having a tough time in Anchorage: a new town, a new job, worried about her cat, lost and scared in a strange city. Part of me dreads calling her because every time I've talked to her recently it's been almost all distressing news. My excitement to share my adventure is squelched by her stress and unhappiness. Stephanie and I have alternately been best friends, or a couple, for many years. Her struggle to be happy is a serious strain on our relationship. But I know she can't help it. We've had so many fun times camping and boating and fishing and hiking! If only she could be happy.

Tom's place is an Airstream trailer and hiker hang-out at Kennedy Meadows. Tom, is "Just Tom," the guy who gave us a ride a few days ago. I use one of his computers to answer email, do a little business from the real world, update my website and try to research snow levels. The latter proves difficult. All the hikers are talking about the deep snow in the Sierra. MeGaTex, a team of hiking pals established on the Appalachian Trail, is planning on forging ahead soon. Others seem undecided. Swift and Buckeye, a young couple, are planning to head into the snows as well, but are stressed because some of their mail hasn't arrived. I've decided to flip to Ashland.

Since I have a canister and ice axe I don't need yet, and they do, we make a mutually beneficial deal: they can use my stuff until Echo Lake and leave it there. When I get to Echo Lake SOBO I'll pick it up just before I need it.

Wyoming and I have a talk. She likes the Ashland plan but I warn her that I will end up hiking on my own because I am primarily a solo hiker. It's my style. We've gotten along exceptionally well, but I'm concerned that if she comes with me she will inevitably end up hiking hundreds of miles on her own. Nonetheless, she wants to go.

SOUTHBOUND

"A venturesome minority will always be eager to set off on their own, and no obstacles should be placed in their path; let them take risks, for godsake, let them get lost, sunburnt, stranded, drowned, eaten by bears, buried alive under avalanches – that is the right and privilege of any free American."

— Edward Abbey, *Desert Solitaire*

There is no public transportation north from Kennedy Meadows so we will hitch. I talk to a local fellow who hangs out in front of the store. He agrees to drive us down to the highway in the morning for $20.

It is a steep, winding descent with few or no guard rails. It's easy to imagine a tire blowing out and plummeting to our deaths. The concern is exacerbated by our driver zooming around the corners, accompanied by audible gasps from Wyoming in the back.

Delighted with our survival we are soon standing along a desert highway with a *MAMMOTH LAKES* sign in hand. It's still early in the morning and nice and cool. A car turns off the road we've just come down and pulls over for us. It's Passant's mom! Passant is a chess whiz and Darko is his thru-hiking partner and girlfriend. Passant's mom brings us to the beautiful little town of Lone Pine.

Hitching to Mammoth, on Highway 395 below Kennedy Meadows

Our next ride is from a butcher and the next a climber and finally an ultramarathoner heading for Reno. He is knowledgeable and interesting, telling us all about the land we were passing through. He drops us near some motels. We choose one. It is a dump. The rooms are spacious but shoddy and the clientele is sketchy. We stand on the balcony looking over the courtyard and the windows of the opposite rooms. "This is the kind of place where you'd see somebody's bare butt in about five minutes," I say. The words have barely left my mouth when an obese naked guy appears at a window.

In the morning we take a city bus back to 395 and pick the most strategic hitching spot. We make awesome signs: one says *SUSANVILLE*, another *PACIFIC CREST TRAIL, NORTH*. But after several hours: no luck. We are stuck. After discussing our options, we head back into town and buy tickets for the Medford bus. It leaves in the evening. With time to kill we get something to eat then check out the casinos. I am not a casino guy, so I go see a movie then watch people on kayaks and inner tubes go through the rapids on the Truckee River.

It's a wearying all-night bus ride with a cast of Greyhound characters but we make it to Medford without incident. We grab breakfast at Bad Ass Coffee, buy some groceries, then walk to the post office to mail off supplies and to rearrange our resupply plan. Wyoming is either smarter than I am or more organized or both, because she gets things sorted out faster than I do. We are hiking hundreds of miles in the opposite direction from what we've planned so we'll need our supplies in the reverse order. I mail the guidebook and associated info I have now to South Lake Tahoe. My package that was to go to South Lake Tahoe is now going to Seiad Valley. Used trail info and unneeded supplies I mail home.

We find the bus to Ashland, and from Ashland it's a pretty easy hitch up to the trail. It is so nice to be back on the trail! It's green and lush with many colossal trees. The trail hasn't been maintained for months so there are huge trees lying across it in places. I don't have decent maps until we get to Seiad Valley, about sixty miles. Luckily we soon meet some people out for a weekend hike and they, very kindly, agree to cache some maps at a road crossing ahead! I roll out my pad and sleeping bag beneath a tree in a green meadow and quickly fall asleep. I awaken to the sound of animals grazing nearby. Deer go bounding off when I sit up.

Today we make good time but hit significant snow around 6,000 feet. When the buried trail parallels a closed road we walk the road for a way. Wyoming finds a rickety aluminum lawn chair and packs it along for a joke as it is the antithesis of lightweight thru-hiking. Our feet are soaked from wet snow. With no fire danger, we make a nice campfire when we camp. Wyoming is smiling as she relaxes on her nice lawn chair, warming her feet next to the crackling fire.

In the morning I crawl out of my shelter into a foggy world of wind, drizzle, and snow. My heart sinks. The point of our "flip" was to avoid most of the deep snow but today we're going to have plenty. Did we jump from the frying pan into the fire? We've just started walking and see fresh bear tracks. I take a photo of Wyoming's hand next to a muddy footprint on the snow. With all the snow and the trail so difficult to follow we begin to make up our own route. We hike cross-country or walk down stretches of snowy logging roads. From a high vantage point, I spot something on a sunny hillside below. I pull my monocular out of my shirt pocket and see that they are elk, the first of the trip. They go loping off when they realize they've been spotted.

Wyoming and I are swapping stories, trudging down a snowy road.

"One time I was floating a river in Alaska, maybe three hundred miles from the nearest road," I am saying. "When I see something at the edge of the water, and it's a full, sealed bottle of whiskey!"

"Really?" she says, amazed. Just then I look down and see a full can of beer sticking out of the snow! I present it to Wyoming and pick up another for myself. She finds a third. What an astounding coincidence!

We reach a wooden sign bolted onto a tree: *OREGON/ CALIFORNIA*. We sign the register located in a metal box. It comes as no surprise that we are the first thru-hikers of the year. After enjoying some snow-free trail we set up camp in a pleasant spot. I pull out my alcohol stove and boil up some water and add it to some rice and chicken to soak. Wyoming makes some mac and cheese. At 6 PM I crawl into my bag and close my eyes.

During the night I hear the hiss of snow on the silnylon of my shelter. I reach up and tap it and hear snow sliding down onto the ground. Towards morning when the light begins to gray I slip on my shoes, put on my jacket and hat, unzip the tent door and step outside. About 2 inches of clean white snow covers the ground and trees and bushes with more snow sifting down. I take a few steps away from my tent to pee then walk back. I grab the tent pole and gave it a shake and most of the snow slides off. It is June 10.

"Hey Wyoming, are you awake?"

"Yeah."

"We've got a couple inches of new snow."

"Yeah, I thought I heard it snowing last night."

I hear her rustling around in her tent. Pretty soon the top of her sherpa hat appears as she crawls out of her tent. She looks around and then looks at me.

"How much do you think it will snow?"

"I don't know. Hopefully it will quit soon. Guess we'll just have to start walking and see how it goes."

We eat a little breakfast as we pack, then head down the trail. At this altitude, we are in the clouds and back into some serious snowpack from last winter. We slog along in the clouds. Snow swirls down in a tunnel of dark trees. It is damp and chilly and eerie. It would be an easy day to become disoriented.

The trail is completely buried in snow now and there are few if any blazes or other indications of where the trail is heading. I look ahead along an opening in the trees. It might be where the trail is, or just a random opening. I stop and pull out my guidebook. Wyoming is already looking at hers.

"Well, the trail should be running roughly southwest," she said.

I glance at my wrist compass. "That's kind of what we've been doing, but I can't tell for sure if this is the trail or not. What do you think?"

"Seems like it might be, but I can't tell either."

"Let's just keep going and pay attention to what direction we're heading and eventually we'll be able to figure it out for sure. One way or another it won't kill us if we lose the trail for a while. We've got everything we need on our backs."

We continue slowly contouring across and up a mountainside. The trees thin until there are just patches of trees on the snowy mountainside, so we can no longer pick out "lanes" in them that might indicate trail. The clouds and snow limit our field of view to only a few hundred yards, making navigation much more difficult. Occasionally we see a sawn-off log or other sign that we are on the trail, but finally we are unable to spot any clues where the trail might be.

Getting out our maps we talk it over. Wyoming points at her guidebook map. "We must be about here somewhere. We camped about there, right?"

I look where she is pointing. "That's mighty close. I think you're right. We've been heading mostly southwest. We've walked about two hours, so under these conditions we've likely come about three-and-a-half miles or so. How about we just say to hell with the trail and continue climbing up and across the hillside until we make the main ridgetop? That's where the trail's heading and when we get there we can just follow the main ridge until we find the trail."

"Sounds good to me."

After another hour we were on top of a ridge. "Hey, Colter, do you think this is our ridge?"

"I'm pretty sure it is. It's heading in the right way, anyway. Hopefully it isn't a spur ridge. It would be nice if we could see a little ways. Guess we can just keep walking and make sure we are heading in the right direction."

It is cold and windy on top and we walk along in the clouds and blowing snow with our hands in our pockets. I am about 50 yards ahead with Wyoming following. Occasionally

I turn around to see if she is still with me. Ahead, I see a frosty sign. "Red Cow Camp," it says, with an arrow pointing west. I pull out my guidebook.

"We must be on the right ridge. I guess the trail is under our feet somewhere."

Huge mushroom-shaped boulders loom ahead of us. Around some of these boulders, and around many of the ridgetop trees, there are large wind-scoured depressions in the hardpack snow. The snow is 15 feet deep or more in places and in the flat light it is sometimes difficult to tell where the ground falls away. Despite the conditions, we are making pretty good time. Assuming we are going in the right direction.

The ridge appears to be turning. Studying our maps we make an educated guess where we are. The snow is still falling and visibility is severely limited. I'm not sure the exact definition of *blizzard*, but it seems that this might qualify.

Hiking in a snowstorm, north of Seiad Valley

"Maybe it's time we just bail off this ridge," I say. "It shouldn't take us too long to get below this deep snow and we should be able to hit one of the roads and figure out an alternate route into Seiad Valley."

"Sounds good to me. I wouldn't mind getting out of all this snow."

We drop off the ridge and are soon happy to find a sign on an old logging road showing we are exactly where we thought. Down the fall-line we hike, oftentimes using the slippery snow to "ski" a short distance. Occasionally we punch through into snow wells where the snow has melted around fallen trees, after which blowing snow has hidden the well. Still, it isn't long before there are patches of bare ground. I am feeling pretty happy with our decision.

As we descend there is less snow but it is wetter as the falling snow turns to a light rain. Our open mountainside is now a brushy ravine. The creek falls more sharply and the walls of the canyon grow steeper. We were forced to repeatedly wade across the creek to continue. I am concerned that we might get in a position where we hit a waterfall with no safe way to get down. We try contouring away from the rushing creek but a cliff pushes us back. Occasionally one of us slips but we always manage to catch ourselves before we get into trouble. The odor of crushed ferns mixes with the smell of the wet forest. A cliff meets the creek on our side. The creek is getting deeper and I am anxious to escape this gorge. We wade across again, and work our way up the hill on the opposite side. It appears that the hillside is flattening out a little bit. I can see signs of recent logging ahead. Logging means logging roads. Wyoming catches up to me and stands with her hands on her hips, soaking wet from head to toe and with the creek roaring below her.

She points ahead. "Doesn't that look like a road?"

We work our way over there and soon stand on an old logging road. It is a steep, lousy road but an absolute piece of cake compared to what we'd just come down. Following it downhill for a half mile we suddenly reach a gravel road. It is delightful to be back to some good walking.

"Want to stop for lunch?" Wyoming asks.

"You know what, I'd like to, but I'm too chilled. How about we motor down this road for a while until we're all warmed up?"

The sun actually starts to show through the clouds a bit, and the rain stops. Just as we decide to eat we come upon a pickup. A guy is inside is a timber cruiser eating lunch. He shows us good maps of the logging roads. He is very familiar with the area and we discuss options for walking into town.

We thank him and leave. Using a copy of his maps we began taking a shortcut down a series of logging roads. The upside is that this route should save us several miles. The downside is a common pitfall of many short-cuts: a significant possibility of confusion. We experience confusion aplenty. There are roads that aren't on the map. Other roads appear to have been renumbered. We are wasting so much time backtracking and trying to sort things out we decide to just head downhill until we hit the main road again.

That is a fine plan until we started hitting sizable patches of manzanita about 12 feet high. They have beautiful glossy-brown trunks but their intertwined branches drag at our feet and legs and packs. Extensive patches of poison oak mean that we had to choose whether to fight our way through the manzanita or brave the poison oak. When we finally stumble out on the gravel road the manzanita has claimed Wyoming's warm sherpa hat which had been drying on her pack.

We are now walking down a quiet backroad. Life is easy and the sun is out and it is a beautiful world. We walk past an old ranch house with a gorgeous wrap-around porch.

"Check out that place," I say. "I love those shady old porches."

Wyoming notices an older fellow working on the fence nearby. "We like your house! Especially your wrap-around porch," Wyoming says. She loves meeting people, especially people like this. Both Wyoming and I grew up on dairy farms.

"Thanks," he replies. "My wife really likes it. That's why we bought the place."

"Cool. How long have you lived here?" she asks. *Exactly what I was going to ask,* I think.

"Two weeks," he says.

I'm surprised. "That's funny. I figured you probably lived here for decades."

As we hike, large trees line the road, and wildflowers accent the rich green of the fields. A large piece of loose metal on a feeding trough creaks back and forth in the wind. A band of horses graze in a field. One watches us curiously.

A graceful arched wooden bridge suspended by steel cables spans the Klamath River. We clomp across, looking down into the clear water trying to spot fish. Fifty yards on the other side we hit the paved road. At a pull-off, we spread our gear to dry and relax in the warm sun. How quickly things can change.

In a few miles, we hike up a logging road and camp along a creek. The snowy ridgetops, 5,000 feet above us, high in the clouds, are just hours and a few miles away, but it seems like a different world. I sleep well.

It's an easy walk along the beautiful Klamath River this morning, past beautiful trees and with eagles soaring above us. An old miner invites us to coffee at his camp. At about noon we hike into Seiad Valley. We get lunch at the cafe and then walk to a campground. The owner is very hiker friendly and shows us around. He is wearing a T-shirt that says "F#@$ the_____" [some local organization he is butting heads with]. I get a shower and we run a load of laundry and watch Schindler's List, which Wyoming hasn't seen. When I pull my clothes out of the drier I find a couple of big holes melted in my nylon hiking shirt. My only shirt. (I end up wearing the duct-tape repaired shirt for the rest of the hike.)

When I run across the campground owner I am reluctant to bring up my shirt but I want to save the same drier disaster from happening to other people.

"Just so you know, that drier is running awfully hot. It melted holes in my shirt."

"Yeah, I hear that a lot," he says.

In the morning we have a breakfast feast but pass on the Pancake Challenge. In the infamous Challenge you get five truly giant one-inch-thick pancakes for $16, and if you can eat them in two hours they are free. Only a few people in history have been successful. To me, it kinda seems like you lose even if you win.

The waitress explains the "State of Jefferson" sign on the post office. Independent thinkers had once dreamt of creating a new state, Jefferson, encompassing southern Oregon and Northern California. They felt a greater affinity for their region than for their state. The idea is still popular, more in spirit than pragmatically.

Today the campground owner is wearing a different shirt. This one says "F#@$ the_____" [some other local organization]. I was hoping to receive my GPS in the mail before we leave here, but it won't make it in time. At the post office, I fill out a forwarding order to have it sent to Etna instead.

A few miles out of town we miss a key turn which adds three or four frustrating miles. Most of the footbridges have been chewed on by black bears. A big blacktail buck bounds nearby. We make a pleasant camp next to a creek. Wyoming shows me how to use a slow shutter speed to get some of those blurred, milky-white shots of nearby rapids. I find a couple of wood ticks crawling up my legs and Wyoming shudders when she finds one on herself as well. Wyoming tries to teach me cribbage but to her chagrin, I'm simply not interested.

June 13

We are climbing steadily, into the Marble Mountain Wilderness and back into the snow. There is some clear trail but most of it is buried. If it wasn't clear to us before, it certainly is now: we will be dealing with significant deep snow despite our "flip" to Oregon. We are learning to not worry about the actual trail when we lose it, but to just use the map to follow the lay of the land along the route. All this snow is somewhat disheartening, but our spirits are good as we stop for lunch. In the warm sun in a snow-free meadow, we admire an incredible view of a rocky peak appropriately named King's Castle.

On a snow-free trail a person can let their mind wander if they are hiking alone, or talk to a hiking partner if walking together. This is much less relaxing. To follow a map efficiently it's important to stay oriented, to identify landmarks, to be aware of time and to estimate distances. I'm an experienced map reader but Wyoming seems to have a natural knack for it. It's nice to share the burden of navigation.

We stand on a ridgetop looking at our maps.

"Where do you think the trail goes from here?" Wyoming says, looking at a snowy drainage ahead of us.

"The map shows it basically contouring along the side-hill."

"Yup."

"How about we just shoot for that clump of trees?"

"Sounds good to me."

We are crossing many steep snowy hillsides where we have to pick our steps carefully. We've been seeing numerous bear tracks and I watch the snow-free hillsides. Finally, I see a small black dot moving.

"There's a bear!" I say, pointing.

"Are you sure?" Wyoming says, skeptical.

"Yup, it's a black dot, and it's moving around." I pull out my monocular and we take a look. Cool!

Wyoming pauses to catch her breath after the long climb to Jumpoff Ridge

Above us lies Jumpoff Ridge. We've dropped far downhill to avoid walking a steep hillside for a couple miles. It is a long, steep, tiring climb, where we are concerned about falling and sliding out of control back down the steep mountainside. I try to weave back and forth, staying near trees that we can use for handholds, and to stay above trees that might be used to stop a short slide down the slope. Wyoming is tense, I can tell. I am, too. Near the top, we pause before our last push over an even steeper snow cornice. Wyoming's face is flushed from the physical and mental struggle of the day along with the bright sun reflecting off the snow. She has been a real trooper.

At last, we reach the ridge top, and we walk along looking for a good campsite. Just ahead a bear comes charging out of the brush!!! It sprints across the trail and disappears over the steep ridge to our right. Wow! We chatter excitedly about our dramatic sighting.

In late afternoon we find decent snow-free spots with some bushes to partially protect us from wind. In every direction are breathtaking views of the snowy Marble Mountain Wilderness. From our sleeping bags we watch the warm alpine-glow of sunset on Black Mountain, looming high above us.

It's 6:30 in the morning. We've already been walking for an hour. It looks like it will be a nice, sunny day. We are hiking over a little rise... BEAR! Right ahead of us! A large, beautiful, cinnamon-brown black bear. We have time to take several photos before he ambles away.

Ahead we see the roof of Marble Valley Guard station and are surprised to find a young couple there, the first people we've seen in a couple of days. They are super nice. Wyoming and I have been considering walking lower trails but are concerned about water levels of the creeks we'd have to cross. They tell us they've done many creek crossing in the area and haven't had any problems. Wyoming and I decide to take a lower route on the east side of the divide.

Most of what little bare ground there is consists of beautiful gray marble rock which gives this wilderness its name. After some easy scrambling, we find ourselves working our way up the last few-hundred feet below the main ridge. If we slip in the wrong place we could easily build up enough speed in an out-of-control slide to hurt ourselves badly. Two people adds some measure of safety in one sense: one could go for help for the other, but it also, in another sense, doubles the odds of someone getting hurt. With more than one person in a party, there is often someone who feels pressure to do things outside their comfort zone. And it's wise to consider that little voice that says, *is this foolish?*

Reaching the top, at last, we find where our alternate trail bails off the other side, buried under more snow. After a long descent, we are finally rewarded with some patches of clear trail. Then, we are happily walking down actual dirt of an obvious trail. Yahoo!

We descend steadily along the Wooley Creek Trail. Somewhere up ahead we have to ford this creek. It looks deep, fast and cold. Nearing the ford we begin watching carefully for good alternates, where the creek is shallow or has logs across it. It doesn't look good.

"What do you think?" Wyoming says, pondering the crossing. "I don't like it. It looks too deep and too fast. And there's that little waterfall just below us. If we fall it's not going to be good."

"How about that spot just upstream?" We walk up there, and it definitely looks better. Wyoming is getting ready to cross.

"I'm going to double-bag all my important stuff," I say, trying to stall her a little.

"OK."

"Have you done many river crossings?"

"In Alaska I've done a bunch." The water swirls around her calves and then her thighs. Halfway across she begins to lose her footing then she is suddenly in the water, being swept downstream. I sprint downstream to the main crossing, hoping to grab her as she passes if she can't regain her feet. I don't see her. I look upstream and downstream desperately trying to see her.

"Wyoming!" I yell, sick with dread. If she got past here, she went over the waterfall, and…

"Wyoming!"

"Colter!" Wyoming comes stumbling out of the brush just upstream from me, streaming ice-cold water and shivering.

"Are you all right!?"

"Yeah. Just a little shaken up."

I help her with her gear and we build a fire. Her camera and radio are ruined, but so what, compared to her life? Luckily her sleeping bag didn't get too wet. I help her build a fire and give her some privacy as she dries her clothes. I try the crossing and make it without too much trouble. Thirty more pounds makes a big difference at holding me down to the creek bottom. Later I bring her my down jacket and we sit looking into the flames of the warm fire.

"That was scary," I say.

"Yeah."

"If you had gone over that waterfall…"

"Let's not talk about it."

"Okay. The creek should be quite a bit lower in the morning after a cold night. Tomorrow it might be doable."

"I hope so." I mark the water level with a stick.

In the morning I check my stick. I can't believe it.

"It might have actually risen a little," Wyoming says. She's right.

We talk about it. If I was alone, I'd continue on with our plan or go back up and walk the general route of the PCT all the way to Etna Summit. Wyoming is more spooked by the steep snow than I am, but not without reason. Our river crossing experience didn't boost her confidence. Looking at the map it makes sense to backtrack most of today. We can go back up over the top and take another trail down to a trailhead, then road-walk into Etna tomorrow.

As usual when I pack up to leave I take a quick look around to make sure I haven't left anything. Just as I turn to leave I notice something: a round gray stuff sack among the round gray rocks. My tent! That was a near miss and another reminder that things like stuff sacks and knives should be bright colored.

With some resignation, we start making the long climb we came down yesterday. It's about 4,000 vertical feet! Not only that, but we will end up hiking all day in the wrong direction. It's dispiriting. Nevertheless, it has to be done.

We are pretty quiet at first, but then we discuss our plans after Etna. I want to climb back up into the mountains after Etna, and Wyoming wants to stay lower for a while. She'll be safer if she stays lower, I'll be happier if I play it by ear. It's hard talking about splitting up our hiking team.

Finally, I say, "Man, what are people going to think if they hear that we headed north together, and I left you all alone? What if something happens to you?"

"They won't say that. We talked about it. Nothing will happen, and it wouldn't be your fault anyway."

As usual, she's a trooper. No blame, no arguing, not trying to lay a guilt trip on me, both of us agreeing that it's for the best. It still makes us unhappy.

The trail is easy except for one spot where an avalanche has swept down a drainage creating a jumble of jack-strawed trees and boulders. We make even better progress when we hit the trailhead and road and by late afternoon make it to Indian Scotty Campground. We find a fine campsite above the river. It's nice to be out of the snow.

June 16, Day 57

It's a day of road walking. Some people hate it, but with roads like this, without much traffic, I don't mind it. There's different scenery, and I like winging it without a guidebook

97

sometimes. A lady out running stops and is incredulous that we are walking another 20 miles yet today to get to Etna.

We continue on past cattle and horses and mules. I stop to take a photo of a cool airy old hay barn, one end open and the other with 2-inch gaps between the vertical planks. We walk through the tiny town of Mugginsville and stop at the Greenview store for lunch (a half-gallon of Cookies and Cream for me!) and sit at the picnic table in the shade to eat.

In the outskirts of Etna, a driver leans out the window. "Are you two thru-hikers?"

"Yes."

"All right! First hikers of the year!" He drives off giving us a thumbs up.

At the post office, I am stoked to find my GPS has arrived. We find a restaurant where I order a taco salad. Wyoming heads to the little microbrew pub and I head for the Hiker's Hut. They are also happy to see the first hiker of the year. Wyoming and I will have the place to ourselves. I take a nice hot shower then use their computer to catch up on email and my online journal.

June 17, Day 56

This is such a nice place we decide to zero here. The gracious folks who own the Hiker's Hut live next door and generously offer to share a big, delicious breakfast. They ask us not to tell our fellow hikers because it's not part of the standard hiker rate.

Wyoming has made friends with the owners of the Etna Brewery, where we eat lunch. They give us a tour of the brewing operation which is really interesting. Furthermore, they are gold miners, and introduce us to their dog, who is recovering from a rattler bite!

There is no Forest Service Office in town but the Fort Jones office kindly offers to send some forest maps with an employee that lives in Etna. She meets me at the Hiker Hut after work. I find it extremely interesting that she only brought up having hiked the whole PCT herself after I specifically ask about the trail! Most former thru-hikers love to "talk trail."

Wyoming and I watch *Coal Miner's Daughter* back at the hostel. Later, she fiddles with her phone, camera, and radio, which have taken a beating from her near miss in the creek. She philosophically points out again that they are nothing compared to what might have happened.

June 18

Today we head our separate ways. Wyoming nearly forgets her map case but fortunately notices before it's too late.

"I'll miss you, Colter."

"I'll miss you, too, Wyoming. Hey, stay safe. I'll see you down the trail somewhere. How about this: if you think you're ahead of me, scratch 'CO' for Colter in the trail, and if I think I'm ahead of you I'll scratch 'WY.' Then maybe we can leave a note with the date and time or give each other updates."

"Sounds good."

We exchange a hug and I watch as she walks off down the street. These few hundred miles are the longest I've hiked with someone.

I've studied the Forest map and, to avoid a long detour, decide to walk a side road to Callahan and return to the trail from there. I enjoy walking this quiet road through ranch country. At one field two huge old workhorses walk with me, curious and friendly, just on the other side of the fence.

Callahan has seen better days but has character and a tiny store. When I use the bathroom, the wall is covered with names. I am amazed when I recognize one name, then several more, all from one of the Alaska Hotshot crews. They must have been working on a fire nearby. Small world!

From Callahan, I climb and climb. Late in the day, I stop for photos of beautiful scarlet snowplant flowers. I camp for the night on a nice flat bed of dry pine needles, alone on the trail again.

In the morning I leave the back roads and enter the Trinity Alps Wilderness. At first there is a clear hiking trail but then there is more and more snow. I ignore the trail and use the map to follow the lay-of-the-land, climbing to return to the PCT, still far above me. At times it is so steep that I zigzag trying to link exposed vegetation or bare rock to minimize the odds of sliding back downhill.

By 9:00 AM it is a world of rock, trees, and snow. I reach the shore of a lake that is several hundred yards across. After evaluating the snow-covered ice, I head straight across. As a life-long northerner, it seems strange to be walking across a frozen lake in California on June 19!

Crossing a frozen lake, Trinity Alps, June 19

I stop for a break in a melted-out spot. Despite the snow, the sun is warm and the log and ground around me are dry. With my tiny Swiss army knife I slice off cheese which I eat with crackers while admiring the scenery.

After hours of climbing I reach the main ridge and stand astride the hidden Pacific Crest Trail, several feet beneath the untracked snow. The view is amazing. To the east, I see what must be the Castle Crags Wilderness. It seems likely that I am the only hiker in the Trinity Alps Wilderness right now. It is a lonely scene. It makes me happy.

Where's my knife? It isn't clipped to its usual spot. It doesn't take long to confirm that it's lying somewhere on the ground back at the break spot where it shall remain. I don't know how I missed its red handle when I got up to go, but I did. Rats!

Since the trail is of no practical use right now, I decide to just wing it until I reach Castella, where the PCT crosses Interstate 5 near a little store. The stress of navigating is almost completely erased. It's easy to follow the route when the route is of your own choosing. From high spots like this reading the map is pretty easy, and if somehow I were to become totally confused, my GPS will straighten me out.

Hiker tracks! Nope, bear tracks. That's the second time today. With the long views, I'm surprised to not see any of the bears making them.

This evening I'm camped tucked back in the trees near Castleton. The mosquitoes were fierce as I set up. Sure is nice to have a netted shelter! I've resupplied from the little store here. In Etna I got an email from Cliffhanger, her and Milk Sheik started their flip from this point, headed south. They are likely about three days ahead of me. Whether Wyoming is ahead or behind is hard to say. With any luck, I should be able to stick closer to the trail most of the time from here on out.

June 21

It's the first day of summer and day 62 on the trail. Not much snow today, but dozens if not hundreds of trees have fallen across the trail in the preceding months. That's one disadvantage of hiking through an area early in the season: most of the work is done by volunteers and they can't be everywhere at once. Usually, the downfall is not a big deal and is easy to step around or over. Other trees are huge, or there is a tangle of several, and that can be a significant hassle. Still, there are long stretches of bare trail and easy cruising. I'm getting some epic views of the white cone of Mt. Shasta rising out of the dark green trees.

There is so much more wildlife here than in southern California. It's now common to see deer. The sound of calling quail is part of the soundtrack of the trail. One morning I heard something ahead and stopped to watch. A blacktail doe stepped out on the trail and looked back. Moments later a tiny spotted fawn stepped out and carefully watched his footsteps as he worked his way down the hill, closely followed by an identical sibling. There are now many mosquitoes at times, mostly in the evenings, along with an assortment of flies and gnats and bees. Not much of a bother for me, though.

A brown phase black bear boldly approaches my camp

This evening I'm camped below the trail. It's good to be in my sleeping bag after crawling over all that deadfall. Light is fading. What's that noise? It sounds heavy. I crawl out of my tent. A large, brown-phase black bear is working his way downhill towards me. We make eye contact. He is unfazed and continues to roll logs and knock apart rotten stumps looking for food, getting closer and closer.

"Hey, bear! *Scram!*" I yell. He is unfazed. I don't care for his bold attitude. I pick up some stones and sticks and wing them his way. He veers off slightly but circles around below my camp with missiles falling all around him. One finally connects with a dull thud. He hustles off and the forest is silent again.

June 24. 1,000 Miles Hiked; 1,656 Miles of Hiking to Canada

I've been hitting stretches of snow mixed with clear trail. There has been only one marginal spot, where the trail crosses a steep, north-facing hillside marked with two sets of tracks: Cliffhanger and Milk Sheik, no doubt. On one long, snowy ridge I notice a butterfly cross in the steady breeze, and then another and another. I look back the way I've come and against the backdrop of white snow I see a stream of hundreds of butterflies crossing by ones and twos and threes. A butterfly migration!

I reach the road at Lake Britton where I pause to watch the water roaring out the bottom of the dam, then walk on to Burney Falls. I haven't seen a hiker since Etna but now at Burney Falls there is a hum of activity. It's no surprise, the falls are truly beautiful. The sign says they are 129 feet tall, but that doesn't do them justice. In the center are two main cascades with a wide veil of smaller falls on each side, plummeting into a blue-green pool. The bright green vegetation contrasts perfectly.

From a distance, I spot what must be two thru-hikers. It's Psycho and Apricots, sorting their supplies at the picnic table. Other than Wyoming they are the first thru-hikers I've seen for nearly three weeks. They offer me a beer and we swap stories. They have exciting news: at Forester Pass, highest point on the PCT, Psycho proposed. They're engaged! I buy some expensive food at the store and get a much-appreciated hot shower at the campground. In the evening I hike just far enough to camp alone among the pines.

Beautiful Burney Falls

Ahead of me is Hat Creek Rim, with its reputation as one of the hottest, driest stretches on the entire PCT. But right now I'm walking along pretty Baum Lake. Fly fisherman make graceful, looping casts. Trout feeding on surface insects dot the lake with expanding rings. Honking geese paddle around and ospreys patrol by, looking down into the water for fish. When I cross the bridge at the old powerhouse an older gentleman watches his young grandson fish.

"Where are you headed?" he asks.

"I'm hiking the PCT."

"The PCT?"

"Yes, the Pacific Crest Trail."

He is amazed that I'm hiking the whole trail, and he had no idea this is on the route of the PCT, despite having fished here many times over the years.

I top off my water containers at the last brook and continue to crank out miles. Just before dark I reach a water cache, set out by generous Trail Angels, surely the salvation of many parched hikers. A latticework of shading dead brush forms a dome over two or three lawn chairs. In Styrofoam coolers are many jugs of water. Milk Sheik and Cliffhanger have signed the log. They tell of carrying sloshing water in their bear canister just in case this cache was empty.

I roll out my sleeping bag and pad a hundred yards away and then watch a spectacular, flaming orange sunset on a drifting layer of molten clouds.

A lunar eclipse is predicted for just after 3 AM tonight so I set my watch alarm and place it near my ear. A large ant scampers over my face and I brush it away. Another crawls up my leg. I quickly put up my netted shelter and am soon drifting off.

I'm sound asleep when my alarm goes off. I look up at the full moon and wait patiently. Soon a tiny bite of the moon disappears and then very, very slowly grows until, maybe an hour later, perhaps half the moon has fallen into shadow. The beautiful sunset followed by this magical eclipse have made this a memorable camp.

June 26, Day 67

It's warm, all right, but I've gotten an early start and the heat is perfectly bearable. Unseen quail call. I take some colorful photos of red Indian Paintbrush and unidentified yellow flowers against a dramatic backdrop of an impressive, snow-clad Mt. Lassen. People sometimes say photos "take you out of the moment," and I suppose they can at times, but I think they help me look for and appreciate beauty. When memory begins to fade these photos can help bring them back, as sharp and saturated as they are right now.

In the afternoon my guidebook shows the trail nearing Subway Cave. I love caves, so I veer over to check it out. What a contrast! From the heat and blazing sun, I descend into the cool blackness of the lava tube. My tiny LED light illuminates the route as I explore hundreds of yards to the other end. Literally a cool side trip!

I hike into Old Station and give the Heitmans a call and in a few minutes Dennis pulls up and whisks me to their house. Here it is a thru-hiker's dream. Laundry, showers, internet access, "hiker boxes" full of excess food and gear, a lawn for tents, even a treehouse to sleep in! Sugar Mama and Compass are also here.

I update my online journal and in the evening we are presented with an awesome meal including fresh fruit and veggies. What a treat!

The Heitmans and we hikers enjoy a fine, filling breakfast and then they give us a ride back to the trail. Compass and I hike together. Her pace is similar to mine and we spend the whole day hiking and talking. In the evening, we camp together.

June 28

It's no surprise, I suppose, that we are back into the snow with long stretches of trail completely buried. Often there are two sets of footprints but we don't know if they know where they are going! Still, there are occasional clues that we are still on the route.

"You're a good navigator," Compass says.

"Maybe. But Wyoming said that you got your trail name by using your compass to find the way in the first deep snow in Southern California."

"I guess that's true."

King's Creek is swollen with icy meltwater and I have that unsettled feeling I got the day Wyoming was swept away. I volunteer to check it out. Cold, fast water rushes around my upper thighs but I make it without incident. Compass follows, carefully setting her hiking poles with each step. We are relieved when the crossing is behind us.

Before noon we've arrived at the backcountry resort of Drakesbad. What an awesome place! Fine food, showers, a hot springs-fed pool, with a discount and warm welcome for hikers. I knew Compass's husband was meeting her here, what I didn't know is that his family owns Drakesbad!

We wash up and then soak in the warm pool with resort-provided swimwear. Next, we hang out at a shaded table waiting for her husband. He arrives right on schedule. That evening I sit at her family's table to enjoy a true feast and tell hiking stories with Compass. Our group is treated as VIPs, with her family owning the place and all. I am unaccustomed to that kind of treatment, but it's rather fun!

Compass is taking a zero with her husband in Drakesbad tomorrow. I set up my shelter at the nearby campground. A young couple next door is setting up their tent and they offer me a beer.

"Are you an Alaska Smokejumper?" he asks, looking at my cap.

"Yeah, I retired a couple years ago."

"My dad worked for the Alaska Fire Service for years."

It turns out I know his dad, and friends of mine were at his wedding a few days ago! A small world indeed.

Two blacktail bucks with large antlers are feeding in the meadow as I hike out this morning. The trail leads past the opaque and steaming waters of Boiling Springs Lake.

Later in the day I study my map and walk off-trail to see if I can find a warm spring. It takes some doing but I find a nearly perfect spot. A small waterfall of warm water plunges into a delightful little pool under a big leaning tree! I soak in luxury. This is the life. I love hot springs!

I've reached the road to Chester where there is a log to sit on and a hiker register. Inside is a note. "Piper's Mom" is offering hikers shuttles into town! I dig out my phone, call her number, and a cheerful voice tells me she'll be here in 20 minutes.

True to her word, a smiling lady pulls up and hops out. "You must be Colter."

Her daughter, Piper, hiked the PCT in recent years. The generosity shown to Piper was so inspirational that Piper's mom became a Trail Angel herself. Hence her trail name. She takes a quick photo of me, which she does with all her hikers, and we are on our way. She has just started her shuttles, and as matter of fact this is only her second one, the first was Milk Sheik and Cliffhanger.

She drops me off at the cafe. I have a large, leisurely meal in air-conditioned comfort. Later at the grocery store, I wander the aisles looking for appealing, calorie-laden food.

To save Piper's Mom the drive back I decide to hitch. I stand with my *HIKER TO TRAIL* sign and in minutes a car pulls over and soon I'm back on the trail.

As darkness nears I am looking for a camp spot but it's steep. As I thread my way over, under and around some fallen trees there is a flat spot of trail. I make it a policy to not camp right on the trail where animals often walk at night and where I might impede fellow hikers. I make an exception here, knowing that neither animals nor hikers are likely to show up at night in this tangle of trees. After setting up camp I check my cell phone. There is a good signal so I call Stephanie and we have a good talk. Then, I dig into my pack and unwrap my treasure, a half-gallon of softening Triple

Vanilla ice cream! I recline on my soft sleeping mat propped up by my down sleeping bag, secure from the bugs by my tent. In extravagant bliss, I eat spoon after spoon of some of the finest, richest ice cream I've ever enjoyed.

A half-gallon of Triple Vanilla ice cream. It's what's for dinner!

Neither man nor beast passed my tent last night. There's a gray post just ahead. In gold lettering is etched the following:

PCT MIDPOINT
CANADA 1325 MILES
MEXICO 1325 MILES

The mileage for the current trail might be a bit off but the sentiment is the same: this is, approximately, the halfway point. The significance is considerably lessened for me, though — for me, the mileage is nearer 1,100. I take the obligatory photo nonetheless. An hour later I take a non-obligatory photo of a weathered sign for "Butt Mountain," sure to amuse kids I know.

Today is Thursday, which, out in the woods, means little. But it is also July 1st. I come upon a stretch of trail with deep snow and no visible ground at all. The snow is hardpacked, though, and so the work comes from route-finding and making sure that I don't go sliding down a hill.

I find a radio station on my tiny radio and hear a song with the line "Daisy Dukes, bikinis..." something, something. The announcer says it's called "California Girls." First I've heard of it.

On the long descent to Belden, I am blocked by an enormous jumble of downfall. I have trouble finding where the trail exits the extensive and chaotic mess. It's so dreadfully difficult I have to laugh. At least it makes a good photo.

The PCT descends thousands of feet, out of the snow, all the way down to the heat along the Feather River and the road to Belden. The Braatens, Trail Angels, have a place nearby called Little Haven. I elect to walk the mile there to avoid calling them for a ride. The road is narrow and unsafe for walking. I should have called but I'm committed now as I walk along, watching for their place...

"Hey there, hiker, where are you headed?" I hear a voice say.

"Oh, just wandering around. Wondering if anyone will put me up for the night." Through the trees I see Wyoming wearing her Hawaiian shirt and beaming, standing next to a lady who can only be Brenda Braaten. They welcome me and Wyoming shows me around. She's had many adventures of her own and has also connected her steps all the way from Etna to this point.

I take a shower and we head down to the local store for a delicious deli sandwich. Tonight I'm sleeping in a comfortable bed in a private room. Nice!

In the morning Brenda is "cooking up a storm" as Wyoming says, bacon and eggs, home-fries, muffins, and apricot juice. The Braaten's are educated, religious, and very generous people.

Brenda drives us back to the trail. Wyoming starts hiking and I go to the post office to look for my package. It's here. I've got pages from Yogi's guide for the next section of trail, batteries, and trail food. I carefully go through my pack and the box. I sort out things that I don't need: old guidebook pages, extra batteries and excess food, an extra Platypus water bottle. I put together a USPS Flat Rate box and send it on to my buddy Griff, enclosing a note to hold it for now.

I walk across the bridge and into the tiny "town" of Belden. There has been, or is going to be, a music festival. These festivals have a reputation of being either an awesome party, or loud and obnoxious, depending on perspective. There are numerous young people showing considerably more style and skin than I am. I grab an ice cream bar at the store to fortify me for the 4,000+ foot climb ahead.

The trail is steep, and there is a hazardous stretch of snow, but it's steady going. A young family approaches me.

"Hey, do you know where Lost Lake is?"

"Sorry, I don't, I'd have to look at my maps."

"That's OK. We've got maps, we'll find it. Hey, are you Colter?"

"Yup."

"Your friend says she's planning on camping at Rock Lake."

"Thanks!"

I finally catch up to Wyoming and we hike together. In the evening she looks wistfully at a lake hundreds of feet below the trail.

"What do you think about camping there?"

"I'd like to camp there, but I don't really want to hike down there and back up tomorrow morning."

Instead, we find a nice flat spot just off the trail.

July 3

"I'll bet we see our first Northbounders today," Wyoming says at breakfast.

"Seems like it would have to be pretty soon, doesn't it?"

At the road, we decide to walk the loop to Buck's Lake. We follow it past nice cabins, the lake, a couple of lodges and a little store where we buy treats. Thru-hikers are loath to pass up food sources. Wyoming replaces her lost compass at one of the lodge stores.

There is a hum of activity at the fire hall where the fire department is having a pancake breakfast fundraiser. Sweet! We are welcomed, make our donation, and are soon enjoying pancakes, sausage, cantaloupe, and juice. The locals are friendly and curious about our hike. Before we leave town I buy a half-gallon of ice cream and share it with Wyoming. I'll bet we've each eaten 3,000 calories today and it's not even noon!

We arrive back at the trail just behind a large gaggle of Boy Scouts. We pass them, then they pass us, and we pass them again. Several lightly laden hikers are hustling down the trail towards us.

"There's your NOBOs, Wyoming!"

It's several young guys, including Wander, Dave (the fellow I hiked with the first day), Lakewood, Bojangles. It's obvious they are having fun pushing themselves and being in front of the pack. They've hiked straight through the Sierra.

"Hey, guys! How was it?"

"It was hard, but fun! Did you guys do a flip?"

"Yeah, up to Ashland. How's the snow ahead?"

"There's still plenty of snow but it's melting fast. How about north of here?"

"Same thing. But it will be nothing compared to what you've already come through, I'm sure."

Then off we go in our respective directions. It's good to have a first-hand report of conditions ahead of us.

The Boy Scouts have caught up. A few guys seem to be keeping their pace pretty easily but some are already struggling. Tomorrow there will be many blistered and disheartened Scouts. We end up trapped in the middle of the mob, not my cup of tea, but finally lose them when we take a long break to let them hike ahead.

We arrive at the Feather River and are relieved to find the Scouts aren't here. A frenzy of mosquitoes descend on us so we quickly set up our shelters, cook dinner, and fall asleep to the sound of the flowing river.

July 4, Day 75

From a beautiful wooden bridge, we look down to a rushing Feather River. Powerful water has swirled stones to grind round holes in the bedrock. Some of the stones are still in place, waiting for the river to rise to resume their work.

We've got a climb of maybe 3,000 feet ahead, so it's good to be starting early, in the cool of the morning. During our steady ascent, Wyoming looks down and spots a reddish salamander on the trail. We check him out then set him off the path and resume our long climb.

It's very warm today, which is great for melting the snow ahead of us, but Wyoming is getting short on water now that we've been on the trail for a few hours. She makes the long bushwhack down to, and the long climb back up from, a spring far below the trail. Just up the PCT, she is frustrated to learn that there is a nice trail to the spring.

It's about noon when we find a hiker that we know, sleeping right next to the trail. It's Crowdog. One good thing about thru-hiking is you can set any schedule you want: if you want to hike into the night and sleep until noon, go for it!

Down the trail, we stop to admire some especially pretty wildflowers — yellow, red, white, purple. When we reach the Quincy-LaPorte Road, we are both low on water and follow the road a quarter mile to a water source that's plotted on the map. At the little creek, we take a snack break in the cool shade. It's important not to get behind-the-curve on water.

Late in the day, we approach a little lake — Duck Soup Pond, according to the map. We decide to camp here. I roll out my sleeping pad and bag on a nice flat spot underneath a tree. Although we are next to a lake there are no skeeters for some reason. Wyoming talks me into playing some Five Card Draw. She's a card enthusiast and an expert player.

Instead of fireworks this 4th of July, legions of frogs croak cheerfully in the lake. From my sleeping bag, I look up to watch a spray of stars twinkling in the black sky.

Good ole Wyoming has gotten up early and gives me a rare cup of trail coffee. As we sip our coffee we look at our maps. A jeep road goes around the south side of Mt. Etna and the trail around the north side. We decide to follow the jeep road to avoid the deepest snow sure to be on the shaded north slope.

The jeep trail works well. After a few miles we are back on the trail but it is steep and snowy in many places around Gibraltar Mountain. The map shows switchbacks going up. We elect to just ignore the unseen trail and pick the safest route up the slope, linking together dry ground and patches of trees when we can. Wyoming is carrying her MICROspikes and she is enjoying the extra traction. We run across a NOBO thru-hiker, Ed. He says there are lots of NOBOs behind him.

We study our maps again and decide to do another lower route for a few miles. There are terrific views of snowy mountains from here, and it's green and snow-free where we are. Ahead are two round-ish brown spots in a meadow. They're moving. It must be bears! Wyoming is looking down so I grab her arm and point and we sink down behind a log to watch the bears through my monocular. They are both brown-phase black bears. Had this been Alaska we would have been thinking they were grizzlies at first. They busily feed their way into the timber and away from our route.

There's a nice flat area near a little creek and we've had a big day, lots of miles and climbing and considerable snow. This will be a good camp. There are a few skeets so I set up my tent but Wyoming elects to cowboy camp beneath the stars.

I feel lightheaded so I take my pulse. It seems erratic which doesn't boost my confidence any, especially since we are out in the middle of nowhere. I check again and it's definitely erratic. This isn't good. It's concerning but there's not much I can do other than try to get a good night's sleep and see how I feel in the morning. What does this mean, anyway? Is my hike over? Is this my last epic adventure? Is this life threatening?

In the morning I talk to Wyoming about it. I can tell she's a little worried but as usual she's a trooper. I consult the map. "You said it's twelve miles to Sierra City? When we get to the road I'm going to hitch into Truckee and see a doctor and find out what's going on."

"OK, Colter. I'll probably spend the night in Sierra City."

"Alright. I'll end up a day or two behind you. Just go ahead and do your thing and maybe I'll catch up later."

It's a pretty easy hike to the pass and the road. I've got a marker and print up a *TRUCKEE* sign. Wyoming and I give each other a hug and wish each other well. I know she'd like to hike together some more. We are a good team and I feel bad but this plan makes sense.

Pretty soon a pickup pulls over and the driver rolls down his window:

"I can take you as far as Highway Eighty-Nine."

"Sounds good." We make the usual small talk as he drives. He drops me off and turns north. I deploy my sign to hitch southbound. I've finally got a cell signal, a weak one, and try to make an appointment in Truckee. It's a tedious process.

A van pulls over. "We can take you to Truckee."

"Perfect." I climb in, still on my phone. "Sorry, I'm on hold."

"No problem."

At last, the appointment is made.

I turn my attention to the driver and his friend. "Where are you guys headed?"

"To a music festival." He explains that they've just been to one and are headed to more. He's a musician. His girlfriend rides with her bare feet on the dash. They are both super nice, just the type of people that commonly pick up hitchhikers: they are young, free spirits with plenty of room for hitchers. I thank them profusely when they drop me off.

I find a hotel and get all cleaned up and then do some laundry. My heart is back to normal which is a good thing because they can't run my tests until tomorrow.

After a good breakfast I walk a mile or so to the hospital where I fill out my paperwork at reception and am soon sent to the examination room. The doctor comes in.

"So you're concerned about an irregular heartbeat?"

I fill him in on all the details.

"OK, we'll hook you up and run some tests and see what you've got going."

After he's had a chance to look things over, he comes back in.

"Everything looks completely normal. You say you're hiking the PCT?"

"Yeah."

"You are obviously in great shape, then."

"I *should* be."

"Did you by chance drink a whole bunch of coffee that day, or drink coffee when you normally don't?"

"Actually, yes. I had a big cup of coffee that morning and I usually don't drink any on the trail."

"Based on how good things look now, your strange heartbeat might have been caused by some temporary electrolyte imbalance. You know what, if it were me, I wouldn't worry about it, just be aware if it happens again. I'd hit the trail and finish my hike. I'd recommend spending another night in town just to be sure." He then asks me some questions about hiking gear. This is all very good news. What if it had been bad news?

After food resupply shopping, I enjoy a good restaurant meal, and decide to hitch back to the trail. It's two quick hitches and soon I'm back on the PCT, relieved to have things back to normal.

What a beautiful, sunny day! A large yellow and black butterfly is feeding on pink and white flowers. I stop and watch it for a long time, so close I can see the delicate scales on its wings.

It's an extraordinary day for wildflowers. It's near evening and the low light saturates their colors. I wander through patches of flowers looking for pleasing combinations of orange, yellow, red and blue.

I'm going to call it a day. My guidebook shows that, despite having hitched all the way from Truckee today, I've still managed to put in twenty miles and climb well over 3,000 feet. I am thankful. Truly grateful. What if the doctor had told me my hiking days are over?

The morning sun is a red ball rising through the trees. The air is cool. Today I'm shooting for Donner's Pass, specifically a Trail Angel's house called Pooh Corner. It's about 23 miles or so. It should be very doable if I don't run across anything crazy. Stretches of the PCT are going to be over 8,000 feet today so I hope the snow won't be too bad.

There are long stretches of snow burying the tread. I'm following the trail when I can, or following tracks of other hikers, or just winging it. Occasionally I pull out my GPS just to make sure it agrees with my navigation.

My energy is sapped by serious butt-kicking snow slogs. When I stop to rest I soak in views of snowy mountains marching off into the distance. Splendid cascades of snowmelt run off huge slabs of flat rock.

Peter Grubb hut is a handsome place, built of stone and wood with a shingled roof. It would be a fun place to spend the night. I'm reading through the hut register, pen in hand, when a day hiker comes in, looking disheveled.

"I need to sign that," he says, pulling the pen out of my hand and beginning to write. I flush with anger but before I say anything, he adds, "I fell down out there, I'm heading for the road." Apparently he whacked his head on something, and he's concerned that it might be serious. There's a day hiker watching us. He volunteers to follow him out to the road to make sure he's OK.

The trail descends to, and passes under, I-80. It continues on through a rocky landscape to Donner Pass, named after the tragic Donner party of 1846. They weren't the first nor the last people to suffer severely from early winter snows. It's a good reminder not to push the season too late on the PCT, either. My goal is to have my hike wrapped up no later than September 30.

At Donner Pass, I call Pooh Corner. A volunteer says he'll come pick me up. It is a long, long wait but I'm happy when he finally rolls up. At the house Bill, aka Pooh the owner, welcomes me warmly. Pooh thru-hiked the Appalachian Trail and has been a Trail Angel here for years. This is a beautiful place, right on Donner Lake with a garage for hikers to sort out their gear. Bill shows me the shower, laundry, and computer and tells me about meal times and basic house rules. Two other thru-hikers are also here, Damian and Golden Child. About 8 PM, Wyoming shows up!

We have a fine meal of brats, corn-on-the-cob, potato salad and more, with brownies for dessert. I roll out my sleeping bag and pad down by the lake, showered and well-fed and content.

July 9

A joyful dog greets me in the morning with a cold wet nose on my neck. This is an awesome place. Wyoming and I decide to take a Zero here. I call my cousin Pam. I haven't seen her in what, thirty years? We make arrangements to meet where she lives, only about a day's walk down the PCT.

It's a feast for breakfast: pancakes, fresh fruit, cheesy eggs. For brunch we have fresh cornbread, syrup, butter, jam, and orange juice. Few people enjoy good food more than thru-hikers.

Wyoming and I take a kayak out for a long paddle on Donner Lake. It's a beautiful, sunny day. We paddle along a beach where people are sunning on the warm sand. It is a marvelous change from our hiker's world of the last three months.

Back at the house, I sort through my gear. All my chores are done, I'm clean, my clothes are freshly laundered, my website updated. Two more thru-hikers come in, NOBOs, French-speaking fellows I haven't met before.

Dinner is another feast and includes appetizers and soup. Everyone volunteers. I'm assigned potato peeling and the preparation of a fancy sauce. People are so different. For me, it's simply not worth the effort to spend so much time preparing an elaborate sauce. But beggars aren't choosers, and we sit down to a meal far better than any meal I've cooked in my life.

Before bed, we play a game of Jenga. One of the players, Golden Child, is a petite college student from the East Coast. She tells about a creek crossing in the Sierra that was so challenging she had to SWIM across. Swimming across a glacial melt creek! Yikes. She seems the type of person who will finish the trail.

Breakfast is another meal fit for hungry thru-hikers. Bill tells us the shuttle will leave in an hour, everyone be ready! I check and double check to make sure I haven't left any gear in the garage or in the washer or down by the lake. I'm all set. The two French-speaking NOBOs are still messing around on the computer. Bill can tell that they aren't going to be ready and asks me to give them a nudge.

"We're leaving in ten minutes," I tell them.

"We *know!*" one says, annoyed. Bill looks at his watch.

Ten minutes later all of us are sitting the shuttle, ready to go. All except the two foreign NOBOs.

"Does someone want to go get those guys, please?" our driver says. I hop out and find the NOBOs still on the computer.

"We're leaving."

"Hang on a minute!" one snaps.

Five minutes later they saunter out and throw their packs in back. Bill is grumpy and I don't blame him. They've ticked me off too. It is incredibly rude to make him or his driver wait when they have been so extremely kind and generous. It must be challenging as well as rewarding to be a Trail Angel. Most hikers are thankful and cooperative with Trail Angels. A few hikers develop an attitude of entitlement, seeming to feel they are on a heroic adventure, and deserve to be treated accordingly. In fact, Trail Angels owe them nothing, while hikers owe Trail Angels their gratitude and cooperation.

Up at the pass, at last, I find a plaque:

GREAT SUMMIT TUNNEL OF THE SIERRA NEVADA

BENEATH THIS PLAQUE THE FIRST TRANSCONTINENTAL RAILROAD TRAVERSED THE MIGHTY SIERRA NEVADA RANGE. THE 1,659-FOOT SUMMIT TUNNEL TOOK OVER 15 MONTHS OF CHINESE MUSCLE AND SWEAT TO COMPLETE. THE CHINESE PAINSTAKINGLY HAND-DRILLED THEN BLASTED THE GRANITE ROCK WITH BLACK

POWDER AND NEWLY INVENTED NITROGLYCERIN… THE MOST DIFFICULT OBSTACLE FACING THE CENTRAL PACIFIC RAILROAD WAS OVERCOME WHEN THE TUNNEL WAS OPENED IN AUGUST, 1867…

Compared to the danger, hard work and racism those Chinese workers endured, how hard is a thru-hike?

I enjoy wonderful ridgeline walking today with plenty of snow in sight, but the trail is almost snow free. I can't resist taking photos of the mountains and wildflowers. Among today's NOBOs I recognize Shades and Max Chill. We exchange trail reports. It sounds like the worst of the snow is behind all of us now. What's left is melting fast.

I leave the PCT and hike down the steep trail to Alpine Meadows where my cousin Pam lives. A pickup is parked at the trailhead. When a tall blonde lady steps out I know her instantly, she looks so much like my aunt.

"Hi, Bruce!" she says.

"Hi, Pam, it's been a long time!"

Pam laughs. Last time we saw each other, we were kids.

We drive down to her house which is right next to a pleasant creek. Just my kind of place. She introduces me to her new little puppy, a yellow Lab named Jasper. He is crazy cute and I play with him as Pam and I catch up.

As we eat, Pam tells me she took a job here at Alpine Meadows so she could ski all she wants, or nearly so. I admire people who take charge of their own fate as much as possible, to live the life they choose. Later we do a grocery store run so I can top off my food supply.

I slept great, with the window open next to a creek it was like being on the trail, except for the nice bed. After a good breakfast I shake Jasper's paw goodbye, give Pam a hug, and set off up the trail to the PCT.

Today is another especially beautiful day. It's trail like this that people imagine when they think of the Pacific Crest Trail. I take a calendar's worth of good photos.

Two tiny figures walk towards me down another spectacular ridgeline. It's thru-hikers, but who? When they are closer I recognize them, Swift and Buckeye.

"Colter! Great to see you."

"Hey, you guys! How was the Sierra?"

As they tell of their adventures, Buckeye says, "Hey look!" I turn around to see a coyote trotting across the trail behind me. Cool!

"We left your ice axe and bear canister at Echo Summit. Thanks for the loan."

"No problem. That worked out great for me, too. Did you need the ice axe?"

"I don't know if we actually needed it, but it was nice to have at some of the most sketchy spots." I make sure I know where they've left my stuff and we say goodbye. Those two are really enjoying their journey.

Thru-hikers Swift and Buckeye near Alpine Meadows

It's afternoon and I'm sitting next to a little brook. Years ago I'd been diagnosed with giardia twice, in different years, each time after drinking backcountry water. Since then I've been very careful to treat or filter all my water. However, before this hike I read an article that made a very convincing case that most backpacker giardia cases are probably not from water, but from dirty hands. The article claimed water testing in the Sierra showed it to be remarkably safe. Because of that article, on the PCT I've been especially careful about clean hands and hand sanitizer. Since hitting the Sierra I've skipped treating some of the cleanest looking water. (I've since learned that these claims by Rockwell and Welch are dated, largely untrue, and refuted by the CDC. Many people become sick from the water in the Sierra, and elsewhere.)

I don't trust this brook though, so I'm holding up a bottle of Aquamira at eye level, counting out drops, when around the corner comes a familiar hiker.

"Anne!"

"Hi, Colter! Wow, how are you?"

"Great. I haven't seen you since... the Anderson's."

"How was the flip?

"Good. And the Sierra?"

"Beautiful. I had a bad scare, though." She tells me about a particularly threatening creek crossing. She fell in and got swept away in the icy water, getting beaten violently on rocks, truly scared for her life. A big hiker grabbed her and helped her out of the water, badly bruised. "I was so scared I was thinking about quitting. I'm glad I didn't, though."

It is nice to reassure her that she'll likely have no more crossings anywhere near that frightening. I tell her about Wyoming's crossing scare, but that was off trail. We eat as we talk. Anne is one of my favorite hikers, but we both have "miles to go before we sleep."

"Maybe I'll see you down the trail, Anne," I say, giving her a hug.

"That would be fun. Have a good hike!" And with that, she hikes up the trail and disappears around the corner.

Thru-hikers Assface, Wolf Taffy, Not-a-Chance,
and The Croatian Sensation, NOBO

I slept well again. I pretty much always sleep well on the trail! Today it really feels like I'm in the Sierra Nevada. The scenery is awesome. I see a sign. Wait a minute, is this right? I pull out my guidebook. I think I missed a turn. I turn on my GPS just to verify. Yup. I'm headed towards Mosquito Pass. I backtrack a bit and hike southeast along Aloha Lake. This is just one of the beautiful lakes today, all with incredibly blue water. Above them, tower spires of gray rock trimmed with bright white snow.

Four fit-looking hikers are walking towards me.

"Assface! Wolf Taffy, great to see you out here. Not-a-Chance! And The Croatian Sensation, I presume."

"Hi, Colter. Looks like your flip worked out OK?"

"Tell you what, we didn't miss all the snow, that's for sure, but yeah, it worked out fine."

It's always fun to chat with kindred spirits.

It's now the morning of July 13, about 7:30 AM. Coming towards me are two hikers that I know, though I've never met them.

"Boston and Cubby! I'm Colter."

"Colter, how are you doing? It's amazing you recognized us." We are fellow 2008 hikers of the Continental Divide Trail. I'd seen their blog from that year, and I knew they were hiking this year. We talk more about the CDT than the PCT. I bring up how they immediately got a ride hitching at Monarch Pass in Colorado, while I had stood there for SIX HOURS. They laugh. The mosquitoes are crazy this morning though, so we cut our conversation short.

At Echo Lake my bear canister and ice axe are waiting for me, as promised. The bad news is that I just added several pounds to my pack. After repacking I walk out to the highway to hitchhike into South Lake Tahoe for food.

At the straightest stretch of road, I hold up my *HIKER TO TOWN* sign, trying to smile without it looking like a crazy, desperate smile. A car is pulling over! I hop in.

"Thanks for the ride!"

"No problem. Are you hiking the PCT?"

"Yup. I'm curious, why did you pick me up?"

"I hiked the Appalachian Trail a few years ago, so I know about hitching into towns."

"That's interesting. I hiked the AT in 2001."

"Yeah? I had some friends hike the AT that year."

"What were their trail names?"

"Sharpshin, and Strix."

"It's a small world, because I met those two on the Continental Divide Trail!" (A very small world indeed. When I return home I'll find a months-old email exchange between the driver and I. He was living in New Jersey. We'd been exchanging info on adventure trips each of us had done. It's remarkable that he happened to be visiting the opposite side of the country AND had come along at the exactly the right time to give me a ride. In the fall he is amazed when I email him about our random meeting!)

At the grocery store, I thank him for the ride. Inside I buy enough food to complete the 76 miles from Echo Summit to Sonora Pass.

From Sonora Pass I'll hitch into Kennedy Meadows, the north one. How can there be two?! I'm also going to buy enough food for the section between Vermilion Valley Resort (VVR) to Kennedy Meadows, the south one. The latter section is something like 175 miles. I'll plan for nine days' worth of food because I want to spend a day climbing Mt. Whitney, as well. So I've got to buy about 13 days' worth of food, at two pounds of food a day, that's heavy AND bulky.

I wander up and down the aisles of the store. Basically what I'm looking for is calorie-dense food that I find palatable. Choices include the following...

For breakfast: Pop-Tarts, instant oatmeal, and granola. I can munch on granola for snacks as well.

For lunch I've got peanut butter, crackers, peanut M&M's, jerky, two flavors of Craisins, Power Bars, ramen and tuna pouches. Many of these items can serve as snacks or desserts, too.

For dinners, I buy a variety of Knorr Sides Plus, better than the regular ones because they have veggies. And of course some Idahoan instant potatoes. A bag of real bacon crumbles will add to the texture and flavor of those meals. Those items will comprise the basis of most of my evening meals. Plus, at VVR, I can look over my food supply and supplement it with whatever they might have in their hiker box.

I stuff as much as I can into my pack. I leave the rest in a double plastic bag and hike over to the library where I get on a computer to update my hike journal. Because of the time limit, I have to hustle so much I get a little bit of a stress sweat going, trying to check my email and all.

VVR only accepts UPS packages. I hike over to the UPS store and pick out an appropriately sized box. I pack it as carefully and compactly as possible, checking and double-checking their address.

Finally, I write my name and address on all sides of the package. They verify the approximate delivery date and give me a receipt. Sweet!

Hiker towns like this, with a lot of hikers coming through, tend to be easy hitches. It's a quick hitch back at the PCT.

On the trail, I meet a couple of NOBO thru-hikers. They said they've had a good hike, except that they got knocked off the trail for a couple of days by giardia. Both of them. From not treating their water. Hmmm.

"It was bad, man. Treat your water. And, hey, if, heaven forbid, you happen to get giardia, ask the doctor for tinidazole. It's apparently new in the U.S. or something. Anyway, the good thing is you take four tablets, all at once. BAM! It works great. Done."

"Thanks, what did you say it was, tini...?"

"Tinidazole."

"Hey, thanks."

It makes me wonder about those babbling brooks where I skipped treating water. I'm going back to treating everything again.

This evening I'm camping in a pocket of timber near Little Round Top peak. This was a big, big day. I walked something like fifteen trail miles, plus to the lodge at Echo Lake and back, plus all my walking around town. AND all that shopping and packaging and mailing and website updating. Yup, I'm whupped.

I'm admiring the rich early morning light on rugged ridgeline when the Israeli girls come striding down the trail, beaming.

"You're walking south now?" one says.

"Wyoming and I flipped up to Ashland. How is your hike?"

"We love it! So beautiful."

When I walk away I'm smiling myself. Everybody likes their positive attitude.

Hours later two tiny figures power up the trail towards me. I can hear them chattering cheerfully as they near. I recognize them from way back in Southern Cal, a thousand miles ago.

"So what trail names are you two going by now?"

"Sweet Sixteen," says the taller one. She's young, but certainly not sixteen.

"How did you get that name?"

"Well, my dad came to visit me on the trail. And he met some of my hiking friends. So he told the guys, 'Hey, you guys know she's only sixteen, right?' So now I'm Sweet Sixteen!"

"And how about you?" I ask the other. She's very short, and a strong hiker.

"Micro Burst!" We all laugh.

This evening I'm camped above the East Fork of the Carson River, admiring some especially dramatic cliffs. Thunderheads are building, towering higher and higher, glowing pinkish-orange in the setting sun. It's one of the most magical sunsets of the whole hike. I sit on my sleeping pad, my arms clasping my knees, until the light has faded.

I'm about five miles from Sonora Pass, treating a quart of water. A hiker joins me. He's going into Kennedy Meadows as well. (I still can't believe there are two Kennedy Meadows in the Sierra!) I kinda wish he'd pull ahead or fall behind because sometimes it's not easy to get a hitch for two male hikers.

Despite my concerns, it turns out to be an easy hitch. The lodge directs me to the showers and laundry and on the way I spot a familiar face.

"Wyoming!"

"Hi, Colter," she says in her soft voice. "It's good to see you!"

"Yeah, you too. Hey, the laundry is over there, right?"

"Yup."

"Tell you what, I'll throw in my laundry and grab a shower and I'll see you in a bit."

After my shower I sit in my rain gear and chat with her, catching up on the trail news.

"So are you hiking out today?" I ask.

"Yeah."

"Me too. How about we hitch back up to the pass together and we can camp together tonight?"

"OK."

In the store I buy a salad and some miscellaneous expensive food and sit outside with Wyoming to eat. When my clothes are dry I change. We walk out to the road. It should be easier to hitch with a female hiker than it is by myself. Seems less threatening I guess.

An older gentleman picks us up. He tells us all about this area. He drops us off at the trail. We thank him and start climbing. The old team is back together! There are snow patches several hundred yards long, and on some fairly steep spots, but this time of day the snow is a little soft and reasonably safe. Under worse conditions, this slope has been described by at least one hiker as "life-threatening." I plant my poles as I walk and Wyoming is wearing her MICROspikes. We watch our step carefully and cross without a problem.

It's fun to hike and chat again. We swap cameras to take shots of each other admiring nice scenery. This is probably about the prettiest time of year. Mountains half covered with snow are more beautiful than totally snow covered OR snow-free mountains. It's no wonder that people love the Sierra Nevada. Our camp is at nearly 11,000 feet, on a gently rolling mostly-flat spot in very fine scree. We set up our shelters among scattered bushes and rocks.

Climbing the south side of Sonora Pass, while SOBO

It's morning. I feel nauseous. This is high altitude, but I should be well acclimated by now. Was it that salad I bought? I'm feeling worse, fast. Wyoming is packing up a stone's throw away.

"Hey Wyoming, I feel really queasy this morning. Maybe it was that salad or something, but why don't you go on ahead and I'll see how I feel."

"I don't want to just leave you here, Colter."

"Please, just go ahead. Sorry about that."

"OK. I hope you feel better, Colter."

The crunching of her footsteps fades. I lay in my tent groaning quietly. When the sun hits, the tent is soon uncomfortably hot. I crawl outside and puke violently. I stagger back to my shelter and grab my sleeping pad and put it in the shade of some bushes and curl up in the fetal position. Suddenly I have to get up and kick a hole in the dirt and drop my pants, and immediately after puke some more. I lie back down, sweating. This repeats, over and over. For hours. I have to move my sleeping pad into the shade as the sun swings around.

Is this food poisoning or giardia? I think this is the sickest I've ever felt and it's not getting better. Maybe I should hike out and hitch into town? See a doctor or at least get something to settle my stomach? The thought of walking the four miles back to the Pass and then having to hitch into town is a terrible thought, but I finally decide that's what I have to do.

Sicker than a dog I pack my gear, stuffing it into my pack haphazardly. I'm hiking, but very slowly. I stop to be sick, repeatedly, occasionally lying down, curled up and sweating. Near Sonora Pass I'm desperate to reach the road so I chance hiking down the fall-line instead of taking the long switchbacks. I have to scramble down some rocks but finally stumble onto the road.

Tables and chairs are set up with a half dozen hikers gathering around, enjoying a feast with their Trail Angel. His car is parked nearby. There are few things I want to see less than a feast right now, and few things I want to see more than a Trail Angel with a car. Oh, thank goodness!

Everyone looks up at me. I turn to the Trail Angel.

"Hi, I'm Colter. Hey, I'm really sick. I think I might have giardia. I hate to ask, but I wonder if you might drive me into Bridgeport."

"Did you hike out of Sonora Pass?" one hiker says.

"Yeah."

"When?"

"Yesterday."

"It can't be giardia, then. You weren't out there long enough." She misunderstands. She doesn't know I'm a fellow thru-hiker, out here for months. I'm too sick to explain. I look at the Trail Angel.

"I don't want to leave all these hikers here," he says, and glances away. I loathe to ask for favors and I'm stunned a Trail Angel would turn me down when I am truly in need, truly sick, but beggars aren't choosers. I turn and walk towards the highway, an outsider among thru-hikers, turned away by a Trail Angel. An unpleasant surprise on both counts.

Two-day hikers walk down the trail to their car.

"Are you heading into Bridgeport?" I say.

"We are. What's up?"

"I hate to ask, but I think I might have giardia and I wonder if you'd mind giving me a ride."

"Giardia? Oh man, that sucks. Sure, hop in."

They are a cheerful pair. Luckily I'm feeling a bit better and am able to answer a few questions about my PCT hike. At Bridgeport, I leave them with my sincere thanks and they leave me with their best wishes.

I check into a room, then walk into town and buy some Pepto Bismol and Gatorade. I make some phone calls. There's no clinic in town and it looks like it's going to be a big hassle to get to one. I'll think about it tomorrow. I'm still feeling a bit queasy, but dramatically better than I was. That was horrible. Really bad. I slowly rehydrate and take a shower and crawl into bed.

In the morning I feel weak but much better. Maybe I'll hang in town today, putter around, try to recover, see how I feel? At the laundromat, I see Fire Marshall and hear an update about his and Zero/Zero's hike. At the grocery store, I buy some bananas.

Back at my room, I read and study my guidebook and make plans and call Stephanie. Things are not right between us. Other than that, I'm feeling much better this evening. Maybe it isn't giardia? Maybe it was just something I ate? If I feel normal in the morning I'm going to hitch back up to the trail again.

I'm able to enjoy a breakfast this morning. My first hitch to the turn-off to Sonora Pass goes well. The second hitch takes longer but soon I'm climbing the same switchbacks Wyoming and I were climbing three days ago.

A hiker I don't recognize approaches me. "Are you Colter?" she says.

"I am. How did you know?"

"I talked to Wyoming. She said to watch for you. She told me to give you this." She hands me a folded paper.

"Thanks! Have a good hike."

"You too."

The note is addressed simply to "Colter." On the back, she has drawn an intricate tree. Above it, she's written:

Hey Colter, Getting to Tuolumne Meadows Tuesday, July 20 and will stay the night. Hope everything's OK. I may do the first section of the John Muir Trail. Hope to see you sometime, Happy Trails. Wyoming.

Kind-hearted Wyoming. Always thoughtful. I feel sorry about asking her to leave me when I was sick, but I don't regret it.

In a couple of hours, I pass that horrible camp where I was so sick. It's nice to leave that behind me and put in some miles of forward progress. In places, the trail is completely buried in snow but it's not a serious impediment. Judging from the reports of NOBOs, the worst of the snow is gone. The scenery is beautiful: cliffs and sparkling snowfields and blue mountain lakes.

This evening, warm in my sleeping bag, there's a knot in my stomach, but now it's from thinking about Stephanie.

Oh, what a day! Dramatic gray peaks punch through glittering white snow into a brilliant blue sky. Along the trail is a sign:

ENTERING YOSEMITE WILDERNESS

Yosemite! When I was a kid, Yosemite meant nothing without the word "Sam," but as an adult I've been looking forward to visiting this magical place for years. I hike through a green meadow along Dorothy Lake, admiring Forsythe Peak which towers above it. A packer riding a mule waves as he passes. He's leading another mule with an expertly packed load, both animals shiny and healthy, manes groomed with pride. Late in the afternoon mule deer feed in the meadow, near another idyllic camp in another stunning valley.

Now, every day is spectacular. Each day is a highlight. I take a break in the shade along an especially beautiful lake, shoes off, socks drying on a handy bush, sweaty feet drying. After more miles, I stop on a high ridge. I sit on my bear canister, eating lunch, studying my guidebook, swigging from my water bottle and drinking in the views up and down the valley.

There are many hikers at Glen Aulin High Sierra Camp, carrying only light day packs or totally pack-free. They have, I believe, had all their gear packed in by horse from Tuolumne Meadows.

I stop to appreciate the aptly named White Cascade Falls, which roars and plunges into the lower pool. Yahooooooo! From here, I climb along the green meadows of the Tuolumne River, admiring a graceful rounded dome in the distance. The seven hundred feet or so of vertical climb over the six miles to Tuolumne seems insignificant on the PCT.

It's fun walking into Tuolumne Meadows but it's strange seeing so many people. I feel like a real veteran, whiskery and tanned, clothing faded, fifteen hundred miles of trail behind me already this summer! It's good to be proud, but it's important to be humble. Some of these people are real heroes, people who save lives, people who are taking a quick break from sacrificing for the benefit of others.

In the little store, I buy some trail food and treats and ice cream for right now. Outside at a picnic table, a guy is talking to a couple young ladies. Where have I seen that guy? He's not a thru-hiker. Finally, I walk over to him.

"Where do I know you from?"

"Peter Grubb Hut, remember? I walked with you for the last stretch down to the road."

"That's right! It's a small world! I thought maybe you were somebody famous or something."

He turns to his friends. "Hey, he thought I was a movie star!" They laugh. "Are you staying at the campground tonight?"

"I'll probably put in a few more miles."

"Why don't you stay here tonight? There's plenty of room for your tent at our site. We'll feed you. Give you a couple of beers."

"Sure. Thanks!"

It was a fun evening. It's good to be social once in a while! This morning I pack quietly and head cross-country to intersect the PCT. At the edge of a meadow a big mule deer buck feeds, his antlers still in velvet. In the shade is another, and another. Three large bucks! Now a fat young marmot is feeding next to the trail, completely ignoring me. Finally, he looks up at me as if to say, *"I'm sorry, can I help you?"* It's always fun to see wildlife.

The PCT climbs higher back into the Sierra, passing 9,000 ft, above 10,000 ft, and then over Donahue Pass at 11,050 ft.

There have been many dramatic stretches of trail, but none more splendid than here in the Ansel Adams Wilderness. Thousand Island Lake is stunning, but it's a reflection of Banner Peak that stops me in my tracks: stone and snow, trees and sky, the colors rich in the morning light.

And oh, the mountain wildflowers: blue and purple and red, orange and white and pink.

Banner Peak, Ansel Adams Wilderness

It's the morning of July 25. I reach Devil's Postpile, once-molten lava that has solidified into geometric, parallel columns of stone. In some places the columns are nearly straight, but in others it's like the straws of an old broom, bent from years of sweeping. It's a truly remarkable and unusual work of nature.

I'm looking forward to a night in Mammoth Lakes. I walk into the store at Red's Meadow.

"Where does the bus stop?"

"Right out there," the friendly cashier says. I buy an ice cream drumstick and wait outside. The bus soon appears, filled with a far different social strata than the Greyhound bus Wyoming and I took out of Reno. Most are people with money and with nice cars parked somewhere nearby. This is just a vacation shuttle for them, as it is, I suppose, for me.

The fellow at the motel desk has a surly attitude. Maybe another hiker has offended him. I try to be patient. It's a long wait but he sorts things out. Oh, what a luxury it is to take a good hot shower, put on freshly laundered clothes and sit down at a restaurant with a full menu! I savor every mouthful.

Well-rested after a night in a real bed, I walk over to a different restaurant for breakfast, update my website journal, and buy groceries to last me until Vermilion Valley Resort, only two or three days down the trail. I'm going to take a zero here in town. I kick it in my room for hours, chowing down on fruit and other fresh food I bought at the store, watching movies and channel surfing. Paradise!

I call Stephanie. She is distressed about her new job and new home and missing cat. I tell her about my hike, but I feel guilty being too enthusiastic about it. It seems unfair that one of us is on a grand adventure and the other is stressed out in the real world. I gently mention that my box to Kennedy Meadows barely made it on time (she'd mailed it about ten days late) and I know she's busy but it would be a bummer if I missed a resupply. She gets very, very angry. She is doing me a favor, how can I criticize her when she's only trying to be helpful? Of course, I don't mean it that way, and of course, that's not what this fight is all about. Something has changed and we both know it and she is scared of what it all means. It makes me sad for both of us.

In the morning I feel sick. Sick like I was out in the mountains. I recognize the pattern of recurring sickness, and the now clearer symptoms: I have giardia. I call and make an appointment and suffer the brutal walk over to Mammoth Hospital, brutal even though I'm heavily dosed with Pepto Bismol.

The doctor walks into the examination room.

"So you are hiking the PCT and are feeling sick? What kind of symptoms are you having?"

I tell him the gory details and about being sick a week or so ago.

"Were you treating all your drinking water?"

"Not all of it." I tell him about the article I read, about there not being enough giardia in Sierra water to get sick. The doctor laughs.

"They can't test a few water sources then claim the water is safe in thousands of untested water sources years later. You've got classic giardia symptoms. I treat many hikers with giardiasis every summer. I'll write you a prescription."

"Can you prescribe tini... I can't remember the name, but it starts with a 't'. It's supposed to be new in the U.S."

"Let me check." When he returns he says, "I've always prescribed Flagyl, but tinidazole looks even better. I'll write you a prescription."

I walk over to the pharmacy in a nearby store and hand them my prescription. I'm am sicker than a dog and stand slumped against the counter.

"Have you got insurance?"

"I've got my Blue Cross number."

"We need the actual card."

"I don't have it here. The hospital just used my number. Look, I'm really sick. Can I come back with the card later?"

"Hang on." She walks away and talks with a supervisor. When she comes back she says, "Sorry, we need the card."

"How about I give you cash, you hang onto it, and then I come back with my card when I'm feeling better?"

"Sorry."

If anger could cure giardiasis I wouldn't need the prescription. Instead, I make the long, sweaty walk back to my hotel room to find my card, then make the long walk back. It's hot and I'm extremely nauseous. I hand the lady my card. She hands me my prescription. I pay for the tinidazole and a liter of 7-UP that I hope will help settle my stomach.

"Have a nice day," she says.

"Yeah."

Finally back in my room, I collapse on the bed and take some anti-nausea pills. Then I eat a banana so my stomach doesn't revolt against the four big tinidazole tablets. I drink a little 7-Up, sipping a little bit more from time to time as I watch TV. Evening rolls around and I'm already feeling dramatically better. Man, what a relief. "You won't get giardia in the Sierra," the article said. "Giardia isn't that bad," it said. Right. I knew less after reading that article than I did before. I'll be treating all my water again from here on out.

It's another zero in Mammoth for me. Just to make sure. Thru-hikers tend to lose weight, and I lost noticeably more weight on my two rounds of giardiasis at Sonora Pass and here. Man, I'm glad I didn't get sick on the trail this time!

Over at the cafe I enjoy a real breakfast. It's a fine day of blathering around town, calling some friends, watching TV, and eating. Recovering from being sick makes me appreciate being well. And all these months on the trail make me appreciate the simplest luxuries we all take for granted.

July 29

It's wonderful to be back on the trail, to be healthy, to be cranking out the miles in this beautiful country. I lost two days to giardia in Mammoth. Wyoming will be way ahead of me. I wonder if I'll catch up to her again? The trail climbs up and up, steadily, snow-free, with countless, gorgeous calendar views of the Sierra Nevada mountains, into the John Muir Wilderness.

After two days of hiking I near Vermillion Valley Resort aka VVR. Two section hikers rest near the trail, one with his boot off, his foot ground to a raw, red mess. I admire his stoicism. More prevention and less stoicism might have served him better, though. Together we ponder his options

139

for boot lacing, moleskin, and sock adjustment, but his main strategy is courage.

When I see the Mono Creek Trail I head down it for the VVR Ferry. I am amazed by the number of hikers waiting here! No other PCT thru-hikers, though. When the ferry arrives we stack our packs and crowd onto the boat, which roars across the Lake.

At VVR I ask for my package and they quickly find it. There's an $18 fee for holding it but there is considerable hassle in handling hiker packages. Every package they hold means less supply sales at their store, so the fee seems reasonable. "Thru-hikers get a free beer!" they tell me.

I sort through my food box, I'm just a little light on food so I check out the hiker box (a barrel, in this case). I find three treasures: a genuine package of freeze-dried backpacker food, a quarter pound of butter, and a package of Ding-Dongs. Score! Now I've got plenty.

The menu at the restaurant looks delicious. I sit at a table of John Muir Trail (JMT) hikers. I decide to splurge on a huge steak, with trimmings.

"Do you want your free beer now?" the waiter says.

"Sure, thanks."

After the meal, I say goodbye to my new friends. When I go to pay my bill, I notice I've been charged for my only beer, the free one.

"I see that you charged for my free beer," I say.

I hand him the bill and he glances at it. "Oh, yeah, I guess we did." Then he turns to the next customer. It's not worth arguing about.

Outside I sort through my whole pack, throwing out trash and excess packaging to reduce the bulk and weight of my food load. This place is a little too busy for me. I'm going to walk back to the trailhead rather than spend the night and wait for the ferry. I carefully pack my food into my bear canister. It's a very, very tight fit. As a matter of fact, there's a little food that won't fit, food the regulations will require me to eat before camping.

My food supply for about nine days and 190 miles

I've packed Knorr Sides Plus, Idahoan Instant Potatoes, Peanut M&M's, Pop-Tarts, instant oatmeal, granola, jerky, Craisins, crackers, Power Bars, bacon crumbles, ramen, tuna pouches, peanut butter, and Ding Dongs, butter, and a freeze-dried meal from the VVR hiker box.

July 31

This will be my longest carry of the whole Pacific Crest Trail, about 175 miles, plus a day trip to climb Mt. Whitney, about 190 miles total. Many, if not most, thru-hikers break down this section by going into either Lone Pine or Independence to resupply. I've decided to simplify my logistics and stay in the mountains the whole way. The trade-off is that I'll have the heaviest starting pack weight of the trip, about 35 pounds walking out of VVR, including food, ice axe, canister and a quart of water. My pack will be lightened about two pounds a day as I eat.

In the cool light of the evening, I see one of the most magical things I've witnessed on the whole trail. Along the grassy bank of a pretty little creek, the water is boiling with the splashing of feeding trout. There are so many of them, feeding so incessantly, that I snap photo after photo, attempting to capture a fish leaping out of the water. It proves to be easy. One shot shows a trout launching away, out of the water. Another photo the curved back of a trout leaping out of the water at an insect. The best shows the wide-open mouth a trout, jumping high out of the water, his red gills flaring, in pursuit of a hatching bug. They are brook trout, with white-edged fins, orange bellies, delicately mottled backs, and sides with beautiful red spots inside blue halos.

It's August! If all goes well, I'll finish the PCT next month. Near the trail is an old hand-built log cabin. Sixty-one years ago, someone stood here with a pocketknife and carved "1949" into the already-aging wood.

At noon I'm looking at Evolution Creek, an infamous name among thru-hikers. For PCT NOBOs this crossing is often daunting. Now, weeks after the normal high water of snowmelt, Evolution Creek is nothing more than uncomfortably cold.

Evolution Valley is incredible. Every time I put my camera away I see a mountain scene that is even more impressive. Without a photo, I might not believe my own memory.

On the shores of Wanda Lake, the low evening light brings an almost supernatural quality to the pink, shooting-star flowers waving gently in the breeze. Across the blue water jagged fingers of bright white snow fill the ravines of the rugged gray peaks, soaring 13,000 feet into the summer-blue sky.

I camp not far away, a very high camp, at 11,500 ft. My gray shelter matches the gray boulders around me. I eat dinner here in hiker Valhalla, watching the mountains until the last sunlight leaves the highest summit.

My Wild Oasis shelter set up below Muir Pass

The morning sun and I reach the top of Muir Pass together. Even now, in the height of summer, it is below freezing. Here is the iconic Muir Hut, a stone structure with a conical stone roof. Inside I look up at concentric rings of stone, skillfully placed, at least I hope so! On the outside of the hut is a plaque:

TO JOHN MUIR, LOVER OF 'THE RANGE OF LIGHT' 1931

On some long-ago day John Muir stood here alone at nearly 12,000 ft, like me. Muir looked out across the same crags, with their cold stone and snow and distant lakes. It is, I think, despite the hut, one of the most purely wild scenes I have experienced on the PCT.

I descend the other side of the Pass, now in the shadows, wearing my gloves and mitten shells. On a pond, crystallized feathers of freezing water have stretched all the way across and fused together in a thin shell of ice. Winter is never far away at this altitude.

The morning sun washes over the mountains above Helen Lake and the trail drops down through Le Conte Canyon. A young Kings Canyon National Park ranger is sitting on a rock slab, watching a twelve-foot cascade of the Middle Fork of the Kings River. A yellow kayak appears above the falls, then paddles into the current and plunges into the pool below. I walk up to the ranger.

"Wow, that's pretty crazy!"

"It is! It sure is fun to watch though," she says, smiling. Another kayaker appears below the cascade, watching as an orange kayak takes the plunge.

"Where did the kayaks come from?"

"They do a fourteen-mile portage over Bishop Pass."

"How high is Bishop Pass?"

"Almost twelve thousand feet."

"Yikes. That is hardcore." I'm told they paddle another 40 miles downstream, dropping 7,000 ft in all! They have to do many, many falls. It is, apparently, the most challenging expedition kayak trip in the country. I'll take their word for it. It must be thrilling, though!

I hike downstream with the ranger, talking thru-hiking and rangering. When she turns off to another river overlook we wish each other well. It is only late morning and I have many more miles to go today, and as much climbing as I can handle. From the turn-off up Palisade Creek, I am at 8,000 feet and have nothing but climbing ahead of me. I pass 9,000 ft. The "Golden Staircase" isn't as dramatic as I had imagined. I laugh when I notice there's a typo in my guidebook, calling it the "Golden Suitcase." I climb and climb, trying to pace myself so I'm not out of breath, so I don't have to stop to rest, but my energy is waning. I climb above 10,000 ft. I pass Upper Palisade Lake at 11,000 ft. As the last sun hits the mountaintops I find a spot to set up my shelter among the rocks, alone in the world, not another human being within sight or sound.

I watch the sunrise from 12,100-foot Mathers Pass. Snow is barely an issue. The basin beyond the pass is especially beautiful in the morning light. The sky is cloudless and blue, the dark shadows accent the ruggedness of the dark gray mountains, the south slopes nearly snow-free. It is windless and quiet except for the crunch of my footsteps and the gurgling of a nearby brook. The whole valley belongs to me.

An hour later I ford the South Fork of the Kings River, wring out my socks and continue on with wet, but drying, feet. The trail drops down to about 10,000 ft but just before noon, I've climbed nearly to the top of 12,150-foot Pinchot Pass. I turn back to look at a greenish blue lake nestled under the peaks. I follow the switchbacks down the mountain. The ford of Woods Creek is easy. There's a swaying wooden walkway suspended from a spiderweb of steel cables. I camp in a secluded spot near a tiny lake. This was a 26-mile day which included two 12,000-foot passes. Not too shabby!

August 4

I wake up as the first light seeps through my shelter. I eat some granola while packing. Long before the first direct sun, I'm already hiking. An hour later I pause at Rae Lakes. There is total silence. The world is holding its breath. The Painted Lady, with her band of black stone, stands over the water as she has for a million years. Her head is in the sun and her feet still in the shadows, all reflected in the trout-dimpled blue water.

It's an 1,800-foot climb from my camp to 12,000 ft Glenn Pass. With a steady pace I top-out, without breaking a sweat, still in early morning. Ranks of blue-gray mountains march off into the distance.

Near noon, close to the trail, is a pretty little falls and a ten-foot-wide creek. I sit on a flat rock of perfect height.

From the side pocket of my pack I take an empty canteen and mix a cap of Aquamira, setting the timer on my watch. The falls rumble. The air smells cold and wet and clean. I set up my stove and windscreen/stove stand, and use a medicine cup to measure my alcohol fuel, then pour it into the stove. I fill the pot half full of water. My watch shows nearly five minutes have passed. I fill my canteen and pour the solution of Aquamira into it, then light my stove and set the pot on to boil. A few minutes later the telltale stream rises. It's boiling. I lift it off just as the alcohol burns out. I pour the hot water into a plastic mug, one of two that serve double-duty by screwing together to protect my stove and windscreen. I add a pouch of instant potatoes and mix it up and cover it to soak for a few minutes. When it's ready I mix in a generous dollop of butter and some bacon bits. From my front shirt pocket I take my spoon, dig in, and blow on the spoonful impatiently. It's hard to believe that something so simple can be so good!

"The Painted Lady" – Rae Lakes, Sequoia & Kings Canyon

From here I have 3,600 more feet of climbing to reach Forester Pass. I'm excited by the challenge, though. Reaching Forester Pass will be a major milestone of the PCT.

I concentrate on pacing. Don't push too hard, don't become winded, but no break until I really need one. With a thousand feet of climbing left I stop at a creek to treat a quart of water. At over 12,000 ft I can feel the altitude, but I've got plenty of energy reserves. There are snowfields, reasonably steep ones, but I either walk in the rocks around them, or follow existing footsteps.

Above me are tiny figures milling around. One stands with his hands on his hips, looking down at me. That must be the Pass! As I near I see they are teenage boys, maybe eight of them, with several adult men. They look proud of their accomplishment, and they should be. At the top, a sign reads:

ENTERING SEQUOIA NATIONAL PARK
FORESTER PASS ELEVATION 13,200 FT.

One of the men offers to take a picture of me, and I happily accept. I pose, poles in hand. He takes the photo, a cliff behind me, two greenish-blue lakes far below us, imposing mountains beyond.
The group is getting ready to leave. One of the boys is complaining about his knee. He's not sure he can do it. It's really painful. He looks around for sympathy. The group leaves him anyway, with just one adult lingering with him. The injured kid finally departs. I follow the last adult over the lip. It is, in fact, nearly a cliff. But, now, the only serious snow-chute left, the one that terrifies so many hikers earlier in the season, is a well-stomped trail. It requires only moderate care to negotiate safely. Earlier in the season, with hard snow and hundreds and hundreds of feet below, a slip could be "harmful or fatal."

147

Me at Forester Pass, highest pass on the PCT, elevation 13,200 feet
Photo is looking south

The main group hustles ahead. After fifteen minutes I look back to see the trail zig-zagging up to the Pass. It is bolstered by stone walls, switchback after switchback painstakingly constructed into the steep mountainside. The main group has completely ditched the complaining kid with his one adult. What if he needs help? But the group has heard it all before. He's the boy-who-cries wolf, the one who finds it more enjoyable to complain than to challenge himself. One by one I pass the group, then the beautiful green lakes. Alone again I walk for miles, into the evening.

As the light fades I set up my shelter on the edge of Bighorn Plateau. Today I made memories. I hiked 25 miles over two high passes, including Forester Pass, the greatest of them all, nearly 6,000 feet of total climbing. Tomorrow I'll tackle Mt. Whitney. From the open door of my shelter, I look across Bighorn Plateau to the peaks of the Sierra Nevada beyond.

August 5

It froze again but I slept warm and well in my down bag. Today I will climb Mt. Whitney. Happily, my pack is nearly ten pounds lighter than it was when I left VVR, now close to 25 pounds and getting lighter daily. I meet two southbound JMT hikers camped near a creek crossing. They, too, are excited to be tackling Whitney.

I leave the PCT to follow the JMT towards the summit, passing beautiful Guitar Lake. This area, from the PCT to the summit and on to Whitney Portal, is heavily regulated due to the popularity of Mt. Whitney. I'm not a fan of too many rules, but here the rules are necessary. I begin encountering a few fellow climbers, resting or slowly ascending. With months of hiking and weeks of being at altitude, I have a huge advantage.

Coming down the trail is a face I recognize.

"Plod, how are you doing!"

"Colter, it's great to see you! So did you do your flip?"

I tell him about flipping up to Ashland, and that I'm about ready to finish California when I reach Kennedy Meadows, only a few days away.

"How about you?"

Plod explains that when he hit the deep snow in the Sierra it just wasn't fun anymore. He went home for a while and is now going to hike as much of the trail as he can before the fall snows hit. It's a prime example of "hiking your own hike." Plod is in great shape. He got a very early start and has already summited today! We exchange cameras to take photos of ourselves posing in front of the fluted, snowy cliffs of a long ridge, with two green lakes in the foreground. With that, we shake hands and part ways.

Climbing Mount Whitney from the PCT

When the trail from Whitney Portal joins my trail a dozen hikers come into view. Mt. Whitney is on the "bucket list" of countless hikers and I will share today's adventure with many of them. It's over 3,600 ft of climbing from the PCT to the summit, and about eight miles one way. As the hours pass, I climb above 13,000 feet. The thinner air is noticeable. Underneath my backpack, my shirt is wet with sweat.

Like my fellow hikers I am watching ahead, hoping I'm near the top, and at last see the stone "Smithsonian Hut" that stands on the summit. I climb until there is nothing left to climb, and stand atop the highest point in the Sierra Nevada, the highest mountain in the Lower 48! The plaque reads:

MOUNT WHITNEY   ELEVATION 14,496.811 FT.
JOHN MUIR TRAIL – HIGH SIERRA TRAIL
SEPTEMBER 5, 1930

That last ".811" feet was the hardest! Camera in hand, I walk around the summit plateau, peering over the edge here and there, down thousands of feet from a dizzying height. To the east are endless miles of high desert. North and south and west are snow and lakes and mountains and more mountains.

It's time to head down. Counterintuitively, it takes much more effort to go steeply downhill all these thousands of feet than it does to hike flat ground. It's especially true when I'm using leg muscles as shock absorbers to avoid pounding my knees too badly. I rejoin the PCT at Crabtree Meadow. A mile or two down the trail mule deer are feeding in a darkening meadow. Thousands of feet above them, awash in bright sunlight, towers Mt. Whitney. Even with summiting, it was a 25-mile day. I am bone tired. My two biggest days of the trip, likely, the last two days, back to back. It's a huge sense of accomplishment. And I am only about three days from Kennedy Meadows!

It's the evening of August 7. In the last two days I've hiked over several passes, including Guyot Pass, Cottonwood Pass, and Trail Pass. I've traveled 55 miles, zeroing in on Kennedy Meadows. These miles have been a little easier, the passes a little lower, with fewer ups and downs between them. Today I lingered in a meadow of gloriously tall Sierra corn lily, with their white flowers, and lupines, with their blue and white flowers. I enjoyed collecting water running from a pipe that trickled merrily into a cattle tank. The pipe means nothing safety-wise, I treat the water anyway.

It's getting dark now, so I pull out my bright little LED microlight and turn on the switch. I watch for a flat place to set up camp. No luck. It's fully dark now and the stars are out. I swing the light downhill to check out a potential campsite and swing it back to the trail directly in front of me. SNAKE! I instinctively jump back.

An enormous snake, maybe four feet long, is stretched out on the trail, banded white and black and red. A king snake and harmless, strikingly beautiful now that I know what it is, now that my heart is slowing.

I walk around him. Soon, I can barely make out a line of trees, downhill from the trail. Should be a flat spot there. I weave around the sagebrush and soon find just what I'm looking for.

I roll out my sleeping pad among the sage and take off my shoes and sweaty socks. From my sleeping bag I look up at a dome of thrillingly bright stars suspended in the silent blackness, their light racing through space at an unimaginable speed for years, or thousands of years, to rendezvous at this meadow tonight. Bats flutter above me. A meteor streaks a long, lingering arc across the sky.

It's an easy hike into Kennedy Meadows, with a light pack and a gentle 800-foot descent over five miles. Walking into KM is like visiting your old high school, the buildings are still there but your friends are gone. There are no thru-hikers, not even any JMTers. I am here with a few tourists.

I order a cheeseburger and fries at the grill. After that long haul from Mammoth Lakes, I enjoy it as only a thru-hiker can. I walk over to Tom's Place (he's a Trail Angel) with some ice cream to check my email and to update my online journal. Quickly scanning through my email, I don't see anything from Stephanie. That really worries me. Normally, Stephanie and I talk every day. On a hike like this I usually call her from every town, and there is always an email waiting for me. Always. That things are rocky between us worries me even more, as our friendship has been so important in her life. It's important in my life as well. I email asking her to please respond, at least so I know she's OK. I walk over to the pay phone and try calling but there's no answer. I call her parents but they're not home. I leave a message asking them to call me back to let me know if they've heard from her. I wish I knew. This is a bad feeling.

At the store, the clerk takes my money for a shower. After getting all cleaned up I walk over to the intersection. This time I'll hitch down the mountain. Soon a station wagon pulls over. I'm on my way, this time at a much more sensible speed than the ride Wyoming and I got! The person in the passenger seat turns to me. "Are you a Christian?" I hear that question fairly often while hitching, when many drivers are looking to save lost souls.

At the bottom of the hill, they let me off on the desert highway in the heat of the day. I'm glad I have plenty of water. I've just gotten my *MAMMOTH* sign out when my cell phone rings, the first time in weeks.

"Hello?"

"It's Stephanie."

"Are you OK?"

"Of course, why wouldn't I be OK?"

"I hadn't heard anything! I was worried about you."

"You weren't worried about me." Our conversation falls off a cliff, fast. This is the angriest talk we've ever had, by far. She wants to take the summer off from our friendship. I think not talking is the worst thing we can do, at least if we want to stay friends. We say sad goodbyes and hang up.

I stand by the road with my *MAMMOTH* sign, sweating from stress and the heat. I don't want to be hiking for two more months, alone in the mountains, wondering what's going to happen between us. There is way too much time to think. And I'm losing my enthusiasm for a relationship that's bringing me nothing but stress and unhappiness for months. Whatever happens, things will never be the same.

It's dusk when my last ride drops me off at Mammoth. I walk over to the motel I stayed at last time, get a room and take a long hot shower. I watch TV for a while then fall asleep.

This morning my mission is food shopping and shipping food drops to Oregon. Originally I was going to do this resupply at Ashland, but due to our flip it makes sense to do it now, while I'm passing through Mammoth Lakes. At the grocery store, I throw in a few treats like wasabi peas and shelf-stable chocolate milk to drink at my resupply points. Each resupply I try to vary my diet a little.

I carry bags of groceries over to the UPS store. I pack a box which I ship to Shelter Cove. Then, I take the remaining groceries over to the post office. On a picnic table outside, I assemble two Flat Rate Priority Mail boxes, one for Big Lake Youth Camp and another for Timberline Lodge. I like this strategy of mailing my own resupply boxes. Plans change (like our flip); it's good to buy what suits my appetite now and I don't burden other people. If, for whatever reason, my hike ends early, I won't end up with weeks or months' worth of Pop-Tarts and Knorr's.

Chores done, I draw up a *HIKER TO RENO* sign and head out the road. My first ride is a young lady.

"Thanks for stopping, I'm Colter."

"I'm Aubrey."

"Did your parents name you after that old Bread song?"

"Yup."

"I like to ask people why they picked me up."

"Your sign. I met a PCT hiker this summer. He's my boyfriend now. He told me all about you guys hitching, so I wanted to help out."

When she drops me off I soon score another ride, this time from a sixty-ish guy in an old pickup.

"So what are you up to?" he asks.

"I'm hiking the PCT."

"So why are you hitching to Reno?"

I explain. He tells me about his life. He'd once been on top of the world, a young guy, good looking, so good-looking that he'd gotten a job as a model.

"I was working as a clothing model for Playboy. I was traveling around the world, Brazil, Europe, always with beautiful women. I actually stayed at the Playboy mansion a time or two."

"Wow. That was quite a life."

"Yeah. But then I started drinking. Got out of shape. Lost my job. My life went to pieces. I've been drinking ever since. My son helps me out." There is a long thoughtful pause. "So what are you really doing out here?" He thought I was, like him, more or less homeless, and the PCT was just a cover story.

Wyoming and I failed miserably on our last hitch out of Reno. Maybe because we were trying to hitch from the edge of the city. I want to start hitching just north of town.

"How far north are you going?" I ask.

"Just into Reno."

"Tell you what, I'll give you ten dollars if you'll drop me off a few miles north of town."

"OK."

What I hadn't realized is it's still a freeway just north of Reno. I give my driver his $10, thank him, and walk down to try hitching at a ramp, not feeling very comfortable about what is probably questionable legally. No luck. At dusk I walk over to a store, grab something to eat, and find a campsite in an out-of-the-way spot in some sagebrush.

In the morning I walk over to the convenience store, buy a cup of coffee, and strike up a conversation with the clerk.

"Tell you what," he says. "I used to hitch all over this country, and you ain't never getting a ride out of this spot. Nobody will pick you up."

"Is there a northbound bus that comes through here?"

"Nope." He sounds confident, but I'm not going anywhere standing here. Back at the ramp I stand with my sign, trying to think positive. After a few hours, I am positive — positive that the clerk knows what he was talking about. Now I am stuck. I need to retreat to Reno.

I try the other side of the freeway and miraculously got a ride from a trusting young mom.

Man, I hate to ride the Greyhound. On my bus seat, I find a pair of absolutely giant panties. I sit somewhere else. Nearby a lady of about seventy is telling someone about her new boyfriend and what a fabulous lover he is, not sparing the details. In the middle of the night, I arrive in Redding. I walk across the street to wait.

My old smokejumper buddy, Murry, gets out of his car, a little stiff-legged from decades of slamming into mountainsides under a parachute. It's great to see him. It's a long drive to his house near Mugginsville, the tiny collection of houses that Wyoming and I hiked through nearly two months ago. As we near his house Murry is telling me about a local bear when a bear dashes out across the gravel road right in front of us! Murry is already going slow and hits the brakes. We hear a thump but the bear and car are unhurt. Remarkable timing on the storytelling! Murry shows me my sleeping quarters and soon I'm zonked out.

I'm going to take a zero here at Murry's. He shows me around his house. He designed and built it with the help of friends. It's a log home, no neighbors, in the foothills of the Marble Mountains. It's open and airy with an awesome view. It features wooden cabinets and nice windows, a split-level loft, wooden beams, beautiful staircases, bookcases, a wood stove. An absolutely beautiful place with cool, rustic outbuildings.

"Murry, I am hugely impressed. What an incredible accomplishment!"

"Thanks, Buck. I did a lot of the work with draft horses. Dragging the logs with them. Didn't even build a road to the house at first."

"It's so quiet up here."

"Yeah, it's nice."

Murry shows me around the area, telling stories, visiting historical sites. In the evening Murry makes us a good, home-cooked dinner. We relax and reminisce and philosophize. He and I share the same worldview: life is a grand adventure, the meaning of life is to live it fully.

OREGON

"No man is a failure who is enjoying life."

— William Feather

e are up early in the morning and he cooks me a big breakfast. A blacktail doe and a spotted fawn walk past the deck. I pack up my stuff and we load up. We drive to the pass east of Ashland where Wyoming and I started our southbound flip. It seems long ago. At the pass, I double-check to make sure I have everything. I thank and shake hands with Murry, then shoulder my pack and head up the trail. I am NOBO again, headed for Canada.

August 14, Day 114. Mile 1,789; 867 Miles to Canada

I am asleep in my camp in the Sky Lakes Wilderness, low on the flanks of Mt. McLoughlin. The sound of my beeping watch alarm seeps into my consciousness. It is 3:30 AM. I sit up and start packing.

This is going to be my 40-mile day. I crawl out of my tent and look up into the black, moonless sky, a perfect canvas for the arching spray of stars in the Milky Way. It's a sight that always gives me a thrill. It is about 50 degrees with a light breeze.

I eat as I pack. At 3:45 I start walking. One hiking pole is stowed in my pack, the other in my left hand. My tiny LED light is in my right.

How hard is forty miles going to be? There's theory, and there's reality. I often see simple math applied to make big mileage look easy, calculations for the potential miles in a single day, or for an entire thru-hike. There's value in those formulas but they can be very misleading.

The theory: Let's say someone new to long-distance hiking has a 70-day window of time off. They'd love to complete a thru-hike. They go out on a local trail one day and see how fast they can hike. About three miles an hour. Easy. So they figure three miles an hour hiking 14 hours a day, say 6 AM to 8 PM. Call it 13 hours of hiking with a half hour lunch and two 15 minute breaks during the day. $13 \times 3 = 39$ miles a day. $39 \times 70 = 2{,}730$ miles. Plenty of miles to do the PCT or the AT. Barely enough to do the CDT, too, if you are an average hiker taking the most common routes.

The reality: Injuries on the trail are common. Most of these are minor injuries, but they often mean time off trail or a slower pace or both. So let's say this hiker loses three days to injuries, one to a day off and the equivalent of 2 more days due to a slackened pace for a week. Now it's down to 67 days of hiking. His calculations haven't taken into account the time it takes for town stops. It takes hours to hitch to town, buy groceries, visit the post office, do laundry, buy new shoes, shower, order new gear, hitch back out to the trail. A town stop can burn half a day, minimum, even if there's no relaxing or time off involved. If he's kept town stops to a minimum, he might have 17 town stops for the summer. A half day per town stop minimum. Let's say he loses eight days. Now he's got 59 days to complete his hike. Mathematically he's not going to be able to cover the miles for either the PCT or the CDT. In the real world it takes a gutsy, gifted athlete to cover 39 miles a day all summer. Snow, steep trail, rain, heat, humidity, physical ailments, mental struggles: all work against the hiker. The record for hiking the PCT at the time of this writing is 65 days. 2,650 miles divided by 65 days is 40.76 miles a day. The record for the AT unsupported is currently 61 days. 2,178 divided by 61 = 35.7 miles per day.

I have far fewer variables to slow me down for this single day's hike. This is a relatively mellow stretch of trail. The weather looks good. I am in peak shape. On this one-day push I don't need to be concerned with exhausting myself for future days, yet I don't want to injure myself by overdoing it. In order to do 40 miles, I need to start early, keep moving as much as possible, and hike late.

The trail is easy to follow in the bright beam of my little LED light. Trees are silhouetted black against the starry sky. I maintain a steady pace of a little more than 2 1/2 miles an hour. With breaks and lunch, I should be able to do my 40-mile day in less than 20 hours. I've heard some outstanding hikers describe a 40 mile a day as "a cruise." And I've heard slower hikers describe 10-mile days as brutal. I've hiked a lot of miles in my life. This will be my biggest day so far.

After an hour a fork in the trail appears. My light beam falls on a sign for the Twin Ponds trail. I check out my location on the map and keep hiking. The air is cool and calm, perfect for hiking. The only sounds are my footsteps on the trail and an occasional click as my trekking pole strikes a rock.

The stars are slowly disappearing. Clouds must be rolling in. Thin gray light creeps above the eastern horizon. I begin to see objects beyond the reach of my light. I shut it off. If I can see well enough to avoid tripping, navigation is easier without a light, so my eyes can adjust to the dark and I can see farther. That bigger picture helps me stay oriented.

Just ahead, below the PCT, a headlamp bobs. Someone must be approaching up a side trail, from Christi's Springs perhaps? Ten yards ahead, just off the main trail, are the gray shapes of two hikers cowboy camping on the ground. Next to them is a tent. Although I want to talk to the hiker coming up the trail, and I'd planned to get water here, I don't want to wake up their whole camp. I keep walking.

At about 7:30 I've walked ten miles. Not bad. I continue a steady pace for another half hour, then sit down for my first break of the day.

I am walking steadily down the trail when a small brownish creature flickers through the trees down low. I walk as quietly as I can, scanning the timber ahead. There it is! Two of them! Two what? They dart in and out, weaving around the trees. They run into a sunny opening. Young pine martens! One of them bounds over to a fallen log with the other in hot pursuit. The lead marten ducks into a hollow and his sibling races around to cut him off at the other end. After a brief tussle of rolling around on the ground, they sprint to a tree. One jumps up and circles around the tree with the other one quick on his tail. After this fifteen seconds of frenzied activity, the forest is abruptly calm again.

I walk down the trail smiling to myself. It looked like they were having fun! As I come around a bend I spot another marten, this one much bigger, obviously one of the parents. It runs across the trail and onto a pine trunk, scurrying up to the lower branches. I walk closer and can see it peeking down at me, with shiny black eyes below foxlike ears. The marten ducks its head behind the trunk and then out again to take a quick look, its darting movements typical of the weasel family.

The hours and the miles pass. I stop to treat a quart of water from a brook. I pull out my little MP3 player and stick in one earbud and surf FM stations for news. The trail follows a ridgeline off and on for miles. I keep losing my station, so I put my player away.

I am admiring the trail contouring around the side of the mountain ahead of me when I notice a trail off to the left. Two sticks lie across the trail in the direction I was going. Pulling my guidebook out of my left front shirt pocket I take a quick look. I almost headed down the wrong trail!

Late in the morning, I am hiking along an open hillside. Three hikers appear over a spur ridge. They have heavy packs, each with a fishing pole strapped on the side.

"Are you thru-hiking?" the first guy asks.

"Yup. How about you guys?"

"We're just out for the weekend. Taking it easy, trying to do a little fishing. His feet are killing him," he says, nodding towards his friend, hobbling painfully up to the group. His friend smiles weakly.

"That sounds good to me," I say. "The fishing, I mean."

"How far is it to Isherwood Lake?" Unless I'm specifically paying attention to how far I've come from a given point, or unless I know exactly where I am on the map and can measure the distance, I usually have only the vaguest notion. In this case, none.

"Boy, I don't know. I don't recognize the name."

"That's OK. We're going to sit down for a bit and we'll figure it out."

At about 11:30 I reach the Devil's Lake Trail. I've come almost exactly 20 miles so far and am still feeling strong. My maps show a brook about two miles ahead. That will be my next goal: water, a hot meal, and a break. The trail follows the ridge gently downhill, skirting to the south of the shale of Devil's Peak. At the next saddle the trail descends an open, north-facing cirque in a series of switchbacks.

The tiny stream trickles across the trail. I find a flat, shady spot, take off my pack, and pull out my cooking pot and a water bottle. From the small pocket on the back of my pack, I take the two small bottles of Aquamira. I put seven drops of each bottle into one of the white mixing caps, and prop it up where it won't fall over while it sits for five minutes. At the brook, bubbles gurgle up from my submerged canteen as it fills. Plentiful skeets go for blood. I fill my cooking pot and start the water boiling.

The mixed Aquamira is now yellow. If it had been clear I would know I'd used drops from the same bottle twice. My watch timer says 5:57. I dump the contents of the cap into my water bottle, then pour a small amount of water in the mixing cap, slosh it around to rinse the last of the Aquamira out, and dump it into my water bottle.

I grab a random Knorr. "Rice & Pasta Blend with Broccoli in a Chicken Flavored Sauce." I open the pouch and dump it into my plastic mug/stove container. I feel around my food bag and retrieve a couple packages of whole-grain sandwich crackers, one peanut butter and one cheese. They are one of my favorite trail foods.

Steam rises. I pour the boiling water over the rice/pasta in my mug, then cover the mug with my balaclava to hold in the heat. I scarf down the rest of the crackers and then turn to another wonderful, if less healthful, trail food. Almond M&M's. The peanut variety are also hard to beat on a thru-hike. Both varieties are calorie dense, delicious, easy to pack, and the nuts are a good source of protein.

Something is coming down the trail. A hiker appears out of the trees and stops when she spots me.

"Have you seen a man with a blue pack come by here?" She has an accent. A New Zealander. Possibly an Aussie. You'd think I'd be able to tell the difference by now.

"No. I was over at the brook for a bit, but I'm pretty sure no one has come by recently. I'm Colter, are you thru-hiking?"

"Yes. I'm Kea. If you see a guy with the blue backpack, please tell him we will wait up the trail for him."

"Sounds good."

"You're a thru-hiker, too?"

"Yup. Have a good hike."

"You too."

I wonder if her friend has taken the wrong turn that I barely avoided. Nearly everyone misses a turn or two, or ten, during the course of the summer.

My food is ready. I blow on the hot spoonfuls. When it is gone I pack up and hit the trail again, fully fueled up.

At 24 miles Honeymoon Creek flows across the trail. According to my guidebook, the next on-trail water source is 22 miles away. Assuming I make my 40 miles today, I'll have 6 more miles to go tomorrow morning for water. I drink the rest of my water bottle. The ground is muddy from horses, people, and deer. Definitely an important spot to treat the water. I walk upstream a short distance and mix some Aquamira. I use my bottle to pour a couple quarts of water in my collapsible Platypus. Then I fill the quart bottle.

I'm fully hydrated now. I'll use two full quarts yet today. A quart tomorrow morning will get me to the next water.

I am still feeling strong, no blisters or pains. Still, I can tell I've put in some miles. Through big pines, I walk. The grating call of a Clark's Nutcracker comes from the forest. Two of them fly across the trail, gray and white and black with heavy bills.

At 5:00 I pass the Jack Creek Trail and the 30-mile mark, and sit down for my last long break of the day. Mosquitoes descend. I rub a small amount of DEET on the backs of my hands and on my cheeks. My remaining food is a bit sparse, but I have enough. Still, another pound of food would be nice.

Thirty-two miles, 35. As darkness falls I catch a flash of light behind me and turn around. Nothing. That's funny. Maybe it was a headlamp off the trail or something. Another flash. I turn around and watch. It is lightning, beyond hearing distance. I keep plodding along. Now I can hear the thunder. It is full dark. The flashes come faster and the rumble is nearly continuous. For the second time today I hike by the light of my tiny LED. A cool wind swirls through the trees. I smell the approaching rain.

On this bare ground, the trail is difficult to see. I pull out my GPS. When it has a fix I look at my position plotted in the green glow of the tiny topo map. Comparing it to my guidebook I can see I am just a hair short of 40 miles. The storm is rolling in fast. I decide to simply walk in the right direction for ten minutes, find a good camp spot and set up. I'll find the trail in the morning.

A cool wind hits as I reach a flat bench. I sweep my light to evaluate the relative height of the trees to minimize the chance of getting zapped by a bolt of lightning striking a tall tree. It looks pretty good here, with no dead trees or large dead branches that could blow over or fall on me. Just as I peg down the last corners of the tent the first cold drops hit. With one last look to see things are secure, I pull my pack inside with me. I am very tired, but it is a good tired. Forty miles for a mortal like me is a hell of a long way.

It is easy to find the trail this morning. It takes less than two hours to hit the pavement at Highway 62. Across the road is a sign mounted atop a stone-and-concrete pedestal. "Pacific Crest National Scenic Trail," it says. On the right side is a map of the PCT's route through Crater Lake with the badly-weathered caption: "A 33-mile segment of the Pacific Crest National Scenic Trail winds through Crater Lake National Park, passing along the west side of Crater Lake, through subalpine forests and pumice fields."

Next to a PCT emblem are these words: "The Pacific Crest National Scenic Trail is a long-distance trail for hikers and equestrians. It extends 2,638 miles from Canada to Mexico along the rugged and often remote crest of the Cascade Range and Sierra Nevada. It is marked and maintained through 3 states, 8 national parks and monuments,

5 state parks, 24 national forests, 25 wilderness areas, 3 BLM districts, plus state and private lands. Each year, a few determined people travel the entire length on foot or by horse." Determined people. A good choice of words.

I follow Yogi's advice to ignore the sign suggesting that hikers take the more indirect route, and walk the shoulder of the highway towards Mazama Village. At 8 AM there is very little traffic. I take a shortcut down a steep hill and follow the driveway into the Village. A few early-birds are walking around or driving slowly down the side roads. The restaurant is my first goal. Where is it?

"Excuse me, can you tell me where the restaurant is?" I ask a couple walking by.

"It's that building right there."

"Thanks."

I follow the sidewalk around to the other side of the building. There are animal tracks molded into the concrete, deer, bear, and elk.

Very realistic looking and a nice touch. Making sure my shirt is tucked in and I am as presentable as possible, I walk in the front door.

"Are you here for breakfast?" a young lady asks.

"I sure am!"

She leads me to a table. About three tables are already occupied. I see a fairly large pack next to a corner table. It looks too big for a thru-hiker pack.

"Let me know when you're ready to order."

"Actually, I hear the buffet is great. That's what I'll have."

"OK, help yourself."

I lean my pack and poles out of the way so no one will trip on them. On my way to the bathroom, I see someone flipping through a guidebook in the gift shop. Mr. T! He doesn't see me.

After washing up I stand in the buffet line looking at a dizzying variety of food. Waves of delicious aromas waft around me. My mouth watering, I get some biscuits and gravy, pancakes and syrup with butter, bacon, and eggs. In a bowl I scoop some mixed fruit, and grab a cup of yogurt for good measure.

Mr. T walks up as I sit down. Might as well make the best of it. "Mr. T! Would you like to sit down?"

"Hey, Colter. Sure." He walks over to his table, grabs a stuff sack, and sits down.

"How's the hike?"

"Pretty good," he says. "I've lost a lot of weight, though."

"I must have lost about twelve pounds myself. You've really slimmed down!"

"But I don't want to lose too much. I don't think I'm getting enough calories. I think it's making me sleepy." He is pulling out food wrappers from the stuff sack and is writing something down in his notebook. "I've been figuring how many calories a day I need to keep up my strength. I'm trying to record every calorie that I eat."

"How many are you thinking you need?"

"For me, it's something like two hundred calories a mile."

"That sounds about right. I think it's pretty hard to get enough calories on the trail. I'm going to try to eat about four thousand calories right now!"

We talk as I eat round one and round two, then I walk over to the showers. I find a scrap of soap and have a good scrub in the hot water. After getting dressed I wash out a pair of socks and a set of underwear.

Over at the store, I lean my pack just outside the door. From a gallon Ziplock, I pull my spreadsheet showing resupply points. The next one is Shelter Cove Resort, 80 miles away. Four days' worth of food will be plenty. Inside, the hiker food selection is pretty bleak, and expensive. Fuel is on my list, too. I don't see any.

"Do you have any HEET?" I ask.

"We did." The cashier turns around and looks. "We must have sold it all. Let me take a look over here." She walks over and opens a box. "Nope, all sold out. Sorry about that."

"I'll get by, thanks. Do you have a hiker box?"

She points to the side door. "Right outside that door."

In the box are many of the usual hiker donations. I find some oatmeal, some peanut butter, and most importantly, a partial bottle of 70% rubbing alcohol. HEET or denatured alcohol burns cleaner but I've often used 90% rubbing alcohol which worked fine, especially when mixed with remaining HEET.

A lady comes around the corner with a grill. "Would this work to cook on?" she says. Wow. She had overheard me asking about fuel and had gone back to her camp to fetch a grill for me to cook over a wood fire. I'd seen that same lady give a sandwich she'd just bought to some section hikers in the store. A wonderful human being.

"I just found some rubbing alcohol and I think my stove will burn it. Thanks a lot, though."

"You're a thru-hiker?"

"Ah-huh. Just got in this morning."

"That must be really fun."

"It is. And a lot of work."

I stash my hiker box treasures, then go back inside. Snack foods are plentiful. Not so plentiful are the kind of foods I am looking for. I end up with a loaf of bread, some cookies, corn chips, a box of cold cereal, a couple pieces of fruit, and some chocolate. I need a couple more dinners. Usually, I tune out expensive freeze-dried foods on a thru-hike. I have to laugh at myself when I notice the freeze-dried foods that I've overlooked. They will be a good change and not much more expensive than the junk food here. I select several. For right now I buy a pint of Ben and Jerry's "Chunky Monkey" ice cream and an apple.

At a picnic table out front, I spread out my gear near the wall. I mix my remaining fuel with the rubbing alcohol. I set up my stove on the ground to test the mixture.

"Hi, Colter."

I look up. "Hi, Uncle Tom! How's it going?" I haven't seen Uncle Tom since Kennedy Meadows when he was briefing team MegaTex on his plan for hiking the Sierras.

"Great. When did you get in?"

"A couple hours ago."

"What are you up to?"

"I'm going to test out this seventy-percent rubbing alcohol."

It takes two or three tries, but it finally starts. A little hard to light, and smoky. But it will work. Uncle Tom tells me he and Pat are taking a day off here in Mazama.

While we talk I sort all my stuff out, throwing away any trash I can find, then repack everything including the food I've just bought. After I fill a water bottle we say our goodbyes and I hit the trail.

It takes an hour to reach Dutton Creek, then it is a thousand-foot climb over two and a half miles to the Crater Lake rim. The trail passes Rim Village, so I stop for lunch. Rim Village is a swirl of activity, cars and motorcycles and RVs going every which way, pedestrians walking to and fro. There is a long line at the lunch counter but I can't pass up this opportunity for fresh food. I select a large salad with lots of veggies and chicken and grab a chocolate milk to wash it down.

Back on the PCT, the trail follows high above the deep blue lake. Wizard Island rises from the water, looking like a small volcano, which it was. A large group of people are having a picnic right on the trail. Coolers and chairs and children cover the path. I weave my way around them. It is strange to be sharing the PCT with so many.

According to signs along the trail, Crater lake is the deepest lake in the U.S. — 1,949 feet deep. The massive volcanic eruption that created the lake occurred about 7,700 years ago. A 12,000-foot volcanic peak, larger than Mt. Hood, was destroyed in a giant eruption 40 times more massive than the Mt. St. Helen's explosion. It is hard to imagine the experience of people living in the area at that time. A huge peak obliterated, leaving a half mile deep, smoking crater in the ground, deadly debris scattered over a vast area, the world carpeted with falling ash.

Crater Lake

I am thinking too much about my unresolved situation with Stephanie. She doesn't want to talk, and we haven't spoken for ten days or so. We once talked every day if possible. We aren't getting it talked out like we always have in the past and that's a big problem. I like to address and resolve problems that are bothering me rather than putting them on the back burner. There is so much time to think on the trail. It's easy to fall into a negative thinking loop. Many thru-hikes are ended by problems like this. I haven't considered ending the hike because of our fight, but at times it's affecting the enjoyment of my journey. I text her to see if she wants to talk. She doesn't. And she doesn't want to ship my packages to me anymore. She wants to see how we feel at the end of my hike, but our mutual trust is gone. Stephanie has been an important part of my life, but this is, I know, the end of Stephanie and me.

While I am still up high along the Crater I call my parents to update them on my adventure. They are thrilled to hear from me. I fill them in on my hike and hear the news from Minnesota. They are always supportive of all my adventures. Next I call Griff, my smokejumper buddy who will be taking over supply shipping from Stephanie. As usual, he is funny and enthusiastic. I ask him to ship my floored shelter and ultra-light air mattress to Cascade Locks. I plan to swap out some gear for the wetter, cooler weather of Washington state. After these calls, I feel much better. Although I know I will find myself thinking about Stephanie from time to time, I'll try to avoid it as much as I possibly can.

The PCT continues along the crater's rim. I marvel at the intense blue of the lake, cliffs rising 2,000 feet above the water. At 5:30 I cross Rim Drive. The trail leaves the lake behind. Six miles later, as dusk begins to fall, I reach the edge of the Mt. Thielsen Wilderness. Amidst the lodgepoles, I find a flat area with a shelter site free of ant hills and downfall. It has been a day of spectacular scenery, two meals of fresh food, and brushing elbows with hundreds of people, and 21 miles of trail.

The next day the primary landmark is steep, jagged Mt. Thielsen, "The Lightning Rod of the Cascades." The PCT passes along its flanks, then descends to Thielsen Creek. There hasn't been any water since the drinking fountain at Rim Village, 26 1/2 long, hot miles ago. Here, a picturesque brook gurgles down through a sunny green meadow studded with volcanic boulders. The sun on the rich green of fir trees contrasts beautifully with the shadowed blue rock and snow on the rugged north face of Mt. Thielsen. I eat a leisurely hot lunch while enjoying this magical spot.

Two hours after lunch the trail crosses a saddle between Howlock Mountain and Tipsoo Peak. At 7,550 ft, a sign identifies this as the highest point along the PCT in Oregon/Washington. The trail isn't difficult here, and the climbs and descents make for relatively easy mileage.

This evening the last sun illuminates long stringers of pale green moss hanging amidst the dark shadows of the evergreens. What is that bright orange object next to the trail up ahead? I finally realize it's the orange light of sunset shining through a hole in the timber onto a bleached log. I am walking through an enchanted forest at the end of a 31-mile day.

I am up before 6 AM. It's Tuesday, August 17. My campsite is just off the saddle above Tolo Camp. I eat a couple of Pop-Tarts and two granola bars as I pack. It is a familiar routine and I am soon cruising down the trail.

The gentle grade of the PCT skirts around Tolo Mountain and Windigo Butte. I reach a fork in the trail. A sign points left to the Windigo Pass Trailhead. Is the trailhead on the PCT? Time to check the maps. A quick glance shows the trailhead is off the PCT so I take a right. Nice to have maps! At the pass is a water cache left by Lloyd Gust. It has a distinct chlorinated taste but beggars aren't choosers. I'm glad to have it. Lloyd has left a note offering to give rides or assistance to any PCT hikers. He's a true Trail Angel.

Summit Lake appears to the right of the trail. A peninsula juts out into the lake. I've already done 17 miles.

I'll cook a lunch and enjoy a nice view over the lake. Clouds have been building behind me for over an hour. Thunder rumbles in the distance. It's going to rain sooner or later. So far, however, I've been on the sunny side of any rainstorm. I walk down to the lake to fill my cooking pot. Ducks paddle around on the clear water. Low clouds begin sweeping just above the lake. Soon my water is boiling. I study my guidebook as I wait for the Knorr's to soak. A few sprinkles of rain hit me, but each time I scan the sky it looks like, for now, the rain won't amount to anything. Miraculously the mosquitoes are scarce and the sun stays out most of the time making for a very pleasant and scenic lunch.

At Emigrant Pass, I think about the "Lost Wagon Train of 1853." It was attempting to take a shortcut off the Oregon Trail when it traversed through Emigrant Pass that October. Lacking accurate maps or a competent guide, this party of over 1,000 settlers became confused as to exactly where their route lay. It turned out the road they were trying to follow was incomplete. Finally, the emigrants were exhausted and starving, with many near death in the cold and snow of the Cascades. Luckily, established settlers found an advance rider of the wagon train at his cooking fire. They mounted a heroic, swift and massive rescue operation, thus avoiding a redux of the Donner Party.

I hike into the Diamond Peak Wilderness. My sunny day is gone. Dark ominous looking clouds roll over the sky. Thunder rumbles steadily and it begins to sprinkle. I am cranking out the miles and keeping tabs of how near the lighting is.

At 6:00 I look back. Serious rain is imminent. I watch for a good camp spot. Off to my right, there is a low finger ridge with a flat "knee" only fifty yards off the trail. There I find nice dry ground that will drain off to three sides. It's safe from water running down from above, too, especially important when using a floorless shelter like mine. There are no dead trees nearby that the storm could blow down on me. There is a ridge well above that will be more attractive to lightning than my spot. Thunder booms louder and louder. In record time my shelter is up and I quickly drag everything inside and zip up the door. In just minutes the sound of pounding rain approaches and soon it is hammering my tarp.

Rather than pushing on and getting soaked, I have set up just in time to keep everything nice and dry. The flash-crack-BOOM of lightning goes on and on. This is one of the most dramatic thunderstorms I've ever experienced. I watch the rain cascading off the fly onto to the ground and draining away. The rain falls harder with a deafening roar. The storm is so dramatic, so loud, and I am so warm and dry, I laugh out loud. I scrounge some cold food and eat while I listen to the storm and watch as the flashes of lightning light up the drenched forest in a frozen instant of light. The odor of the sodden pine needles reminds me of other storms on other adventures.

I count the seconds between flashes of lightning and the following thunder, dividing by five to estimate the number of miles. Some strikes are less than a mile away. At least twice I jump when a deafening thunderclap follows a bright flash by a fraction of a second. What did primitive people think at times like these? What did they think was the cause of such violence? No wonder children and dogs are frightened! I am glad I'm not camped along a ridgetop.

Now the lightning abates, the rain slackens. I drift off to sleep. My subconscious awakens me when I hear the sounds of footsteps outside. It is something big. Bear? Elk? Then I recognize the sound of squishing-wet shoes and hear the metallic clink of a hiking pole hitting a rock. I feel for my watch and press the light button. The faint green glow shows it is after 10 PM! Apparently someone has gotten caught in the storm and has decided to keep pushing since they are already wet. Likely they are chilled and plan to walk until they warm up and then set up camp with the rain having passed. I didn't envy whoever it was.

The next morning I am skirting around Diamond Peak with its steep, rocky hillside. Last night's rainstorm has created many little brooks. I water up at one of them and push on, passing a series of little lakes, some of them nearly hidden in thick forest. One is aptly named Hidden Lake.

At about noon the jeep road at Pengra Pass appears out of the trees. I pull out my maps and take a right. A rumbling steadily grows. A long train is headed down the tracks that skirt Odell Lake. I watch the last cars file by the crossing then walk the short distance to a paved road which leads to Shelter Cove Resort. The supply box I shipped from Mammoth should be waiting for me there.

After a minute or two, I see an unfamiliar hiker coming towards me. He said he is a southbounder coming from Shelter Cove.

"Did you see any other thru-hikers?" I asked.

"Two couples. Lloyd is driving them into town. Did you see them? They left just a few minutes ago."

"Drat. I must have just missed them. Was it by chance Cliffhanger and Milk Sheik?"

He says it was Charmin and Hasty, with Hiker 816 and Meryl.

"Hiker 816? Any idea how he got that name?"

"Well I think the story is that he'd written on one of his resupply boxes 'Hiker 8/6.' Like, you note that you're a hiker and the arrival date. Anyway, the person he was hiking with said, 'Why does your box say Hiker 816?' The slash looked like a '1'. Later, at least one more person glanced at the box and asked the same thing. That was it, he was Hiker 816."

After bidding our goodbyes I've only hiked a few steps when a pickup slows down as it draws even with me. I know I am less than a mile from Shelter Cove but I figure, what the heck, might as well take a ride. The driver stops and rolls down his window.

"How's the hike?"

"Great!" He is looking down at something and I am ready to accept his kind offer and throw my pack in back. He holds something out the window.

"I lost my dog. Here's my number. I'd appreciate it if you'd give me a call if you see him."

"Sure." He drives off.

Fifteen minutes later I reach the campground, walking between a varied collection of tents, RVs, and trailers. People sit on lawn chairs sipping beers, or lean over charcoal grills flipping burgers, looking up at me curiously. I think I might be invited to chow down on a burger while regaling them with riveting and amusing anecdotes about life on the trail, but no such luck. And I'm not a Yogi-er at heart so I make it to the office without any fresh burger juice on my shirt.

A young lady is working the cash register.

"I'm Colter. I'm a thru-hiker. You should have a box for me here, Bruce Nelson is my real name."

She pulls out a clipboard.

"I can spot you thru-hikers a mile away," she says, smiling. "Nelson, you said?"

"Yup."

"I don't see it. When did you mail it?"

"Ahhh, let me see, the tenth? So what's that, eight days ago?"

"How did you send it?"

"UPS. They said it would take something like four days."

"Are you sure you had the right address?"

"Yup. I called here to verify the address while I was standing in the UPS office filling out the paperwork."

"Well if it's here, it would be on this list."

"Hmm," I say. "Let me make a call."

I walk outside and dig through my paperwork for the shipping receipt. They'd told me to call if I ran into any problems. I soon have them on the line. I give them my tracking number. "It says it was delivered on August fourteenth," they say.

"Alright, thanks! I appreciate it."

I walk back into the office.

"They have delivery confirmation for the fourteenth."

"Well that's strange."

"Where do you store your packages? Do you mind if I dig around and see if I can find it?"

"No problem, I'll get the key. Hang on a second."

As she heads back to the cash register, she glances down and pauses.

"Here it is! I don't know what it's doing here and why it isn't on the list. But we found it, anyway."

"Thanks! No problem. I'm just glad to get it."

I ask about showers and laundry and follow an employee who unlocks the laundry building. He points out the shower building a few steps away.

I dump out my pack and carefully sort out everything that can be washed. In the laundry building, I quickly strip off my dirty clothes and put on my rain gear. Into the washing machine go two pairs of underwear, two pairs of socks, pants, shirt, and shoes.

Stepping next door to the showers I dig out the quarters I'd gotten at the office, but I need more than I'd anticipated. I dig through all my stuff and find just enough quarters. I take off my rain gear and plunk in the quarters and get ready to scrub like mad because the shower will only run three minutes, not long when you're filthy. The shower ends while I am rinsing. Going ultralight means making small concessions on luxuries such as towels. My Kick-Off bandana is my towel.

I put my rain gear back on and walk over to the laundry building. The door is locked! Did I lock it some way? Did someone else lock it? I walk back to the office, in full rain gear on a sunny, warm day. My outfit makes perfect sense in the thru-hiking world, but I'm getting some strange looks from some campers in shorts and t-shirts.

When my laundry is done I simply pull it out of the washer and put on. Nylon clothes dry fast in the sun. My shoes will be damp for while, but that's part of the game. At the store, I buy a Drumstick cone and a can of Pepsi. When I step outside someone is drying gear on a low fence near the lake. As I walk up a young woman with wet hair is going through her gear.

"Hi, I'm Colter. Are you thru-hiking?"

"Hi, I'm Kentucky Blue. I'm not thru-hiking this year, but my friend is."

"Who's your friend?"

"Guthook."

"Really?! Where is he? I haven't seen him for a thousand miles."

"He should be back in a bit."

"I saw you in Mazama, didn't I? I didn't see Guthook then, though."

"Yeah, that was me."

"Colter!"

I turn around.

"Hey, Guthook! How's the hike?"

"Great!"

It's been days since I've seen another thru-hiker. We exchange the usual information: who and what we've seen, who is ahead of us and who is behind us, the best trail magic, and what we expect to find ahead of us. Guthook has taken his own path in the beard department. It's standard to start the trail clean-shaven and grow a full, bushy beard on the trail. (At least for guys!) When I first met Guthook he had a full beard. Now he was sporting a nicked but otherwise smooth face. The transformation is amazing.

"They couldn't find my package," he says.

"Really? They couldn't find mine, either, at first."

They had looked high and low but apparently Guthook's package really isn't here. He'll have to buy expensive food from a limited selection here. He is naturally quite disgusted after having gone to the time and expense to ship quality food to himself.

As we talk a chubby golden-mantled ground squirrel comes hopping out. He watches carefully as Guthook and I eat, reaching up with his little paws, making little grabbing motions.

"Aw, go away, I've seen much cuter than you," Guthook says. I laugh. Just then a clump of crushed peanuts drops off the cone I am eating and the squirrel scurries over, picks it up, and scurries away.

"Looks like he's been eating well this summer," I say.

"Well, I'm headed out. I'll see you down the trail."

"All right. Have fun."

I walk through the campground and towards Willamette Pass. Just after crossing the road there is a trailhead. A fellow walks up to his car as I approach.

"How was the hike?" I say.

"Good. Are you doing the PCT?"

"Yeah, how about you?"

"I'm actually working out a plan to ride it on horseback."

"Wow! After seeing the trail, I think that would be harder than walking it."

"Do you need food or anything?"

"I just resupplied, but thanks."

"Sure, how about an orange?"

"That would be great, thanks."

We talk about his plans and he asks some questions, especially about the Sierras. We say our goodbyes and I began the long climb out of the pass. When I get to Lower Rosemary Lake I meet two hikers heading my way.

"Are you thru-hiking?"

"Yes. How about you guys?"

"We are just hiking around this area. Where are you from?"

"Alaska. How about you guys?'

"No kidding. I'm from Fairbanks!"

"Well it's a small world, because I'm from Fairbanks too."

"People think it's funny that Alaskans are down here hiking, but this is beautiful country."

I reach the intersection to Maiden Peak Ski Hut. I want to check it out. It's supposed to be nice and shelters along the PCT are a rarity. It takes me a minute to find the right trail, but then it is a short walk to the hut. Compared to the typical shelter on the Appalachian Trail it is palatial, an 8-sided log structure with wooden shingles and a nice overhang over the doorway. Inside are tables and chairs and even a wood stove. On the wall are posters explaining how to identify lynx and wolverines. "Rules of the House" requests visitors not leave garbage or food that would attract animals. On the table is a logbook. I sit down and snack while I flip through the register. There is an entry from Wyoming, who is about three days ahead of me. She says hello to Anne and me and that her hike is going well. Among the many other hikers I recognize are Swift and Buckeye, formerly known as Justin and Melissa. They are the couple that had borrowed my bear canister and ice axe. They are about a day ahead of me. It is clear they were enjoying their adventure. They report braving the mosquitoes by swimming in a nearby lake.

This would be a marvelous spot stay, especially in the hard rainstorm last night. I still have a couple hours of daylight left, so after a nice break I head down the trail.

Shortly after passing the Maiden Creek Trail I am dropping down a gentle hillside when I hear the distinctive whine of turbine engines. An aircraft is approaching, low. With last night's thunderstorm and the Redmond, Oregon smokejumper base being only 50 miles or so away it's probably a smokejumper aircraft. A minute later, I see it, a Sherpa jumpship, flying low over the timber about a mile to the northeast. I watch it through my monocular, hoping to see them jump, but after a couple of orbits it disappears to the south, the sound of its engines slowly fading. The only sounds are once again my footsteps and a gentle breeze in the treetops.

After walking another mile down the moderate slope I hear a plane coming from the south and soon it is passing overhead. The plane banks into a slow left-hand turn, the kind a smokejumper plane makes when everyone is looking out of the left side windows and the jump door, attempting to spot a smoke. I see its open jump door but try as I might I can't see any smokejumpers.

The plane orbits overhead and I watch for streamers. Wind streamers are crepe paper, usually yellow, red or blue, ten inches wide and twenty feet long. They are used to determine wind speed and direction and to detect down-drafts. After finding a fire the smokejumper spotter (jumpmaster) will radio dispatch for the go-ahead to man it. The plane will circle as the spotter and jumpers look for the safest jump spot within a reasonable distance of the fire. Ideal is a large, open, rock-free meadow at a safe distance from the fire, on a calm or low-wind day. Rarely is the jump spot ideal. Picking the best spot means choosing a combination of lesser hazards.

Then I smell smoke. I hadn't seen the haze of drift smoke from up high. There is a small fire nearby, the fire they are looking for. I walk straight into the light breeze expecting to see a puff of smoke from the base of a lighting-splintered tree trunk.

I know from my years of smokejumping that fire reports can be undependable. People mistakenly report wisps of low-lying clouds, blowing dust or even clouds of pollen. Sometimes a tiny smoldering fire is there but it proves nearly impossible to spot from the air.

They have made several orbits and still no streamers. But now I know what they don't: there is definitely a fire here. I can smell it. They will soon leave if they can't find anything. I dig out my cell phone to report the fire. The signal is weak but I get an answer:

"Nine-one-one."

"Yes, I'd like to report a wildfire."

"Sir... you'd like to report..."

"Yes, can you hear me?"

"... fire... repeat."

"I'd like to report a wildfire near Bobby Lake."

Then the call was dropped. My phone rang moments later.

"Hello?"

"... called... information..." I glance at my phone. No service.

It's easier and cheaper to put a fire out when it's small. I look up at the plane and know what is going on: the spotter is kneeling at the open jump door, scanning the forest below, the roar of wind filling the fuselage. The jumpers are sweating in their padded suits, helmets in hand to prevent them from rolling out of the open door, faces next to the row of windows, looking for the fire. I am between two worlds, the world of smokejumpers where I lived for over two decades, and my present world as a thru-hiker.

The Sherpa levels off and heads north, the sound of the engines quickly fading. My weak phone signal is gone.

Just before dark, I find a good camp spot in open Lodgepole pines. There is level, dry ground. There are no rocks and a carpet of pine needles, with good drainage should it happen to rain again,

Mosquitoes buzz around my head. My bandana hangs from beneath my ball cap, around the back and sides of my head. It does a remarkably good job of keeping them off my neck and face, but I frequently have to brush them off my hands. I pull the food bag out of my pack, then the sleeping bag, tent, stove, and spare clothing bag. Last I pull out my sleeping pad which is carried as a vertical, hollow cylinder in my pack, the other items stuffed inside. The cylinder keeps the frame-less pack from slumping and transfers weight to the hip belt.

I set up my alcohol stove. From my food bag, I select a pouch. The package says, "Rice and Pasta blend in a soy sesame sauce with carrots, peas, leeks and red bell peppers." These Knorr's are a staple for thru-hikers. Found in most grocery stores they are light, easy to prepare, and taste good. I prefer the varieties that feature dried veggies. Most have about 450 calories. Hikers often add butter or olive oil to boost the calories. I tear off the top of the pouch. I pour it in one half of the plastic canister, now serving as a bowl.

Turning, I find the level spot and roll my pad out, curved side down. I lay down on top of it. It's good to have a small hollow at your hips so I feel around until I find a little hollow, reorient my pad and lay down again. Perfect.

Leaving my pad where it lies, I position my shelter over it. I stake out the front corners, then step around and stake out the back. I grab a hiking pole, extend it a few more inches, and then flip the pole tip up and put it in a grommet at the inside of the shelter's peak. After raising the shelter and positioning the pole's handle on the ground, I stake out the front guy-line, then stake out the back corners. I am home for the night.

From under the shelter, I retrieve the sleeping pad and reposition it inside. I pull my sleeping bag from its stuff sack and give it a few good shakes. Unzipping the door I throw the sleeping bag inside and quickly zip up the door to keep the mosquitoes out. I set my fuel bottle out of reach of the shelter to prevent the possibility of grabbing it and taking a swig during the night when I am half asleep. I put a water bottle within easy reach.

White steam swirls up from the stove, pushing up a corner of the lid, indicating a rolling boil. I pick up the Foster's can by the insulated cozy and by the very bottom of the windscreen, which stays cool, and pour the boiling water into the rice/pasta. From its home in my left shirt pocket I take my Lexan spoon, stir the water and pasta, then screw on the other half of the canister, covering it with my balaclava. Lastly, I wrap the windscreen around it. The sealed canister, balaclava and windscreen combination serve as another cozy. In lightweight backpacking a cozy is used to retain heat, and avoid simmering, thereby saving on fuel.

I gather all my loose gear into my pack which I set just inside the door, then put the soaking food just outside the door. Taking a few steps, I take one last pee then crawl into the shelter and pull my pack inside with me, zipping the door shut. Mosquitoes buzz outside the netting. Dusk is falling. I shine my LED light around the inside of my shelter and kill a half-dozen that followed me in. I pull my shoes and sweat-dampened socks off. I use the dirty socks to brush off my feet and scrub away toe jam from between my toes. I give the socks a good shake outside then throw them on the sloped netting inside where air can circulate all around them during the night. Then I dump out my tiny clothing stuff sack and put on my sleeping socks. This is a new habit, a good one: keeping a separate pair of dry clean socks just for sleeping. Pulling on those clean socks is a favorite part of my day.

I take my GPS out of my other front pocket and turn it on and set it to the side. I put my down jacket and other spare clothes in a stuff sack for a pillow. My shoes are out of the way near the foot of my sleeping bag. My GPS now has a fix and I label my campsite P 8-17, standing for Pacific Crest Trail, camp of August 17th. I plot camp on the guidebook map with my pen: 8-17.

I turn off my GPS and unzip the door and quickly grab the hot food. Carefully propping it up where it can't fall over, I zip the door shut again and kill two mosquitoes that have managed to sneak in. After stirring my meal one last time, I lean on one elbow and lift a spoonful. It is still too hot to eat without blowing on it. I am hungry and the food tastes great. Doing dishes consists of scraping out the bowl and licking off my spoon. For dessert, I have a handful of Craisins and some Peanut M&M's. I pull on my balaclava and zip up my bag. In minutes I am sound asleep.

It is a typical quiet night. Camped off the trail in a remote area like I am, there are no car horns, no human voices, no sound of television, no dogs barking.

About 2 AM I awake needing to pee. I crawl out of my tent and walk a few steps in the pine needles. Looking up through gaps in the pines, the clear black sky is sprinkled with bright stars. An owl hoots nearby. I crawl back into my shelter, drink some water, and soon fall asleep again.

I wake up to a barely perceptible gray light. Without looking at my watch I know it as about 5:40. I sit up and put on my down jacket. Sleeping socks off. Hiking socks and shoes on. I've worn my hiking shirt and pants to bed. It looks like a clear morning. I take a quick photo of my camp. Camps are good memories.

Back on the trail, I watch for a high spot where I might find cell reception. I try several times but no luck. Finally, I have a bar or two. Directory assistance gives me a number for fire dispatch.

"Dispatch."

"I'm a retired smokejumper. I'd like to report a fire along the PCT."

"Which fire? There are several fires along the PCT."

He's already ticked me off. "It's a fire near Bobby Lake."

"We know about that one."

"The one I'm talking about is on the west side of Bobby Lake."

"We've got people on it."

"Smokejumpers?"

"Yes."

"OK, thanks." I hang up.

When I first saw the plane, I was hoping a couple of smokejumpers would leap out and I would be there to meet them on the ground.

I'd help them fight the little fire and we'd sit around the campfire that night, telling jump stories and laughing. In the morning I'd help them get their 'chutes gathered up. It would be just like old times.

Once the plane had flown away, it was Plan B. I thought I'd call in the fire, dispatch would thank me, and a jump plane would be rolled. The two or four jumpers fighting the fire would be told that a salty old jumper had called it in. I'd be a hero. Instead, dispatch just wanted me to go away as fast as possible, even before they knew for sure what I had to tell them. I had to laugh. I wonder when they dropped those jumpers?

My friend Johnny Mac, a long time Alaska smokejumper now living in Bend, is waiting for me to call. He picks up right away. We agree to meet at 08:30 tomorrow at Elk Lake Resort.

My mind wanders as I follow the winding trail. *Plan B,* I think. In my mind, I see the emergency cut-away handle smokejumpers have on their parachute harness in case their main parachute malfunctions. On that handle, one smokejumper had taken a Sharpie and written "Plan B." I laugh out loud thinking about it.

I take a side trail the short distance to Charlton Lake, cooking oatmeal as I sit looking out over the water. Smoke drifts lazily from a smoldering campfire near a tent 100 yards away, barely visible through the trees. Thru-hiking is not camping. They sat around a campfire last night. They're still sleeping in. They'll get up whenever they wake up. I go to bed at dark. I am hiking every day before sunrise.

Thirty minutes after sitting down I am walking again. There are dozens of lakes and ponds along the PCT today. That seems surprising as the area is generally volcanic. Volcanic areas tend to have less standing water because the ground is porous. I stop for a photo at a Three Sisters Wilderness sign. It is a lovely, clear day.

There are gentle rises and descents and more lakes and ponds and plenty of mosquitoes. I have a high tolerance for mosquitoes but today I put DEET on the backs of my hands and on my face, the rest of me protected by clothing.

Towards sunset, I approach the Old Skyline Trail and decide to take the next good campsite I find. I've come about 30 miles today. There is a considerable stretch with no good campsites. I've found that potential campsites that look good from a couple hundred yards often prove too rocky, wet or steep. Nonetheless, when I see a flat area in the open trees a hundred yards downhill from the trail I walk down to check it out. There is plentiful downfall in the area, but I soon find a nice, dry flat spot without any dead trees within falling distance of my shelter.

This morning, August 20, I need to hike six miles to Elk Lake Resort by 8:30. As the sun hits the meadows frost sparkles in the grass.

Four miles fly by. I am standing at a trail junction in an old wildfire burn above Elk Lake. After quickly checking the map I cruise down to the lake and am soon walking up to the resort. It is still only about 7:40 and there isn't much activity. To my dismay, the door leading into the restaurant is locked. I sit on a bench looking out over Elk Lake. Sailboats and fishing boats are tied up along the docks. Steam rises off the warm water. A volcanic peak, presumably Mt. Bachelor, looms not far away.

A young man walks out of the lodge.

"Do you know what time the restaurant opens?"

"I'll bet if you knock on the door they'll get you some food," he said.

"Thanks. I'll give it a try."

"The hiker packages are out back if you sent one here. There's a hiker box, too."

"No package, but I'll check out the hiker box, thanks."

I take a look at the hiker box and find a couple of organic freeze-dried meals. Variety is the spice of life!

The restaurant door is unlocked when I walk up. The lady behind the bar says, "Sit anywhere you like. Coffee?"

"Yes, thanks."

I sat down and looked around. Log walls and beams. Snowshoes and historic photos. My kind of place.

"What kind of music do you want to listen to?"

"I don't care, whatever you like."

"Pick something."

"Ahh..."

"What's on your iPod?"

I had to laugh. "I guess that's a good way to find out what people really like. Old stuff, mostly, I guess. Springsteen, Bonnie Raitt, Eagles."

She turns on an oldies station. I order a big breakfast and flip through my guidebook while I wait. Soon she sets out a large plate of eggs, bacon, wheat bread, and fruit. It looks awesome.

"Have you had many thru-hikers come through this year?"

"Yeah, quite a few."

A hiker comes in and asks about some first aid supplies. She takes him back to the corner and shows him what they have. I talk to him briefly. He is doing a long section of the trail, northbound. I suggest he check the hiker box for first aid supplies as he hasn't found what he is looking for.

I pay my bill, thank the waitress. Outside I sit where I can watch the driveway leading to the lodge. Right on time, my friend drives up.

"Johnny Mac!"

"Buck, good to see you."

We are both beaming as we shake hands. His kids hop out of the car and there are introductions all around. As we drive into Bend John asks about my hike and I ask about his family. His kids politely participate in the conversation.

John gives me a tour of his home. He has a separate guest house with everything I need, bathroom, kitchen, shower, laundry. From the deck, I can see the Three Sisters. After getting cleaned up I walk over to the main house. I show him some of my photos.

"You've got some nice shots there."

"Hey, I'm not the one who took the most famous photo in the history of firefighting." He laughs. While fighting a fire in Montana back in August, 2000, he was riding in a pickup driving over a bridge across the Bitterroot River. He spotted some elk standing in the river with a backdrop of flaming mountainside. "STOP!" he yelled and jumped out, taking only a moment to snap the shot. In no time the photo had appeared on dozens of websites and been forwarded countless times via email. Since then it's been featured in hundreds of places, including magazines and book covers.

"I was just in the right place at the right time."

"Yes, but you recognized it was a great shot, and actually took the photo. A lot of people would have done neither."

We have a nice dinner with his wife and kids, eating outside in the warm dusk. They tell me about their life and

Bend, here at the foot of the Cascades, surrounded by high desert.

At 09:30 John and the kids drop me off back at the trailhead. I "connect my steps" from where I'd hit the paved road, then take the alternate Horse Lake Trail to where it intersects the PCT.

As the trail climbs, drift smoke from distant fires hangs in the air. It seems appropriate, somehow, because my links to Oregon are largely through firefighting. Many years ago I came West to work in the Prineville District, at a tiny Guard Station next to the equally tiny desert town of Hampton. One weekend three co-workers and I drove to the mountains to climb South Sister, which today, thirty years later, still towers above the Pacific Crest Trail. As a flatlander, our climb of South Sister was a thrilling adventure. We left the hot desert and climbed 5,000 vertical feet past glaciers, far above treeline to the 10,358 feet summit. I remember the jubilation of standing on the summit in the cold wind, the world sprawled far below me.

The PCT crosses a large, treeless flat below South Sister. It is an unusually pleasant stretch of trail. Moderate temperatures with a light breeze keep the mosquitoes at bay. The trail is gentle with open views of a series of volcanic peaks towering above wildflower-carpeted meadows. It is a fine day to be outside, to remember, to ponder the future and to revel in the living moment.

At a trail junction next to a large pond three hikers are having a discussion. It is Saturday. Numerous weekend hikers are on the trail, taking advantage of the weather. After months of hiking, most thru-hikers are skinny, weather-beaten, and wearing faded clothing. I can tell they aren't thru-hikers. We exchange our hellos. A few steps later I see Mr. T sitting next to the trail. There is no polite way to avoid him. Instead, I sit down in the shade ten feet away.

"Mr. T! How's the hike?"

"Not too bad."

As we talk I prepare my cooking gear and fill my cooking pot at the pond. I sit back down, put some water on to boil, pull out my food bag out and lean back against my pack.

"So what do you do in the real world?" I ask.

"Retired military," he said.

"What branch?"

"Army."

"What was your specialty?"

"Infantry. I trained as a paratrooper but I got hurt."

"I was in an airborne unit in the Alaska National Guard," I said. I think that did it. It changed the way Mr. T and I related to each other.

I finished eating before he did. "See you down the trail."

"OK."

The miles roll by, with the Three Sisters towering to the right. The trail traverses lava fields and pumice flats, lush meadows, and stands of hemlock and fir.

Two southbounders approach. They are out for a long weekend. "How far to the next water?" one asks.

"I wasn't really paying attention, but let me think." I pull out my map. "The next creek has water. Looks like it's about a mile."

"Thanks." We all sit down for a break. One is from Minnesota, a large-animal veterinarian.

"I grew up on a dairy farm in Minnesota. Large animal vet, that can be a hard job."

"Yeah, but I like it. When did you start your hike?"

"I started April twenty-first. That's good you like being a vet, it's an important job."

"Wow. That's epic. Any big adventures, bear attacks or falling off a cliff or anything like that?"

"Giardia was probably the biggest challenge."

"I had giardia once. In northern Minnesota on a long backcountry trip. I was sick and I knew it was giardia. I knew that horse wormer kills giardia. I went up to a farmhouse that had horses in the pasture and said, 'This is going to sound like a funny question, but do you have any horse wormer?' I explained I was a vet and what it was for. He had some and gave it to me. I called my brother, he's a physician. We worked out how much I should take. It worked great!" (People, don't try this at home!)

Just then Mr. T walks up. "Hey, here's some hiker trash!" he says.

"Hi, Mr. T," I reply. The two other hikers are muttering under their breaths after he passes.

"Sorry about that," I say. "That's just the way he is." I try to explain that "Hiker Trash" is kind of a badge of honor in the thru-hiking world and that Mr. T, unfortunately, simply has a knack for pissing people off.

Near Obsidian Falls pieces of black volcanic glass begin to appear. Above the falls the ground is littered with fractured obsidian. It is now early evening, just after six, and the low sun glints off the shiny stones.

Rounding a corner I can see several peaks rising in the thin smoky haze to the north, Mt. Washington, Three-Fingered Jack and Mt. Jefferson, the tallest, ribboned with glaciers. Glacier Creek babbles through one of the prettiest meadows of the whole trip: lush green grass richly-strewn with pinkish-red Indian Paintbrush, yellow Cinquefoil, white Yampa. The air is heavy with the sweet fragrance of the blue and white flowers of Lupines. I drop my pack and take my camera out, stepping carefully as I look for a perspective that will do justice to the colorful beauty of the meadow. Just as I sit down Mr. T walks up. I am glad he didn't show up earlier.

"I was just taking some photos of these wildflowers."

"Wow," he says. Pulling out his camera, he holds it out at arm's length and snaps off two or three shots.

We are both leaving, so, for the first time, I walk with Mr. T. I am hoping to find a campsite along White Branch

Creek. I stop to take more pictures and Mr. T hikes on. Towards evening, when the trail turns up the creek, I see Mr. T just ahead at the creek crossing, looking at his guidebook. He looks up and says, "I was going to camp around here, but I haven't seen any spots, have you?"

Break in a meadow of blue lupines and red Indian paintbrush

"Nope, nothing. I'm going to keep cruising until I see something." I climb steadily. When I glance back Mr. T is following again. A large glacier on the slopes of North Sister appears to the south. There is a visible trail running up the mountain straight ahead of us.

"Hopefully that's not our trail," I say, pulling out my guidebook.

"Yeah, me too."

"Looks like we take a left, kind of across the slope. I'm glad we don't have to make a big climb yet tonight."

We are crossing a lava field as the sun sinks to the horizon, blazing crimson through the thin smoke. I take my camera out. Black silhouettes of scattered fir trees, living and dead, loom in the foreground. Above, wispy clouds are pierced by the rays of the setting sun. To the east the slopes of North Sister are bathed in a rosy alpine glow, accented by white glaciers, ravines in black shadow. The light is magical.

A friend of mine, a professional photographer, once said, "Light is everything." A scene in poor light is just a photo. Perfect light can bring the shot to life, lending an almost supernatural quality.

The color is draining from the sky. I put my camera away. I pull out my little LED light and hurry down the trail to find a campsite. Mr. T is ahead of me a few hundred yards. The light from his headlamp bobs down some switchbacks.

When I catch up to him it is dark, and he says, "Hopefully this isn't one of those situations where we get in a chain of events that ends up with somebody hurt. Like when we are tired at the end of the day and it's dark and we are hurrying to a campsite."

"I think we're OK. It's dry, we know where we are, we're warm, we've got lights, and we aren't exhausted."

At the bottom of the hill is a trickle of water. We walk until the terrain starts flattening out. I find a campsite. Mr. T is setting up a hundred yards away. A bright, three-quarter moon is rising over the peaks, casting black shadows on the ground. I fill up a quart bottle of water and treat it. I set up my shelter, swatting aggressive mosquitoes, and eat some cold food. Twenty minutes after finding my spot I crawl in my bag. Over at his tent Mr. T is doing his camp chores.

The morning is cool. The trail skirts a lava field and passes barren Yapoah Crater. Low hanging clouds drift slowly overhead, brushing the treetops. They part just enough at Scott Pass for me to look back at the snowy slopes of North Sister. The PCT leaves the forest and crosses a rough lava field. To the south, across the jumbled lava and scattered trees, the Three Sisters tower; to the north, Mt.

Washington, Three-Fingered Jack, Mt. Jefferson, and Mt. Hood, along with lesser peaks. It is a place for long views.

Cars flicker past low spots in the lava as I near McKenzie Pass. I cross the highway and walk out onto more lava on the other side. At the trailhead, there is a small water cache left by Trail Angel Lloyd Gust. My guidebook shows it is nearly twelve miles to Big Lake Youth Camp. That's my next water source. A minimalist on carrying water, I decide to not deplete the cache but to push on to Big Lake. The trail passes through an island of green trees. I stop and look at the edge of the lava, frozen as it cooled 3,000 years ago, so recent in geologic time that the lava is still sharp and abrasive. I imagine the molten lava glowing orange, smoke boiling up from burning trees as they are slowly engulfed.

The trail crosses another enormous lava field towards Mt. Washington. Scattered in this sea of stone are green, dead and dying trees. Rock cairns sporadically mark the trail. I take out my MP3 player from my shirt pocket and scan for stations and recognize the sound and cadence of This American Life, a favorite radio program of mine. People are fascinating. Most people have interesting stories if you ask the right questions. The program skillfully gleans stories worth hearing. For me, it's like reading a good book that brings me to another world for a while.

I sit down for a snack then follow the trail down a thousand feet through ragged trees and into an old forest fire. The trail follows another giant lava flow for a few hundred yards before beginning a long climb along the southwest flank of Mt. Washington. I reach a campspot which my guidebook identifies as Dry Coldwater Springs. On oxymoron, it seems.

A couple walks slowly up the trail towards me, scanning the ground.

"See any tracks?" I ask.

"A few," the fellow says.

"Are you scouting for elk?"

"Deer. The archery hunt starts soon."

I ask them about Big Lake Youth Camp and they say it's not far. At the trail junction, I leave the PCT for Big Lake and fifteen minutes later see buildings through the trees.

I find the headquarters building and set my pack down and walk into the office. Two young ladies are discussing something they are looking at on the computer screen.

"Hi, I'm Colter. You should have a package for me here."

They glance up, but before they can speak, a tattered bearded hiker I don't recognize looks up from another computer and says, "I'll show you where the packages are. Have you heard about the fire closure?"

"No, what's up?"

"They've closed the trail up by Olallie Lake."

"I don't even know where that is. How far up the trail is it?"

"Forty miles or so, maybe."

He brings me downstairs to stacks of packages, as he tells me what he knows about the fire closure.

I am looking for the food I mailed to myself from Mammoth Lakes, and a care package my mother has sent me. Many names on the packages I recognize, but most I don't, especially if their trail names are missing. After scanning through the packages twice I am still missing one. I start over again, more methodically, and at last find the missing one. It was turned sideways and with the label facing away. Many hikers put an identifying mark on each side of a package, say, a green X. Not a bad idea.

At the top of one stack is a box with Anne's name on it. I take it down and write down the date and a quick note, telling her all is well and wishing her good luck.

Scooping the packages up I head upstairs to the deck and sit down out of the way to sort through my treasures. With my tiny knife I carefully slit open the box I'd sent from

Mammoth, pulling out my guidebook information, spare batteries, and toilet paper.

Two hikers walk up and sit down. I recognize Charmin. "Hi, Charmin! It's Colter. Are you still having fun?"

"Hi, Colter. Yes! It's been really great." Looking up at her friend, she says, "This is Hasty."

"Hi, Hasty."

As we talk, three more thru-hikers appear, heading back out to the trail. I don't recognize any of them, but we introduce ourselves. They are Foxtrot, Baby Steps, and Flashback.

I open a carton of shelf-stable chocolate milk and drink it slowly. That hits the spot. Another carton follows the first. Charmin looks on enviously. My mother's package is heavy. It's like Christmas. Naw, better than Christmas. She's sent a large Ziplock full of chocolate fudge. She knows I have a sweet tooth, so she's also made me some peanut brittle. Obviously she read my website where I mentioned a three-pound bag of peanut M&M's being a favorite, so she's included one in the box. From the box I mailed from Mammoth, I pull out another three-pound bag! Along with the usual granola, peanut butter, crackers, pasta, rice and whatnot, there will be ten pounds of chocolate for the next segment of trail! Ten pounds! Granted, that is a crazy amount of chocolate, but there are 106 miles between here and Timberline Lodge. What I don't eat will be a fine treat for the next stretch. It would be deeply *wrong* to not bring it with. All of it. Ten. Pounds. Of chocolate.

Mom sent me other small items I'd asked for as well, a few Ziplocks, several rubber bands, and a half dozen safety pins. The latter range in size from tiny to enormous. The largest is nearly 5 inches long! Charmin smiles as I ponder the giant pin.

"It's cool, but I don't know what I'll do with it."

"I've never seen a pin that big!"

"Do you want it?"

"Sure! I mean, if you don't want it." I toss it over to her. Beaming, she plays with her new prize.

Downstairs I run into Boat, whom I haven't seen since the long-ago McDonald's at Cajon Pass.

"Boat!" I exclaim. "Is Sojo here?"

"Hi, Colter. No, Sojo got off the trail in Lone Pine. He was having fun, but I think he just missed his wife."

"That's too bad, but I'm sure it was the right thing for him. He's plenty tough enough, that's for sure. Where's the drinking water?" Boat points to a sink.

The Walking Sisters are down here doing their laundry. I don't know them beyond having met them briefly on the trail in California. Their dad did the trail not long ago which inspired them to hike the PCT themselves.

"What are your plans for the fire closure?" I ask them.

"That's what we were just talking about. We don't know yet, how about you?"

"I'm just going to keep walking and play it by ear. Things change so fast I think it pays to stay flexible."

I finish repacking on the deck. As I'm leaving, another hiker says, "What are you going to do about the closure?"

"I'm going to keep going and see what happens. How about you?"

He ponders this for a moment and says, "Maybe. But what I don't want to happen is to get there and have to backtrack for twenty miles."

The guidebook doesn't show a direct route back to the trail, so I wing it from the maps. Fresh tracks on the dirt road ahead of me show other hikers have chosen the same route. As I walk I think about my stop at Big Lake. Hiking groups are interesting. There was the Foxtrot group and the Walking Sisters group, for example. Groups form and drift apart. A few stick together for the rest of the trail. Some last for only a day or two. It is hard to believe how many thru-hikers were at that brief stop. Nine maybe? I think I'd only seen two or three thru-hikers actually on the trail in all of Oregon. A stop like that proves I'm an introvert at heart. Finally all those thru-hikers to talk to, and I'm already back on the trail!

Huckleberry bushes flank the trail, many with the first blushes of fall color and bearing ripe berries. I pluck and eat targets of opportunity as I pass. They are tart and sweet, fresh food, loaded with vitamins. Close to Santiam Pass two objects appear on the trail ahead of me, one red and one blue. Trail magic! A note on top of one of the coolers says, "Your mom just called. She said you need to be eating more fruit and veggies... Chipmunk and Napster." There is a garbage bag and a note saying everything would be gathered up in a few days. Inside the coolers is wonderful trail magic: fruit, carrots, tomatoes, and sodas, along with other goodies. Snacking on carrots and sipping a Pepsi, I sign their trail register, thanking them for their generosity.

At the Highway 20 trailhead, a sign has a poorly photocopied map of the fire closure area. I look at my guidebook. It's still a day and a half ahead. They warn of fines for scofflaws. I ponder calling my friend Johnny Mac to see if he can plan an alternate route for me, but decide against it. There is a local Forest Service phone number listed so I try to call for a clarification and update, but the office is closed for the day. I take advantage of the outhouse then hit the trail, climbing steadily into the Mt. Jefferson Wilderness.

A dog comes charging around the corner, happily trailing his tongue, joyfully rushing up to greet me. His owner, a fit, middle-aged woman, runs around the corner, apologizes for the dog and keeps on cruising, the dog rushing to catch up.

It is near dark on a ridgetop on the south flank of Three Fingered Jack. There's a nice level spot near the base of a thicket of trees, well protected if the wind comes up. It's chilly. No skeets. I'll cowboy camp. Kicking a few cones away I roll out my sleeping pad and pull out my sleeping bag, give it a few shakes, then lay it over the pad. Camp is set up in a minute. After putting on my down jacket and balaclava, I turn on my GPS which speeds the plotting of my camp on the map. A 28-mile day. It seems like a long time since I was camped with Mr. T this morning.

August 23

It's morning. I turn to look southeast from the ridgeline. The first rays of the rising sun touch Mt. Washington and the Sisters. Even with broad swathes of burned timber, it is beautiful. I pull out my camera and take a photo, then another one as the light quickly changes. Three-Fingered Jack looms to my right as I contour around its massive flank. I gaze in awe at the rugged spires of the mountain, gray and red bands of stone, below them fields of snow with enormous scree slopes, scattered trees climbing up to the ridge on which I stand.

I set down my pack and find my mini tripod and attach it to my camera. I search for a bit and find a flat rock, then set up my camera. I put on my pack, set the self-timer, and attempt a natural looking pose. In the photo, my blue shirt nearly matches the sky. I look thin but content. It is a perfect early morning in a perfect setting in a magical wilderness.

The hiking conditions are ideal, cool with a light breeze. The trail follows ridgelines for miles, providing constantly changing views of Mt. Jefferson, looming ahead. I stop to take another photo. The pattern of snowfields, the shape of the peak itself, the patchwork of trees and the ridges keep me admiring the view.

Two people are lying down on the trail ahead. They are kicking at a boulder in the middle of the path.

"Need some help?"

"Sure!" We all grab the boulder.

"One, two, THREE!" We give a mighty shove and the boulder starts rolling then bounds down the steep slope, ricocheting off trees.

"Thanks. Are you thru-hiking?"

"I am. How about you guys?"

"Just checking out the trail," the lady answers.

"Well thanks for the trail work, then."

By mid-afternoon the trail is following the west flank of Jefferson, making a couple of easy creek crossings. As the scenery unfolds I watch for the spot where we parachuted to a forest fire in the Mt. Jefferson Wilderness years ago.

In the door of the jump plane, I had looked out across some of this very scenery. Even in the deafening roar of the wind and engines, the adrenaline of the impending jump seemed to make the colors even more vibrant.

Orbiting in our jump ship someone spotted the smoke curling up from the trees. The jump spot was an easy choice, a meadow a few hundred yards from the fire. My jump partner pointed out the outfitter tents just off the meadow.

The spotter leaned out of the door, studying the landscape. He pulled his head back in to talk to the pilot. The spotter turned to us and held up 4 fingers. Four of us, including me, would jump. The first jumper got in the door with the second ready right behind him. Suddenly the first jumper was gone, and two seconds later the second.

The spotter turned to my partner and me, holding up two fingers. "Two jumpers." We stood up in our jump helmets and bulky padded suits.

"Are you ready and are your leg straps tight?" We nodded our heads yes.

"OK, hook up." We hooked the heavy metal snaps to the overhead cable, then move forward towards the spotter and open door.

"Did you see the streamers?" I shook my head yes. "Did you see the spot?" Yup.

"OK, there's only about two hundred yards of drift, so you'll have plenty of forward speed. Make sure you don't overshoot the jump spot. The hazards are the big trees around the spot, especially the dead ones. Watch for the rocks in the meadow. Any questions?" We shook our heads no.

The spotter looked me in the eye and pointed at the open door. "OK, get in the door." I swung into the door and looked down to make sure my reserve handle and main parachute handle are in place, then leaned towards the front of the plane so the spotter could see the ground. My gloved hand covered my reserve handle to prevent an accidental deployment. The roar of the engines and wind was deafening, the air a mixture of sweet mountain air, smoke, and turbine exhaust. The spotter checked to make sure my static line was OK. "You're clear." He did the same for my partner.

His head out the door, the spotter's cheeks flapped in the 100-knot wind. He scanned the ground and gave the pilot a slight course correction over the mic. The spotter pulled his head back in and said, "Get ready!"

I put one hand on either side of the door and leaned back. The spotter slapped me on the back and I leaped out into the wind blast in a tuck, counting:

"Jump thousand, look thousand, [looking at my handle] reach thousand, wait thousand, PULL Thousand!" I yanked the handle and looked up, seeing the drogue pull out my main parachute, a chaotic mass of flapping cloth which blossomed open, without damage or tangles. I glanced around toward the fading sound of the jump ship and saw my jump partner's chute opening.

"YA-HOOOOOOOOO!" I yelled. I grabbed an orange steering toggle and pulled it down hard, corkscrewing down several hundred feet so my partner and I won't be landing in the meadow at the same time. I watched the smoke drifting briefly to see what the wind was doing, then flew upwind of the meadow a few hundred yards. I looked up and located my jump partner once more, then slowed my parachute and flew a half circle around the jump spot. Several horses, tied near the edge of the small meadow, milled nervously, looking up at me and tugging at their ropes. When I arrived straight downwind of the meadow I turned to face it, and slowed my parachute and aimed for the center of the clearing. My heart pounded as my feet slipped past an opening in the towering trees. I made a slight adjustment to avoid rocks in the meadow. The first two jumpers stood next to their crumpled parachutes, getting out of their jump gear, watching me land. I flared my parachute and when I stood up from my landing turned to see my jump partner land nearby.

"Everyone OK?" said Romero, the fire boss. "Yeah!" we answered, one by one.

The Sherpa swung around and on the second pass began dropping our cargo by parachute, including tools, food, water, and sleeping bags. The outfitter appeared out of the trees and marched up to us, wearing a cowboy hat and jeans.

"Who's in charge?" he demanded, red-faced.

"I am. Rene Romero, sir." Rene offered his hand.

"You *cowards!*" the outfitter said.

Rene was a tall, powerfully-built jumper of Pueblo descent. "I'm sorry, what do you mean?"

"This fire should be allowed to burn."

"Maybe so, but we are just the infantry." Rene explained how fire policy is made with input from the public and land managers. The cowboy responded angrily, while Rene kept his cool — which de-escalated the situation.

We walked down to work the fire with shovels and pulaskis. "Hey, Rene," I said.

"Yeah, Buck?"

"I wonder what he thought of your hat?"

Rene took off his ball cap and looked at it, laughing. It said: *Kill Whitey.*

"I didn't even think about it."

Rene, of course, was wearing the hat as a joke for the smokejumpers' benefit, not thinking about having to deal with the public in a situation like he'd just been in.

The four of us began the hard work of cutting a fireline, clearing brush and logs and other fuels around the edges to stop the fire's spread, then working our way inwards. We joked as we worked, good friends in a beautiful wilderness. We were "living the dream" and we knew it.

At the end of a long shift, we walked back to the jump spot by the light of our headlamps to gather our gear and get something to eat. The outfitter walked out with a flashlight.

"Hey, I was wondering if maybe you guys would like a steak and a beer. I got an extra wall tent, too, that you guys could sleep in." Rain looked imminent, so we happily accepted. We gathered our gear and stashed it in the tent then sat down to a fine meal and a beer or two and lots of laughing. The outfitter had become our good pal. It began to rain, harder and harder. There was the sound of approaching horses outside.

"That'd be the hay," the outfitter said. "I'm going to help them unload." We followed him out to unload hay in the cold rain, getting soaked from head to toe. The outfitter liked us even more, then.

The next day, we carefully checked to make sure the fire was out. Our heavy gear was loaded on horses. We hiked out on this very Pacific Crest Trail where I now stand, many years later.

The light is beginning to fade. I'll camp at the next good spot. I find it few hundred yards later, a pretty bench below the trail. I hiked 29 miles today.

As usual, I wake up within a few minutes of 5:45 and begin to pack. Today I'll get to the fire closure. I hope I'll be able to walk through it or to figure out a good detour that won't add a lot of miles. I really don't want to do a backtrack or accept a ride. The trail crosses Whitewater Creek and then Jefferson Park, a vast meadow with clumps of weather-beaten mountain hemlock and heather. It is clear and sunny. I admire the grandeur of Mt. Jefferson in the morning light. Coming out of the park there is a climb of over a thousand feet. Looking back where the trail crosses a hillside meadow I see Mt. Jefferson soaring into the blue sky, a gentle breeze nudging the grass and heather. The colors are saturated, blue, gray, green and white. This moment is the distilled essence of the Oregon PCT.

North slope of Mt. Jefferson

From the top of the ridge the trail descends into a large, treeless snowfield with Mt. Hood in the distance. There is a thin haze of smoke but no smoke columns. Perhaps the fires have been controlled. Luckily the snow isn't particularly steep. I follow other people's tracks, who themselves have been following other people. Pretty soon, judging from the scattered trails, nobody knows where the trail is. Looking at the map, it's easy to see the lay of the land and where the trail is heading. I ignore the existing tracks and pick out my own route.

Soon I am back below treeline. The sky is getting smokier. Small, individual columns of smoke rise here and there. Some of them are very close, because I can see the movement of the rising smoke.

I hope the trail isn't closed. If so maybe there is some way to "accidentally" avoid seeing the signs? I am nearly holding my breath with anticipation. Ahead is the gravel road. Across the road is a piece of wide yellow & black tape stretched across the PCT. There are two signs:

The Olallie Lake Scenic Area is Closed Due to Fire
This Includes all Roads and Trails within the Scenic Area
THANK YOU FOR YOUR COOPERATION

There is a handwritten note posted below it:

PCT Hikers: USFS is running a shuttle 9 AM to 6 PM

Daily until closure Is lifted. Please wait here for a ride around the closure area.

:) Thanks!

Rats! With 25 years of wildfire experience I know I can walk the trail in relative safety or reroute as necessary. But there is no reasonable way I can claim I haven't seen the warnings. What are the odds that anyone will actually see me? Would they actually fine me if they caught me walking on through? Would I be setting a bad example? I look at the signs again. Twice they thank me for being cooperative. Drat.

The "Official Route" of the PCT varies. During the fire closures in southern California, the detour became the official PCT. With an emergency closure like this, a designated shuttle then becomes the official PCT. But I've been connecting my steps the whole way. There is another hand-drawn map showing two routes around the detour. Long road walks. The shortest reroute is going to add something like 12 miles.

I'll walk the shortest detour. My maps don't cover the detour so I take a couple of photos of the detour map, then sit down to orient myself. A helicopter is dropping a bucket of water on a hillside a mile or so away. There appears to be a number of separate fires in this small area. None of them are burning very hot at the moment.

After several miles, there is a roadblock manned by a yellow-shirted forest service firefighter. He is talking to several people in an SUV that have driven up just before I got here. As I walk up, the firefighter says, "Did you see the sign?"

"The one about the closure and the shuttle?"

"Yeah. You didn't want a ride?"

"No, I decided to walk it."

I ask a couple of questions about the detour, but he doesn't know much more. From being on the other side of the firefighter/civilian interface, I know that often firefighters don't know "the big picture" at first. There's often a "fog of war" involved, especially in a fast-moving fire. People on scene may not be locals familiar with the area, and the extent of the fire may not be known yet.

It's easy walking. It's hot. The air is hazy. No flames are visible, but the most dramatic fire activity will likely be in the afternoon. After an hour or so of walking there is a trickle of water off to the left of the road. I fill two quarts. I find a pleasant break spot by a giant log in the cool shade of massive trees. I cook lunch and relax.

When I get back to the road a Forest Service vehicle pulls up. "Are you hiking the PCT?" the driver asks.

"Yup." He pulls off on the nearby logging road. "Do you want a ride?"

"I thought I'd walk it. Are you the shuttle?"

"Yes." The shuttle is running hours late. It is nearly 1 PM and it is the first shuttle of the day. Someone in the passenger seat leans forward. He has a wide-brimmed hat. Young and skinny. He has thru-hiker written all over him.

"Are you thru-hiking?" he says.

"Yeah, I'm Colter. How about yourself?"

"Me too, I'm Hui."

After they have driven off, I head down the road again. Once or twice a car honks just as it reaches me and makes me jump. It is their way of saying hello, usually with a wave or a thumbs-up. An old VW Microbus drives by with the passenger giving a peace sign out the window.

The map shows that the side road the detour follows cuts back sharply in my direction. A shortcut would save me considerable road walking. Getting a good compass bearing I head into the forest. There is more brush than I'd expected. Shortcuts often result in floundering around in brush, encounters with deep ravines, and other unpleasant surprises. But in only a half mile I hit the side road I am looking for. A column of smoke billows up a couple of miles ahead. A beat-up old SUV comes driving slowly towards me. They slow and stop. A guy in a dirty tank top rolls down the window. A heavy woman with flowered dress sits in the passenger seat. Two little kids in the back are yelling something to me but I can't make it out.

"Are you heading to Olallie Lake?"

"North of there, yes."

"The road is closed up ahead."

"Thanks. I'm hiking the Pacific Crest Trail, and this is the designated reroute."

"Yeah, but they just closed the road. They won't let you through."

"All right. Thanks for letting me know."

"No problem. Do you need anything?"

"I think I'm all set, thanks."

"OK, then, have a good hike."

I pretend to study my maps until they are out of sight, then continue down the road, keeping a sharp eye ahead. If the road is blocked, I'll cut into the forest and head cross-country. The fire is building. An impressive column of smoke now rises a mile or so away. It's leaning away from me for now, meaning the fire is mainly moving away. The smell of smoke is heavy in the air. It triggers the old excitement from my firefighting days.

Side roads fork off the main road here and there. The right-hand roads are all closed with ribbon. My road crosses a beautiful stream with a perfect camp spot. I refill my water bottle. Sitting in the shade next to the road I pull out my GPS and study the photo of the map.

After getting a good fix I decide to do another cross-country shortcut that should preclude the possibility of getting turned back at a roadblock.

I start out on a logging road. It has been made impassible to vehicles, with innumerable mounds of dirt pushed up by bulldozers. Then the logging road fades away in an old clear-cut. It's back to genuine bushwhacking. For a long stretch it is fairly easy going through a forest, then steep terrain and brush forces me down along a brook. I try to find the best way through, crossing the rust-colored brook several times, using brush to pull myself over fallen logs. I start angling uphill and reach an old clear-cut with a logging road running the right way. Score! I am now passing the fire. A black smoke column boils into the sky. It's now a crown fire, burning through the treetops.

I use a log to cross a slow, dark, deep creek. I cross the Olallie Lake road, still hiking cross-country. It is nearly dark. The final hill is tough going, steep and littered with fallen trees. Finally, on a hillside steep as a cow's face, I see the trail a few feet away. I am triumphant. The closure is behind me. I hurry down the trail looking for a flat spot. The fire is a safe distance away. The air is nearly smoke-free. The mosquitoes are out. I set up my shelter with an orange sunset filtering through the trees. It is good to be back on the trail.

August 25

It is warm and clear. Or it would be clear if not for the smoke. Area fires spread yesterday and in the cool of night smoke has settled over the landscape below, as far as the eye can see. I hear a weather report on the radio calling for highs of 100 degrees out on the flats to the east. They say that yesterday's fire I skirted has grown to about 500 acres, and there is a complex of fires in the Warm Springs reservation totaling about 25,000 acres. They warn of numerous closures of roads, campgrounds, and rafting areas.

There are more and more of the old Pacific Crest Trail System markers. They are a white metal diamond with green lettering and feature an evergreen tree in the center. They've been here for decades, many rusty and partially grown into the tree.

The smoke lifts. Out in the desert flats, far to the east, wispy columns of smoke rise.

Mostly the trail is in the timber with limited views. Shafts of sunlight pierce the smoky air. My water bottle is dry so when I reach Clackamas Lake I swing into the campground. There are horse corrals and many horses and horse trailers. In the campground families have gathered, families with the look of genuine ranchers. Boys practice roping wooden steers. Western shirts and cowboy hats and cowboy boots are worn with the casualness of people who are living the life, not playing a role. A water spigot is next to one of these groups, so I stop to fill my bottles.

"Have you heard anything about this closest fire?" I ask a cowboy sitting on a nearby lawn chair.

"Not really. We're keeping an eye on it, but we figure if it gets dangerous they'll let us know."

"All right. Well, enjoy your day."

Children watch me curiously as I walk down the camp road.

They aren't unfriendly, but I am an outsider.

I hit the paved road and turn right looking to rejoin the PCT. Two fellows in their late 20s or early 30s have just set their packs down next to their car.

"How was your hike?" I say in passing.

"Good. The trail is in rough shape, though. Really dusty."

"That's a bummer. Is that the PCT right there?"

"Yup."

I walk a short distance into the forest and sit down for a break. Soon two women come riding down the trail. The horses spot me and watch with a wary eye. The women, about 60, are wearing riding helmets. They sit comfortably on their horses but by their clothing I can see they are not part of the rancher group. As they approach they stop their horses.

"Hi there," the closest lady says.

"Those are some beautiful horses."

"Thanks. I've had this one for a couple of years. He was a mustang."

"Really? He was a wild horse?"

"You wouldn't know it, would you?"

"No. Where did he come from?"

"Eastern Oregon, I think."

"That's interesting. I used to work with the wild horse program in Wyoming."

"Is that where you're from?"

"No, I still spend some time there, but I worked there for one summer. I live in Alaska."

"Alaska! Wow. So are you thru-hiking?"

"Yup. I started in late April."

"Amazing. So what is it, like two thousand miles or something?"

"A little over twenty-six hundred."

"That's quite an undertaking, it must be quite an adventure!"

We talk a few more minutes and they ride away. The trail parallels a brook. It does not seem to be in "rough shape" to me. A family with several small children approaches. A four-year-old leads the way, marching along with an exaggerated stride, waving a stick above his head. A gleaming sword to him, no doubt. His father and I talk about the local fires, while glancing up at an orange sun in the smoke-veiled sky.

The trail parallels Timothy Lake, for miles, a pleasant change of setting. I pull out my MP3 player and tune in a radio station. There's a story about a six-year-old severely injured in an auto accident. He lies in a coma for two months, and when he awakens tells the story of his trip to heaven and back. I am skeptical.

Fisherman slowly cruise the lake, or anchor in quiet coves. Teenagers in swimsuits run across the trail on the way to the lake. There are yells of children and distant laughter. Crumpled beer cans lie here and there. Several places along the trail in partially hidden spots are piles of dirty toilet paper. There are plenty of outhouses in the campgrounds just up the hill. Are they lazy, selfish, or just don't know any better?

The beauty returns on more remote trail along the water. I sit on a rock outcropping and look out over the lake. An opaque layer of blue smoke stretches across the water, orange where the smoke thins and the sun seeps through. There's a narrow band of blue sky on the western horizon.

At about 7:00 PM the PCT crosses a creek on a picturesque wooden footbridge. At the next intersection I sit down, weary, and study my guidebook. This is mile 2092.8, and I started at... mile 2063. So that's almost 30 miles. I'll look for a good camp spot. After another half an hour I find one. I cowboy camp in big, open timber. As I lie in my sleeping bag I make plans for tomorrow. My friends Fitz and Steve are going to meet me at Timberline Lodge at 1:30. I haven't heard from Fitz for a few days. If I start walking at 6:00 tomorrow morning, that gives me 7 1/2 hours to cover the 17 miles to the lodge. That's definitely doable, but I'll have to watch the length of my breaks.

In the morning I walk a short distance off the trail looking for a spring. I stand looking down at a small boggy seep wondering if this is the water source. I look at my guidebook again and by carefully rereading what it actually says find a nice spring with a resident frog.

The trail traverses the northeast side of a long ridge and I look northward towards Mt. Hood. It reminds me of photos of Mt. Fuji. The peak thrusts upward into a pale blue sky, glaciers falling away on all sides with a few wisps of clouds around them. A carpet of green trees begins a mile or so below the summit. In the foreground, running towards the mountain, is meadow, showing the yellow-green of early fall colors.

I am surprised to hear my phone ring, fumble for it, and answer, "Hello?"

"Buckster!"

"Hey, Fitz."

"Look, man, I'm an idiot. I was calling the wrong number the last few days and leaving a message with the wrong guy. I finally got ahold of him, which is how I finally figured out it was the wrong number. Sorry about that."

"Not a problem. So what do you think, are you guys coming up?"

"Absolutely. We'll meet you at the lodge at thirteen-thirty, just like we planned."

"Perfect. I'll be there."

That is good news. I had been slightly anxious because I want to see those guys but didn't know if something had come up.

Just short of Wapinitia Pass on Highway 26 I see the beautiful sight of a red cooler. On top is a note. The family of a fellow thru-hiker, The Graduate, lives nearby. They've left goodies and soft drinks for his hiking compañeros. I flip through the register for familiar names while sipping a cold soda. Wyoming, and her new hiking partner, Otter, were here two days ago. After signing the register I cross the pass.

Less than two hours later the PCT crosses Barlow Pass, a major landmark on the Oregon Trail. Originally, settlers reaching the gorge of the Columbia would float their wagons downstream, a very dangerous passage. When Sam Barlow arrived at the Dalles, the beginning of the float, there were 60 families waiting to pay the high toll. A ten-day wait was expected. So Sam Barlow looked for options. With the help of many others, he scouted and constructed a crude road. In places, wagons had to be lowered down the steep road with ropes to prevent them from running away. The Barlow Road became a key link in the 2,000-mile Oregon trail. It had a reputation of being the most arduous 100 miles of all. Two years ago it was a cold, rainy day in the desert near South Pass when I crossed the Oregon Trail while hiking the Continental Divide Trail.

I cross the pavement of Highway 35 just after 11 AM. Two and a half hours left to meet Fitz. It's five miles and over 1,800 feet of climbing to the lodge. I scan for radio stations to occupy my mind. The news comes on. It says the bodies of two Mt. Hood climbers, missing since last December, have been found and will be flown off by helicopter today. Soon, I can hear the helicopter on its grim mission.

I climb and climb. Mt. Hood comes into view. I take a photo of the peak with yellow and blue wildflowers in the foreground. A cold wind hits. Sand blasts my face and grinds between my teeth. Then, there it is, Timberline Lodge. Years ago two friends of mine met here and later married. I'd been hearing about the Lodge for years. I'd imagined an "Old Faithful"-style log lodge set in mature timber. Instead, it's literally at timberline and looks like a European chateau, perhaps, with a steep roof and impressive stonework out front. I'm early, so I swing by the Wy'east store.

"Is this where I pick up my package?"

"Are you a thru-hiker?"

"Yeah. Bruce Nelson. My trail name is Colter."

The cashier, a young fellow, consults a clipboard. A huge St. Bernard walks up and sniffs my leg. He smiles in a mellow stupor. Two little girls, maybe 4 and 6, squeal with delight as they bury their hands in his thick hair. The dog seems oblivious. The parents listen as the girls excitedly describe what it's like to pet the enormous beast.

"Here it is." The cashier hands me the package.

"Thanks!" I step out the door to look for an out-of-the-way spot.

As I sort through my package a thru-hiker walks up.

"Don't tell me..." His name is on the tip of my tongue. He taps his sunglasses. "Shades! How are you?"

"Great. I haven't seen you since the Sierras."

"When did you get in?"

"This morning. Daredevil is here, too. Her parents are meeting her." We catch up while I sort out my stuff. I throw away the empty box and all the trash I can find. In the bathroom I wash up as best I can, enjoying the warm water even if it's only on my hands and face.

Through the arched stone doorway, I walk into the spectacular interior of the lodge. There are huge wooden beams and posts and stonework. It should be full of drunken Viking warriors belting out songs. On the balcony of the second floor, someone is leaning over the railing with a beer in his hand.

"Buck!"

"Fitz! You guys want to come down here or do you want me to come up there?"

"We'll see you down there." Seconds later Fitz and Steve stride in through the door, beaming.

"Buckster, man it's great to see you." Fitz steps forward and gives me a big hug. I feel slightly uncomfortable. I haven't had a shower in days.

"How are you doing, Steve?" We shake hands warmly.

"Great, Buck. How's your hike going? And hey, do you want a beer?"

"Sure, I'll have a beer, but what I really want is the buffet lunch!" We get a table and I head over to the buffet to have a look. It is a staggering sight. Roast beef, fresh veggies, fresh bread, fresh fruit and more rise high on my plate. We sit around a small table, a beer for each of us and my feast before me.

"Buck, we thought we saw you crossing the road about an hour ago. I said 'Hey, that must be Buck!' We drove up to talk to you but it was somebody else."

"Do you know who it was?"

"Yeah, it was Mr. T."

"That figures." I fill them in on the story of Mr. T.

Together, the three of us are 30-year-old smokejumpers once again, tough, confident and laughing. "Jump stories" flow steadily.

"I don't think I've seen you since Dow's wedding, Fitz. What was that, like, fifteen years ago?"

"I think so."

"How about you, Steve? When did I see you last?"

"I think it would have been on Chip Houde's fire in the Brooks Range. Remember that fire?"

"I sure do. We laid out thousands of feet of hose from a creek to the fire and then we started up the flanks and it started raining like a bastard and pretty much put it out. After all that work!"

We finish eating and drive down the mountain to Steve's house. He shows us around. On the wall is a beautiful print of smokejumpers landing in the mountains.

I turn to Steve. "A few years ago I walked into the Redding base and was walking around their parachute loft," I say. "There was a painting of smokejumpers parachuting to a wildfire in dramatic mountain terrain. *This* painting."

"This is the best smokejumper painting I've ever seen!" I said when Bruce Ford walked up.

"You think so?" he said.

"It really captures the experience. Who painted it, anyway?"

"I did."

"Yeah, right." I glanced down to the corner of the painting. *B Ford*, it says.

Bruce is an amazing guy. He can speak fluent Mandarin, Russian, and several other languages. He's also a sculptor and mathematician.

I take a hot shower and change into some clean clothing Steve has loaned me. Steve shows me around his house. Bamboo is growing in his yard. It is amazing that bamboo can grow just a few miles from permanent snow and ice. Fitz and I run to the grocery store for ice cream, a six-pack of beer, and some ingredients for dinner. Later, we eat the delicious Thai meal Steve has made, and then talk for hours.

August 27, Day 127. Mile 2,111; 545 Miles to Canada

After breakfast, I say goodbye to Steve. Fitz drives me back up to Timberline Lodge. There is a large gathering of people, preparing for the Hood-to-Coast relay running race.

I unload my pack.

"Buck, it was great seeing you."

"You too, Fitz. I really appreciate you making the drive. Thanks for lunch yesterday. Say thanks to Steve again for me." I sling my pack and head up the hill to the trail. A jovial announcer works the running crowd on the P.A. Back on the trail I pass under a ski lift and continue hiking around the mountain, towering to my right. Soon all the hubbub is behind me.

Ahead of me is a sign: "River Crossing Safety on Glacial Streams." It tells of a woman who drowned while crossing the Sandy River just ahead, in August of 2004. It gives some good advice on safe stream crossing, such as scouting for the safest crossing and using a hiking pole for balance.

Far to the south Mt. Jefferson and the Three Sisters loom above a rumpled blanket of blue forest and low-hanging clouds. I stop to look at the hillside to my right. Water trickles down stones covered with lush green moss. Stringers of jelly-like algae dangle, slowly dripping cool water.

A walkway has collapsed on a steep stretch of mountainside. It now looks like a chute designed to sweep hikers off the trail and down the mountain. I walk around it and continue on.

The PCT crosses a series of gorges, most with a magnificent view. Many of the creeks are milky with glacial minerals. One is named, fittingly, Milk Creek. I cross the Sandy River without incident. When I reach a pleasant meadow the sun has come out. After a few snacks, I stretch out in the warm sun and doze for half an hour.

With the sun touching the western horizon the trail reaches an old, unused logging road. I consider setting up camp right on the road where there is already a fire ring, but the ground is hard. Back up in the trees there is plentiful downfall in some places, and unstable-looking standing trees in others. After ten minutes of considering the options I drop my pack in a stand of thick lodgepole pine, and roll out my pad between clumps of bear grass.

It's morning, not yet 7. Dad's birthday. I'm standing on the trail, taking a long look northward to three great peaks:

broken-topped Mt. St. Helen's with a leaning plume of steam near the summit, a snowy Mt. Adams, and Mt. Rainier, 100 miles away. In a few days I'll have walked there, to Mt. Rainier National Park.

At Indian Springs campground I take a side trail to intersect the Eagle Creek Trail. It's an alternate route to the official PCT, one that most thru-hikers take because of the amazing scenery. I reach the Eagle Creek Trail and see another hiker looking at his maps. We strike up a conversation and discover that we'd met at the restaurant at Elk Lake. We head down the trail together.

There has been some impressive trail work done on cliffy mountainsides. We swap cameras to take photos of each other, then take more pictures of the numerous waterfalls. Ahead is a roar. We round the corner to see Tunnel Falls, plunging 175 feet over the cliff. The white cascade contrasts beautifully with the green moss and ferns on the wet, gray stone of the cliff. The deafening noise and color and motion is thrilling.

I turn to Dave. "This might be the coolest single spot I've seen on the whole trail!"

"It's awesome!"

Over Dave's shoulder, I see a young lady walking briskly down the trail.

"I'm Colter. Are you a thru-hiker?"

"Yes. I'm Daredevil. Are you thru-hiking?"

"Yup. I don't think I've met you before. This is Dave. He's out for a long section hike. How did you get your trail name?"

"I'm not sure. I don't take dares and I'm not a devil."

"Do you want me to get a video of you walking through the tunnel?"

"Sure!" Daredevil hands me her camera and shows me how to operate it. Then she turns and runs down the wet cliff-side trail, maybe two feet wide. A fall would be fatal. Now I know why she is called Daredevil.

Me at Tunnel Falls, Eagle Creek Trail

We swap cameras and she takes video of me walking through the tunnel. When I come back Dave goes ahead and gets photos of Daredevil and I passing behind the falls, cool mist swirling around us as we enter and exit the tunnel.

When we reach Dave we all stand and look back for another minute of magic, then head down the trail. "See you in Cascade Locks!" says Daredevil over her shoulder as she motors out of sight. We are seeing day-hikers now. Most groups ask the same question: "How far are we from Tunnel Falls?"

There's a steady stream of entertainment, more beautiful falls, and more people watching. Most hikers are enjoying themselves immensely, but others are clearly suffering, nursing their feet, or puffing, hands on knees. Now we feel guilty when they ask, "How far?" because it is several miles with a big climb ahead for them.

At the trailhead a dark-skinned, gregarious gentleman with a heavy accent stops to ask me about thru-hiking. He rounds up his family, including his thirteen-ish daughter and a couple of her giggling friends. He is genuinely fascinated by the idea of hiking the whole PCT. I'm happy to tell him some stories and answer the usual questions about food, shoes, and bears.

Dave and I walk towards town. We spot Bridge of the Gods, the gateway to Washington, the last state of the Pacific Crest Trail. Walking down the street in Cascade Locks we run into a young, wiry thru-hiker I don't recognize. We stop to talk. A middle-aged woman comes hurrying up the street with her camera. She asks if we'll take a picture of her posing with her hiker. Her eyes shine. She obviously has a huge crush on him. She has just met him during his visit to town.

I walk into the Pacific Crest Pub and ask about getting a room. They tell me the hostel isn't yet open for business. They are holding my packages, though, and I wait while they locate them. "Do you guys have Wi-Fi here?" I ask when they set my packages down.

"No, sorry."

At the Eastwind Drive-In, they say they don't have Wi-Fi and they don't know who does. My laptop is in one of my packages and I want to go online with it and order some shoes, update my website, check my email and get caught up on business. It's Friday afternoon. I don't want to wait until Monday to mail my computer and some other stuff home. Dave, who lives in Seattle, generously agrees to mail my stuff for me. I get in line to order us some burgers and fries. Daredevil is in line right in front of me, her head on her father's giant chest.

"Hey Daredevil, do you know that man?"

"Just met him in line," she laughs, then introduces us. After Dave and I eat our burgers I jump back in line for one of their famous giant soft cones. The ice cream towers to an astounding height. In line I meet Freebie, who hiked the PCT last year.

"Why do they call you Freebie?"

"People just give me stuff."

Dave and I head over to Pacific Crest Trail Days which is being held on an island in the Columbia River. Freebie walks with us. A hiker walks up to us and asks,

"Anybody want some Forest Service maps for Oregon?"

"Sure," says Freebie. He smiles as he turns to me with his maps. "See?"

At Trail Days they are selling raffle tickets as fundraiser. Normally not much of a raffle-ticket buyer, this time I purchase a long coil of them to support the cause.

It's a thru-hiker reunion. Apricots and Psycho, the couple that got engaged on Forester Pass, are here, also Max Chill, Shades, Plain Slice, Little Engine, Slim Jim, Hasty, Charmin, Hui, Zero/Zero, Fire Marshall, The Hiking Sisters, and Chocolate Bandito. Trail Angels like Donna Saufley and Georgi Heitman are here, along with many past thru-hikers and PCT supporters of all kinds.

I sit on the grass, open my boxes, empty my pack and attempt to sort things out in an orderly fashion. People keep coming by to talk which is distracting. I need to focus. I want to get this done before the drawing, so I can send my extra stuff back with Dave. I've got an inflatable sleeping pad and a lightweight, floored shelter I'll swap out and use in Washington. Finally, I'm done. Relieved, I join the biggest group of thru-hikers.

Squatch is the emcee. He's perfect. He knows all the old-timers and understands the hiker world. He's unusually quick-witted. Squatch has made PCT videos, is a comedian, and has section-hiked the entire PCT.

Hui wins something. "You look like a thru-hiker!" Squatch says of Hui, fit and tanned. The thru-hikers see who it is and people are yelling, "Hui!" Hui raises his arms in triumph from winning the prize and even more-so for the goodwill of his fellow hikers.

Another number is drawn and as the fellow approaches, Squatch says, "Are you a thru-hiker?" And then, answering his own question, "Naw, too big of a gut." The crowd laughs, slightly uncomfortably.

I win some kind of little pouch of unknown utility. When I sit down, one of the thru-hikers says, "Am I the only one with more than four numbers on his ticket?" We all laugh. Squatch explained at the beginning that he'd only read off the last four of the long string of numbers on each ticket.

There are a lot of prizes. I win a wool hat. The lady behind me is admiring it, so I give it to her. Then I win a nice pack. Some members of the crowd seem to be getting envious of those of us winning multiple prizes, but my luck is likely related to all the tickets I bought. By the time I win a bear canister I hope I don't win anything else, and don't.

Dave takes my stuff I want mailed. I thank him, and we say goodbye. That evening, a crowd gathers to watch *Wizards of the PCT*. It captures the spirit and humor of his very social hike. Afterwards, I make the long walk in the dark to the bathrooms. Walking out is Golden Child, whom I haven't seen since Donner's Pass. I enjoy the conversation but need to pee desperately.

Back at my shelter I stand looking out over the mighty Columbia River, which slides by in the near darkness. Chocolate Bandito comes walking up and I talk quietly to her as I brush my teeth. She is short and cute. We discuss her "stalker." A middle-aged fellow had seen a photo of her on the internet and was driving up and down the trail in Southern California trying to find her. She was relieved to never run into him.

WASHINGTON

"Life isn't about waiting for the storm to pass.
It's about learning to dance in the rain."

— Vivian Greene

August 29

I'm walking down the main street of Cascade Locks on a quiet Saturday morning. A cafe is open. I walk in and glance around. A bunch of locals. A table of three hikers: a section hiker, The 3rd Monty... and Mr. T. I can't politely avoid Mr. T so I set my pack out of the way and join them. Monty says White Beard, her husband, is sick today. The rest of us enjoy a big breakfast.

After breakfast, the grocery store is already open. My spreadsheet shows my next planned resupply is White Pass, about 148 miles and 7 days away. Soon I'm back out in front of the store, packing my food. I shoulder my pack and head for the bridge. At the toll booth, a lady sticks her head out.

"Is there a toll for hikers?" I ask.

"Just go on across. Have a great hike."

I walk across the wide bridge on the coarse steel grid, looking down through the bridge floor to the river below. Along the banks are Indian fishing platforms, where salmon are scooped up during season with long-handled nets. A tugboat with several heavy barges slowly works its way upstream. I keep a close eye out for cars as I cross because there is no separate walkway.

"Welcome to Washington, the Evergreen State." I stop to take a photo. The last state! I glance down and see a lost headlamp. I pick it up and put it in my pack. There's a faster, flatter alternate that follows the road from here, but I'll take the official route. Ripe blackberries line the trail. I stop and pop the warm sweet berries in my mouth. Soon my fingertips are purple. A young buck deer feeds among the bushes. He wanders away unhurried as I approach.

The trail crosses a clearcut. A clearcut? On the PCT? I take a photo of the trail with a large, fresh stump in the foreground. The fall colors are coming on strong. My camera frames especially-beautiful clumps of shiny blackberries, contrasted against the orange and bright green leaves. Then I pop the sweet berries into my mouth.

From Cascade Locks, the lowest point on the PCT at 140 feet, my guidebook shows the trail climbs over three thousand feet in the next twelve miles. I notice a huge slug on the trail. It's about five inches long and dark brown. When I pick it up it has a surprising heft.

My pack is slumping. It's annoying. Until today, I'd used my RidgeRest as a pack frame by rolling it up in a vertical tube inside my pack and stowing my gear tightly inside it. I swapped my RidgeRest for an air mattress so I've lost that frame effect. It is a problem to ponder. Considering my options, I decide to use one of my graphite hiking poles to serve as a frame. I unscrew one into two halves, and try slipping the halves into two loops on each side of my pack, next to my back. Two of the loops are barely too tight. I take out my knife to pick a few stitches. Someone's coming up the trail.

"Colter!"

"Hi, Pat. How's the hike?"

"Great. What are you doing?"

"I'm going to use one trekking pole for a kind of frame for my pack. It's collapsing on me."

"You are going to sacrifice a pole for that?"

"I think it will be worth it."

We hike together discussing where we crossed paths last, when we expect to finish, and updating each other on news we've heard about fellow hikers.

"So what's your favorite thing about thru-hiking?" I ask him.

"Easy. Crawling into my nice, warm sleeping bag at the end of the day."

"Seriously?"

"Yeah. I like to walk fast and get to my camp early and relax. It's like my reward for putting in the miles."

"That makes sense. It's definitely one of the best parts of the day, that's for sure."

"How about you?"

"The adventure of the whole experience, I guess. Hey, check out how fast the fall colors are changing," I say, using my pole to point out the colorful berry bushes.

"I hadn't noticed the colors changing yet," Pat replies. That surprises me. But we all notice different things about the world around us, depending on our interests. How many unique minerals and plants and other cool stuff have I passed without noticing?

We maintain a brisk pace as we talk. Pat tells me about the world of a business office and his theories on working with people. He's got a NeoAir pad, like the one I swapped out for in Cascade Locks. He gives me advice on avoiding punctures, like waiting until it's in the shelter to inflate it.

Towards the end of the day, we start looking for campsites. Just before dark there is a nice, flat spot, clear of brush, with just enough room for one tent.

"Why don't you take that spot?" I say. "Go ahead, you found it."

"I'll keep going a little farther. There'll be another spot."

"All right. See you tomorrow."

I'm not being picky but there are no campsites visible in the next half mile. Or mile. Or two miles. Now it's dark and my newly found headlamp (serendipity!) shows nothing but a steep hillside, or brush, or both. Every time I leave the trail a short distance to check out a possible spot, it's completely unsuitable. Three miles, four, five. Finally, the terrain gets flatter and I wander around until I locate a marginal but workable spot. I want to just sleep out on the ground but there are no stars visible, so I'm concerned about rain. Based on Pat's advice I want to keep my fragile pad inside my tent so I set up my tent, crookedly.

During the night there were a few sprinkles of rain, but it doesn't amount to anything. Just before nine I arrive at Trout Creek, with an arched bridge in the beautiful cedars. There is a pleasant bench with a beam table. Pat arrives as I eat breakfast. We compare experiences. He's already eaten and keeps cruising.

Back on the trail it starts raining. And continues to rain. A beautiful rainbow appears over the soggy forested mountains, but quickly fades as the sunlight disappears. It rains nearly continuously all day until I find a camp spot just past a spring. I quickly set up. There are voices near the spring. It sounds like Zero/Zero and Fire Marshall. I peel off my wet pants and soggy socks. I pull on my nice dry sleeping socks, crawl into my warm bag and listen to the rain on my tent.

It rained all night. It rains as I pack up. With the steady rain, there is little temptation to stop. I'm not cold, I'm not soaked, just wet around the wrists and ankles and neck. I plod steadily. Now and then I pause to pick clumps of huckleberries. A white beargrass blossom draws my attention, its dozens of delicate and intricate white blossoms radiating out to form a nearly perfect sphere.

It rains without letup. Ahead I see a couple packing up beneath a tree 20 feet from a bridge over a narrow clear creek.

"This would be a great spot for your lunch. It's dry under this tree and we're hitting the trail," they say.

"Thanks. I think I'll take you up on that. What do you think of this rain?"

"We're from Washington. We're used to it."

The ground is perfectly dry beneath the tree. I get some water from the creek. I put on my down jacket and boil some water. I read my guidebook while my food soaks. It's nice to be out of the rain for a while.

Back on the trail, the rain is incessant but it keeps me moving. I pass a perfect campsite under a beautiful canopy of a giant cedar. It's already occupied by two tents. The next good spot protected from rain will be my home for the night. For a long way there aren't any big trees, and big trees are what I want. Finally, I find a place where I can tuck my tent underneath a spruce tree. Setting up out of the rain is nice. Getting out of my wet stuff and into dry stuff is even better.

It's September 1! I started in April. May, June, July, August. This is the sixth month on the calendar, the month I'll finish. It's raining. Still. I put on my cold wet pants and my cold wet socks and my cold wet shoes. My shoes squish as I plod along in the fog and dripping trees. Ahead of me is a family of three, a couple and their teenage daughter. All are overweight. They are soaked in their blue jeans and cotton hooded sweatshirts. Huge sleeping bags in tattered garbage bags are tied to their packs. They pause and have a brief discussion, but they are too far away to hear. They are not having fun. If they camp tonight they will be having even less fun. I hope they have a car waiting at the next road.

Just before the road are two large barrels. "Trout Lake Abbey" is written on the white cover of one with a black marker. "Use 2×4 to open." Leaning against a tree is the 2×4, which I use to unscrew the lid. Regardless of where the Abbey stands on heaven and the afterlife, they have brought me heaven on earth here and now. It's an incredible cornucopia of the finest unattended on-trail Trail Magic I have ever seen. Oranges, apples, grapes and drinks and treats of many varieties. My sweet tooth takes control. I have a small package of peanut M&M's, a cappuccino, an orange, and a pudding cup. While I eat, thankfully, I read some of the label-maker messages on the cans:

MAY YOUR JOURNEY BE ALL THAT YOU WANT & MORE

PEACE ON YOUR JOURNEY

MAY ALL BEINGS FIND PEACE

And the pragmatic:

TRASH ONLY IN THIS BIN

I leave them a sincere note of thanks. I walk away, feeling as if I've just been hugged.

At a footbridge crossing a rusty looking creek, I glance at my watch — 11:45. My water is just starting to boil when I hear footsteps. 3rd Monty and Whitebeard. They are in good spirits, but elect to push on to the next (less rusty) water for lunch. They follow my eyes upwards. A patch of blue sky.

Has the rain stopped? The trail winds through the mature timber. Fog drifts across the soggy ground. Two horsemen come down the trail, scouting for elk. In mid-afternoon, a patch of brilliant white snow appears low in the sky. The clouds break. A large patch of Mt. Adams appears in bright sunlight and slowly the whole mountain rises from the dark forest, glaciers gleaming, into the blue sky.

After days of rain, my heart soars now that the sun is out. I almost feel like laughing. The trees stop dripping. Patches of dry dirt appear on sunny trail. A small rectangular object lies on the path. A camera card. I put it in my pocket. On a spur ridge, I find a nice spot and get something to eat. There is a good chance that another thru-hiker has lost the SD card. If so, someone's going to be happy to recover their priceless photos. I put the card in my camera. It's blank.

A fellow is coming up a side trail. He is startled to see me.

"Are you on a trail crew?" I ask. There had been some fresh work nearby.

"Yes. We just got in today. They packed in our camp for us on horses."

"That's the way to do it. I appreciate all the good work." An old yellow lab comes running joyfully down the trail to meet me. "How are you, big guy? You like trail work, don't you?" He wags yes. He's part of the crew.

Late in the day, I'm crossing a wide creek-bed scoured out of the northwest slope of Mt. Adams. It must be 200 yards across. Upstream is the white summit of Mt. Adams. It's 6:15. The days are much shorter now. It will be dark in about two hours. Miles are important if I want to avoid as much Washington rain and snow as possible. But this place is awesome. If I stop now I can dry all my stuff. For the view, I'll have to camp in the riverbed. I find a spot well above the channels that would first start flowing in the case of a hard rain. On that high point is a patch of fine gravel, perfect for putting up my tent.

I pull everything out of my pack. I fluff up my sleeping bag and drape it over a boulder in the direct sun. I lay out all my spare clothing to dry. I pull out paperwork and weight it down with stones. Plastic bags are turned inside out. My tent goes up. The door is tied open. I blow up my air mattress inside my tent. Everything is drying. Make hay while the sun shines.

I walk down to the creek for a couple quarts of water. Back at camp I set up my stove and start some water boiling. I go around and check the drying gear, flipping it over and rearranging it to maximize the drying. I screw my camera onto its mini-tripod, walk down-slope and set it on the rock for a portrait of myself in my little camp against the mountain.

Cooking dinner at camp on the west flank of Mt. Adams Shelter is my Lunar Solo

As the sun nears the horizon, a magnificent alpine glow appears on Mt. Adams. The warm orange light flows and deepens. To the west, the sky is a fiery orange. The sun sinks into a bed of clouds on the horizon. As the orange drains from the world I know that I'll remember this sunset for the rest of my life.

September 2

It's clear again today. I keep looking at Mt. St. Helens and thinking about the drama of its eruption. It's hard to imagine what it must have felt like to be experiencing it as it happens. How big will this eruption be? Will the ash reach here? Will it bury us?

A friend of mine was with the U.S. Army Rangers when the eruption happened. George told me the story years later when we were in the Army National Guard together. They were training in the mountains when they heard a boom and saw a mushroom-shaped cloud rising. The ash began drifting down over them. They covered up in their ponchos and lay down.

"How long do you think it will take us to die?" George finally said.

"I don't think it will hurt us any, as long as it doesn't get too deep," his Sergeant said.

"But won't the radioactivity kill us?"

"I don't think there's any radioactivity in volcanic eruptions."

"Volcano? Wasn't that a nuclear bomb?"

"No, you bonehead. That's Mt. St. Helens. They've been talking about it erupting for weeks. Don't you listen to the news?"

"No. So we're not going to die?"

"I don't think so. Not from radioactivity, anyway." My buddy was an outstanding soldier, but soldiering was his life. He paid no attention to current events, so he was totally unaware of what he was seeing. In a way, he had experienced two apocalyptic events — the eruption of the mountain, and what he thought was the beginning of nuclear war.

When I round a corner, I stop dead in my tracks. There is a wonderful view of the cold blue glaciers of Mt. Rainier. There is a colorful mountainside in the foreground with a wedge of dark timber for contrast. The autumn colors are subtle shades of red, orange, yellow and bright green. My photo is a slight zoom. Perfect. Suddenly I have a feeling of déjà vu. I look at the scene, the photo on my camera, then pull out my guidebook and laugh. The photo I've taken matches the book cover, taken from the same vantage point at the same time of year.

"Goat Rocks Wilderness, Gifford Pinchot National Forest." So says the wooden sign. I'm excited to be here. The Goat Rocks have a reputation of being one of the most scenic spots on the trail, and I've arrived on a clear day. I meet a hiker heading southbound. We talk briefly then head our respective directions. The trail makes a long, steady climb along a steep slope then descends to Walupt Creek.

The trail crosses a ridge. There is a wonderful view of rugged cliffs of the Goat Rocks. A cold wind saws across my face. I drop my pack and put on my rain jacket and balaclava. Below me, at the edge of the timber, I spot a large bull elk. His antlers sway as he feeds.

Over another pass I see the trail running far into the distance, along the hillside and around the head of the valley. The timberline is much lower here in Washington and at this elevation, 6,400 feet, only scattered trees grow. It's chilly, and the sky is gray again. It's time to camp but it's a steep mountainside. But where the trail starts rounding the head of the valley is a flat spot and a creek. I stand in the cold wind and look up on the mountains. A band of white mountain goats, nannies and kids, graze placidly. The air feels as if it could get stormy. I orient my tent door away from the wind. The western sky blazes. The mountain goats grazing among the cliffs fade from white to gray, then disappear as dusk falls.

Still above timberline this morning I look back towards the cliffs at the head of the valley. The creek steps down the lush green valley in series of delicate cascades. I pass outstanding campsites. Sometimes a person compromises on a campsite when there's an ideal spot ten minutes up the trail. But it's fun discovering and not knowing everything ahead.

Something catches my eye. Three camouflaged hunters are sitting on a nearby vantage point, looking over the vastness with binoculars. One of them is about fourteen. They must have gotten up very early indeed. They have undoubtedly already seen some goats, probably a deer or two and possibly bear and elk. They too are feeling the magic of this wilderness.

The vistas are spectacular, as are the wildflowers. I admire western anemone, looking like little white haystacks. There are Blue Lupines and reddish-pink Indian Paintbrush, all on a green carpet backdropped by the glaciers of Mt. Adams. It's achingly beautiful.

Two plump hoary marmots are feeding near the trail. Make that three. Four. They have fluffy tails and dark faces and whitish capes. They become suspicious when they see I'm looking at them. One flattens himself into a furry puddle on a nearby boulder. Another black-masked rascal peeks around a massive rock. Do they ever notice the scenery?

Mt. Rainier appears when the trail crosses a ridge. Soaring well over 14,000 feet, the glaciers and rock on the great mountain are bathed in a cold, blue, early-morning light. Many people say that experiences like these must be shared to be appreciated. But not for me. I am happy to be here alone this morning.

There are signs. "Pacific Crest Trail Hiker Route," says the upper sign, pointing right. "Pacific Crest Trail Stock Route," says the lower, pointing left. I guess it means the faint trail going straight ahead, contouring the hillside. The map shows I can avoid a 500-foot climb by following it. That's what I'll do.

Soon the trail hits a steep hillside of icy snow, the Packwood Glacier. I gauge the slope and look to see where

I'll end up if I start to slide. Far enough for it to get really ugly. There is scattered gravel and stones. At first I use them for traction, but soon I'm down to pure snow, frozen hard. I kick out tiny grooves and set the point of my hiking pole carefully before taking a step.

I'm relieved to hit a rocky trail again, but soon there's another snowfield. Most of this snow was hidden by the topography. With great care, I cross this snowfield, too. But after following the trail a short distance another snowy slope appears. This one even steeper. Old tracks go straight across, too melted out to be of any use. They've crossed in the afternoon, when the snow was soft and much safer. I look up and down the slope. Two hundred yards below, the snowfield narrows to half its width, and there's a boulder at the midway point. After working my way down I still don't like it. I test it by going out a few steps, but carefully go back.

I find a pointed stone weighing about three pounds. It fits nicely in my hand. I reach out, chop a step, then plant a foot, repeatedly chopping and advancing until reaching the boulder for a rest. By the time the rocks on the other side are near, my chopping hand is cold. I remind myself not to become careless. A slip here would still be bad news. When I get to the other side I'm sweating. Back up to the trail, I climb. The Knife Edge is within sight. But before I reach it there is another steep snowfield. Sonofabitch! I start climbing, hoping to avoid the snowfield. I simultaneously reach the ridge, a blast of cold wind, and clear trail. If I'd taken the high route, or had an ice axe, or MICROspikes, been later in the season, or crossed when the snow was soft, it wouldn't have been a problem. But I made it. Out of the wind and in the sun I sit and snack, an incredible, sunny, 270-degree vista spread before me.

It's a joy walking along the Knife Edge towards Mt. Rainier. A mountain goat feeds on the opposite slope. There are thrillingly steep drop-offs in places, but I feel perfectly safe, just by keeping a more solid stance to allow for the buffeting of wind. I am so thankful to be here on a pretty day. Ahead, the trail tread winds northward along the Knife Edge, a white snowfield on the right and dark green trees on the left, with stunning Mount Rainier rising in the background. I take a photo, then another. This will be one of my best memories of the trail.

At last, the trail bails off the Knife Edge to the east. It's short notice, but I decide to call my old smokejumper buddy Rod Dow. He had talked about meeting me at White Pass or Snoqualmie Pass. Let's see. It's about 10:30, and there's about... 15 miles to go to Highway 12. I should be able to be there in 8 hours. I sit down and make some notes. When I call, he isn't home. I leave a message:

> *Hi, Rod, this is Buck. I'm getting down to White Pass at about 7 tonight, September 3. If you can meet me there, please bring me some food if you have time. Ten pounds of food total. Surprise me, but no cans or stuff with water in it, or raisins. Include some granola bars, Peanut M&Ms, jerky, a small jar of peanut butter, and five pouches of Knorr's Pasta or Rice Sides. Also two AAA batteries and water treatment tablets if you can find them. Oh, and a couple pieces of fruit and a pint of Ben and Jerry's. I'll try calling later. Thanks, Rod.*

It's a fairly steep descent, above treeline, so it's scenic. At a beautiful brook, I stop for a break. Water gurgles cheerfully. Purple, blue, red, pink, white and yellow wildflowers, bees buzzing around them, are sprinkled throughout the lush green grass. The PCT contours downward along a hillside and across a major ridge. The mountain panorama is absolutely gorgeous. I almost expect the Von Trapp family to appear before me. I pass a couple of young hikers talking to a middle-aged gentleman and his teenage daughter. The young guys are checking her out when they can avoid the dad's gaze, and she's enjoying the attention. I say hi and keep cruising. The trail falls over 2,500 feet from the Knife Edge to Tieton Pass. Losing that altitude over those five miles or so is easier than climbing it, but still tiring.

I try to call Rod again.

"Hello."

"Hi, Rod, it's Buck. Did you get my message?"

"I did. But I erased it somehow. I can make it at seven. Give me your list again."

He wants more specifics on food choices to fill out my list. I make a few more suggestions and tell him not to worry. Just wing it.

I reach the trailhead at Highway 12 at about 6:40. I walk out to the road, find a good spot to sit, and watch for Rod.

A pickup pulls off the road and does a U-turn and comes back to me. It's Rod and his twelve-year-old son. He pulls up, smiling.

"I told Julian you'd be waiting here."

"How're you doing? Hi, Julian."

Rod pulls into the trailhead parking lot with me following on foot. When he gets out, I say, "Before I forget, remember that bet we had about the helicopter landing on Leonard's fire?"

We take turns telling the story to Julian. We were on one of the greatest fires ever. Fun-wise, that is. Lots of stupid contests and practical jokes. And hard work, too, particularly at the beginning, before it was "caught." When it came time to fly out, Leonard called dispatch and they said the helicopter would be there at 1800.

"I can tell you when it WON'T be here, and that's at eighteen-hundred," I had said.

"Would you like to bet?" Rod said.

"Sure."

"Obviously you'd have to give me some odds. How about, if it doesn't get here at six o'clock, I give you five dollars. But if it DOES, you give me five hundred."

Now this was food for thought. Helicopters rarely showed up on time. Sometimes a little late. Sometimes hours late. Sometimes a whole day late. It was a gamble, but I wanted to make a point. It was worth the risk.

"OK, but we've got to make some ground rules."

"Fine. I'm saying the helicopter skids will touch the ground in the minute from eighteen-hundred to eighteen-oh-one. If it does, you owe me five hundred. If it lands at any other time, I owe you five dollars."

"Alright. But we have to agree that nobody here does anything to affect the landing time. No lying down out in the landing spot or asking them to fly over to check something out on the way in or anything."

"Deal." We shook hands. Now this caught the interest of the jumpers. Naturally, what they wanted to happen was for the helicopter to land right on time and for me to have to cough up the big money.

Eight smokejumpers sat around the landing spot in the scrubby black spruce of arctic Alaska, swatting skeets and glancing at their watches. Then we heard the sound of distant rotors. 1750. It was going to be close! As the sound grew louder the time wound down. At 1755 the helicopter appeared. I admit it, my heart was pounding. The ribbing would be as bad as the financial beating if I lost. Naw, worse, because it would last for years. But the helicopter scouted the fire long enough that it was several minutes after 1800 when it finally sat down. That was close!

As we talk Rod pulls out the food he has brought. Everything I'd asked for and a whole lot more. Burgers, fries. Corn on the cob. Fancy cheese. Yogurt-covered almonds. Gatorade. Fancy, healthy crackers. We talk as it gets dark and I gorge. Rod is, as usual, incredibly generous.

"So, Rod, all this food is for me?"

"Yup, all yours."

"Thanks, man, that's great. But I can't eat it all."

"No problem. Just leave what you don't want to carry."

"OK. But I can't really afford to just GIVE away food, you know? This is some high-quality stuff. I figure you owe me at least thirty bucks!"

Rod laughs.

We talk until dark. Then I pack up and Rod stows the extra food. Free of charge. We shake hands and I head off down the trail, in the dark, to look for a spot to camp.

Morning is foggy and cool, but not raining. Yet. It's Sunday. There are several groups of hikers heading back towards the road, most in good spirits and enjoying their hike. A lake appears out of the fog. A stand of evergreens rises out of the mist on a peninsula, a beautiful scene with a melancholy feel. I haven't heard from Stephanie in weeks. It starts to rain. I hunker under a tree to don my rain jacket. I eat some of the goodies Rod gave me.

Several horses are coming down the trail. I step well downhill of the trail to allow them to pass. An older lady on the lead horse gives me a scathing look, which puzzles me. A following rider gives me a friendly greeting. I interpret that as a way of saying, "Ignore that grumpy old bat."

At a creek ford my feet are dry so I cross on some logs, fifty yards downstream. I sit down to cook lunch on the sunny bank. A tiny toad hops away when I stoop down to scoop up some water. Then another. When I look carefully, there are a dozen within a short distance, making tiny, weak hops. I pick one up. It is about the size of a fingernail.

As I eat a leisurely meal horses approach the bank from the opposite side, looking for the best crossing. The Grumpy Old Bat is leading the charge. She gives me another scathing look. Probably sitting too close to the trail or something. "Do you want me to move?"

"You're all right," says her companion. The horses easily wade the stream, one of them getting a good drink. I cringe as the horses stomp through the area where many of the little toads are hopping madly about.

Crossing an open hillside later, I look down to see a golden lab intently watching me. He's tied up next to a wall tent a couple hundred yards away. Every time I look back he's still looking. His owner comes around the corner and we talk. He's scouting for elk.

"I haven't seen many. And I don't know what's happened to all the berries. Most years I can pick all I want. Right here. Right next to the trail."

"Maybe it froze when they were blossoming."

"Yeah, maybe." Looking back, I can still see a now-tiny dog, standing up and wagging his tail in anticipation.

"He loves coming out here," his owner says, smiling.

Miles later a hiker comes walking up the hill. His umbrella is up and he's looking down at the trail, deep in thought. I can't help but wonder why he's carrying an open umbrella when it's not raining. Or sunny.

"How's your day?" I say.

"Awesome. Thanks. Are you a thru-hiker?"

"Yeah. I'm Colter."

"Hi, Colter. Man, that's AWESOME that you're a thru-hiker. When did you start?"

Frankly, I am honored he is so impressed and interested.

"April twenty-first."

"Nice. How has it been?"

"It's been a great adventure. Lots of snow. That made it harder. But a good experience."

"Man, that is so cool."

"How about you? Where are you headed?"

"Mexico. I'm a southbounder."

"That's funny. I'm glad I asked before I bragged myself up too much."

"No problem, man. I love hearing the stories from the northbounders."

"How do you like your pack?"

We have the same model.

"Pretty good. I like it."

"Looks like it's slumping some for you. It wasn't a problem for me when I used my RidgeRest as a frame but then I sent that pad home. I'm using one of my poles for sort of a frame." I show him.

"Looks like it's still slumping for you."

I laughed. He was right. One of the pole halves had slipped partially out on one side and my pack has started to slump. I drop my pack and straighten it out.

"I've got to work on staying humble. Have you seen Wyoming? Younger lady. Short red hair?"

"She's only a couple hours ahead of you."

"You mean you saw her two hours ago?"

"Yup."

I have to think. Two hours ago. So they had each walked two hours in opposite directions. She was about four hours ahead now.

"U.S. Boundary NPS," says a vertical sign. Mt. Rainier National Park. At a vantage point I can see the huge mountain, mostly shrouded by clouds. Along the edge of the meadow, something moves. I stop and watch. It's an elk. Then another and another. My monocular shows a whole band feeding. A calf rushes up to another elk, trying to trigger a game. It whirls to chase the calf, which goes speeding off, looking back to make sure it's being followed. It weaves around some trees startling another group of elk. The game ends as suddenly as it began. I skirt around the elk to avoid scaring them.

I'm over 25 miles for the day. It looks like rain. Clouds are drifting over Dewey Lake when I arrive and find a good camp spot. I take pride in getting a perfect, taut pitch on my tent. If it pours rain, no problemo.

It's a damp morning. Clouds hang over the lake. Condensed fog drips from the trees. It's chilly. The wet vegetation smells like fall. I stuff my tent in an outside pocket and start hiking, eating some granola bars on the trail. After a while, I hear cheerful chatter. Two thirty-something women come blazing down the trail, in shorts and t-shirts in the chill, gloves on their hands. They talk and laugh without letup.

"See anything good?" I say as they approach.

"We saw a band of elk, but we usually don't see many animals, we yack too much!"

"Keeps the bears away though!" adds her friend as they breeze by. When they are gone I'm still smiling. Those two are enjoying life.

When the trail tops out on an open ridge a distant bull elk bugles. I stop and listen to make sure. The bull bugles again and another one answers. On the opposite hillside are scattered yellow-brown dots: feeding elk. Through my monocular, the bull tilts his head back and bugles. Several seconds go by before I hear it, the rising, piercing whistle. It's always thrilling. Especially the first elk bugle of the fall.

As the trail descends the bulls continue their bugle challenges. Clouds sweep in. They obscure the peaks and slowly descend. It starts sprinkling a cold rain. I cross the highway at Chinook Pass. I was hoping to find a restroom here but I don't see one. Instead I head well off the trail in a thicket of dripping trees and kick a hole in the needles and soft earth. After covering up the hole again I wash up with hand sanitizer. It's then I notice a red cooler back across the road. Coolers are good. Back I go. The sign says:

PCT Hikers!!! Help yourself
Enjoy and Happy Trails, Rhyme and Reason

And, on a smaller sign:

For Thru-hikers ONLY. Sorry! Thank You!

Bless them. There is a register which I sign, but my hands are cold and stiff so I keep it to a simple: *"Thank You! Colter 0800 September 5."* Wyoming and Otter were here late yesterday. A beautiful red apple and a can of Pepsi are my prizes.

I cross the pass for the third time. In a short distance there is a large parking area, abuzz with activity on this Sunday morning. I laugh at myself when I see two nice, dry restrooms.

Ahead are a string of hikers, all women. They step aside to allow me to pass.

"Good morning, ladies."

"Good morning. Are you a thru-hiker?"

"Yup. How far are you headed?"

"Just to the top. When did you start?"

"April twenty-first."

"April!" She turns to her friends that can't hear. "This guy has been walking the Pacific Crest Trail since April!" They all appear duly impressed. "I'd love to do that," she says.

"Judging by your pace today, I don't see why you couldn't."

"Maybe. But I've got some older pets I have to take care of and... well."

"You're out here hiking. Maybe you can have the best of both worlds."

Fifteen minutes later a hiker comes hustling down the trail towards me. It takes me a moment to place him.

"Chris?"

"Colter, right?"

"Yeah. I haven't seen you since the kick-off!" Back then he'd had a huge pack and seemed slightly unsure of what he was getting into. Now he has a small pack and is lean and mean.

"Do you have a trail name?"

"Turbo."

"How do you happen to be hiking southbound?"

"I was running out of time to get to Canada before winter. So I flipped up to the border."

"That sounds smart."

It is a good day for wildlife. A hoary marmot with a fluffy, rust-red tail feeds on the trail, fifteen feet away, shoveling grass into his mouth with both front paws. He glances up at me, unconcerned. His look says, *"What are YOU looking at?"*

Later, a clump of grass goes scurrying through the boulders. I am baffled. What did I just see? The green clump of grass leaps up on a rock and pauses. It's a pika, his mouth stuffed with a small haystack of food for the winter. I laugh out loud.

"Eek. EEK!" Another tiny pika is perched on a boulder, his shiny black eyes staring at me. His stubby round ears belie his kinship with rabbits.

It starts to rain. Then stops. And starts again. There are good views, then the clouds sweep in and hide everything. I put my raincoat on, take it off. And repeat. It's fine. Variety is the spice of life. White dots are dispersed across a steep rock face. Mountain goats! One, two, three... fourteen! White is good camouflage in the snow. Now, not so much. They cross the rock faces with complete confidence.

At 6:00 PM I cross a small bridge and see Urich Shelter at the corner of a meadow. There are several people there. I'm concerned it's non-hikers who have come in to party, this being a weekend. Instead it's Dicentra and Hoosier Daddy, here with Trail Magic. I met both of them at Kick-Off. Dicentra welcomes me and offers me some hot chili on this cold evening.

There are about four hikers. I don't recognize any of them, which is surprising. Maybe they are section hiking or something. I see Wyoming listed in a notebook.

"When did Wyoming leave?" I ask.

"She didn't. She's still here," Dicentra says. "Why are you reading my notebook?"

"I'm sorry. I assumed it was the shelter register." But she's not offended.

Outside, I see Wyoming's red head. When she is just a few feet away, I step out from behind a tree.

"Wy-oming!"

"Hey, Colter. I thought you might catch us today," she says in her soft voice, beaming. We give each other a quick hug. Last time I saw Wyoming was a thousand miles ago. There are a myriad of questions we have for each other. How was the second hitch to Ashland? (Tough) Are you having fun? (Yes!) She introduces me to Otter, whom she's hiked with for a while now. He likes to get up crazy early, and make hot coffee which he delivers to her tent. Sounds like a pretty good hiking partner!

I put up my tent along the edge of the meadow, well away from all the activity. Back at the cabin, someone has built a warm fire in the stove. The Graduate introduces himself. Our small group of hikers sits in the warm near-dark and talks about the trail. Being thru-hikers, we start heading to bed around 9, aka "hiker midnight."

It rains hard during the night. In the morning the meadow is soaked with rain and dew, with rain still dripping off the trees. Dicentra has promised pancakes, but I'm not sure when she'll wake up. I pack up my soaked tent and the rest of my gear and head over to the shelter. Pretty soon Dicentra comes over and makes us coffee, which I drink as I talk to Wyoming. I'm thinking about leaving but Dicentra says the pancakes will be ready soon. Soon a huge, steaming pancake is on my plate, covered with butter and syrup. Awesome! Everybody chows down with the pancakes being replaced as fast as we can eat them. When I'm done eating I do a little cleaning up around the cabin, then put on my raincoat and pack and head for the door.

Wyoming in front of Urich Shelter
Dicentra on left, The Graduate on extreme right

"Thanks," I say to Dicentra and Hoosier Daddy, and, "See you down the trail!" to Wyoming and the rest of the hikers.

It is a wet day. High bushes crowd the trail. They are drenched with rain and shed a continuous cascade of cold water down my legs and into my shoes. It's chilly, even wearing both my raincoat and rain pants, plus gloves with mitten shells. This is logging country. Much of the time I'm walking through old clearcuts in various stages of regrowth. The clouds are "on the deck." It's a day of putting in the miles. It's not all glory and eye-popping views and people slapping you on the back. Sometimes it's a sodden, cold slog. All day long.

Still, there are things to appreciate. I take a photo of the trail winding through massive, fog-shrouded trees, a huge tree trunk, draped with moss, hanging over the trail. I take another of blaze-orange maple leaves against a green hillside. There are plump huckleberries close at hand.

It's tough to find a good spot to camp. I settle for a spot in the wet grass near a road crossing. A few feet away some bonehead has scattered crab shells.

Man, is it wet! It rained through the night and it's still raining this morning. It's been 100% humidity since the day before yesterday. I slept warm and dry, though. That's what's really important. It's too chilly to sit around for breaks, so I walk and walk. There are red sumac berries contrasting beautifully with lush green leaves. And there's Devil's Club! *Oplopanax horridus*. *Horridus* shows a certain lack of scientific detachment from the scientists bestowing the name. Yet, the name is appropriate. The stalk is encircled by spines, which often break off and cause irritation in the skin of the unwary.

I try to give Rod a call to ask if he wants to meet me at Snoqualmie Pass. It would be good to restock, shower, run errands, update my website, check email, dry everything out, and to hang out with Rod and his family. No signal, though. My MP3 player is also on the fritz, working only sporadically. The humidity must have finally gotten to it.

At a lake, there is a fire ring. Atop it is a soggy cotton sweatshirt, singed green wood, and an unburned tag from a tent. It tells a story. Enthusiastic greenhorns walked in from

Snoqualmie for Labor Day Weekend. It rained. A lot. They had a new tent and for whatever reason it didn't keep them dry. The wet cotton sweatshirt got soaked and cold. They tried to start a fire, but it was raining and they were using wet wood, which wasn't going to burn anyway. They fled, abandoning the sweatshirt. I can't help but laugh, but right now I'm not having that much fun myself.

At last, the sound of I-90 drifts up from far below and the ski lifts appear. I leave the trail and head down the slope. Things are quiet around the many ski schools and businesses associated with winter sports. I call Rod to let him know I'm at Snoqualmie Pass. He says he'll meet me at the cafe. Good ole' Rod.

I squish my way over there and study the menu, ordering a large pizza and cup of hot cocoa. It's good to sit down. I only sat down once, briefly, all day. I definitely don't mind the wait. It's nice and warm. I plug in my phone to charge, then sort through some of my stuff while sipping hot cocoa and waiting for the pizza. The young lady tending the register has an accent, German I think. She's a people person. She says two thru-hikers, a young couple, have ordered a pizza and will be back soon. From her description I'm guessing it's Passant and Darko, whom I haven't seen since Sierra City. Sure enough, they soon walk in and we catch up on trail news as their pizza is boxed. They take their pizza to chow down in their motel room. Finally, my pizza is ready. Far more than I can possibly eat and very hot. PERFECT!

Rod and his son arrive. I hop in their truck and we drive eastbound on the interstate. I offer them some pizza and they try a piece but it's a kind of barbecue chicken pizza and they don't care for it. I'm not offended because that just means I'll have to eat the whole thing myself.

We drive up the long driveway to Rod's house and I marvel again at the beautiful log construction. Rod did most of it himself and I'm hugely impressed every time I see it. On clear days Mt. Rainier can be seen through a gap in the trees to the west.

I hang my gear to dry, then take a shower and throw my clothes in the washer. We have some ice cream and peaches while I wait for my clothes. Rod's wife Lisa comes home. She graciously makes sure Rod has seen to everything I might need.

Despite a good dinner, later in the evening I'm hungry for more pizza and open the fridge to grab a piece.

"Hey Julian, do you know where the pizza is?"

"No. Maybe it's in the freezer."

Rod walks in. "Hey Rod, what happened to the pizza?"

"Oh, I threw it away."

He's a kidder, I know. "Seriously, where did you put it?"

"No really, I threw it away. I didn't think you wanted it."

"Ouch."

"Sorry about that."

"That's OK." I'm stunned, though. Half of a large pizza! Few but thru-hikers would truly understand the tragic loss.

In the morning we have a huge breakfast and I pack up my clean dry stuff and say goodbye to Lisa. Rod, Julian and I drive to the grocery store and then to a burger place so I can chow down again on the way to the trailhead. It looks drearier as we near Snoqualmie and sure enough it starts to rain.

"Thanks, Rod, I really appreciate it," I say as I climb out.

"No problem, Buck. It was great seeing you. Have a good hike."

What a loyal, generous friend Rod has been.

Man, is it wet again. Raining off and on. 100% humidity and dripping trees and bushes. Dampness creeps in around my wrists, around my rain jacket hood, up the cuffs of my pants. A good rain jacket and rain pants are priceless. The wet trail reaches a knife-edge ridge in the cold drifting clouds. It has a spooky feel. A good place to watch my step.

252

Well before dark, I begin watching for good campsites. It's been steep and I'm concerned that if I'm too picky it will be tough to find a spot. When I see a faint side trail leading up to a possible bench I climb up to investigate and find a good spot. Soon I'm out of my wet clothes and into my dry long underwear and socks and my balaclava, nestled into my warm sleeping bag.

September 9

Another wet day. There was no scenery yesterday with all the clouds, but today there are occasional brief glimpses of spectacular peaks and lakes of the Alpine Lakes Wilderness. I think about how far it is to the next resupply, and when I might finish the Trail. I reach a creek. Lemah Creek according to the Atlas. Mile 2424 of the PCT. It shows southbound mileage too. I'm only 231.8 miles from the Canada border! Wow. Only on these long hikes does a walk of 200+ miles seem like a relatively short distance.

My next stop is Stevens Pass. Like most thru-hikers I plan to hitch to the Dinsmores, famous Trail Angels. There should be a resupply box that my mother sent waiting for me there, as well as the shoes Johnny Mac had shipped to me. Stevens Pass is at about mile 2477, so... 53 miles. Today is Thursday the 9th, so I should arrive there on Sunday the 12th. Allowing for my Dinsmore's and Stehekin stops I should make it to Canada around the 21st or so. The end is in sight!

No rain this morning. Yay! A deer feeds near the trail, keeping an eye on me but otherwise unconcerned. I snack on some thimbleberries leaning over the trail. Some fireweed has blossomed all the way to the top, a sign that summer is ending. Fall is coming on fast. I can see it and smell it and feel it. Some peaks are visible today. My morale soars when sunlight glistens on the wet mountainsides. It's a 2,500-foot climb in the 10 miles from Waptus Lake to the crest near Cathedral Rock.

Ahead, a hiker comes powering down the trail.

"Jaybird!!" I yell.

"Colter! How's it going?"

"Awesome. How about you?"

"Great. I flipped up to the border." He'd gotten shin-splints and taken some time off the trail. He's decided to flip to avoid potentially heavy snows in Washington later in the season. He is hoping to finish the trail before winter hits in Northern California.

"So have you decided to admit that free will is an illusion?"

He glances at me, remembering, and laughs. "Never!"

Soon I look up to see another southbounder. For some reason, he's trying to take a photo of me.

"Did you get it?" I ask.

"Do you mind going back a few yards?" he says. I head back a ways, then come towards him again. "Got it, thanks! I'm Boots."

"Hi, Boots. Colter."

"I'm trying to get photos of all the hikers. See that tree there? It sort of looks like a woman leaning over with her arms out. I wanted that in the shot." Boots has hiked most of the PCT himself in long sections. He hands me his journal which I read thru for familiar names before signing myself. He's given his tarp to someone he thought needed it more than himself, therefore his sleeping bag is soaked and has gained several pounds. Yikes!

I hear the roar of a rushing stream. I climb up on a boulder to look for the best crossing. Hikers have made a crude bridge out of short parallel logs, in a narrow spot between two big boulders. There are two unsecured stick handrails above them on each side. Just beyond is a similar crude bridge across a second fork. The first bridge doesn't budge during my crossing. Nor does the second. Piece of cake.

Crude log bridges on the Washington PCT

In the morning my tent sags in the wet. Condensation is beaded up inside the fly. Raindrops linger on the outside. I pack up my sleeping bag and gear inside the tent, avoiding the damp walls. After breaking it down I shake it violently several times, droplets flying everywhere, then stuff it in its sack with cold hands.

In an hour, the trail comes to a junction. The map shows the old Cascade Crest Trail takes a more direct but steeper route than the PCT, but rejoins it later. On a whim, I decide to explore the old trail. Initially, I'm somewhat confused by trails running down to the nearby lake and campsites. It's clear the trail hasn't been maintained in quite some time. It's barely above freezing and the dense huckleberry bushes overgrowing the trail are heavy with clinging rain. Each step knocks a cascade of ice-water onto my already aching cold feet. Looking uphill I see a long climb ahead of me. I sit down on a rock and unsling my pack, digging out two plastic bags. Taking off my shoes I slip the bags over my wool socks then put my shoes back on. It makes a huge difference. My wet feet slowly warm as new cold water runs off the plastic bags.

At the gap, clouds screen distant mountains, but I can see the rocky draw that descends to the PCT and the deep blue of Glacier Lake far below. As I near the intersection I see the back of a sign. When I turn around to read it, it warns not to take the route I've just come over, the trail is abandoned. I laugh.

Crossing a divide I use the tip of my hiking pole to write *CANADA* in the smooth soil, with an arrow pointing northeast. A short distance later the sun begins to soak through the clouds and into the indigo blue of Trap Lake hundreds of feet below.

I turn around to see two hikers hustling up the trail. "Pat! Shades! How's it going?"

"Hi, Colter. How's your hike?"

"Kind of wet. Have you guys had lunch yet?"

"No."

"How about we stop at the next good spot?"

"Sounds good."

We walk as we swap trail stories, then drop our packs next to a log in the trees.

"Looks like your pants have taken a beating," I say.

Pat laughs and looks down at his legs. His blue rain pants have several long rips on each leg, the flapping tatters partially held together by duct tape.

"I found them in a hiker box."

We are all headed to Stevens Pass today, but I plan to go to the Dinsmore's and they plan to stay in Skykomish. We swap some of our remaining food.

Back on the trail, we hike a steady pace for miles. It's fun to talk trail again. Along a lake, there is a palatial tent with a large blue tarp set up as an awning. Someone calls out to invite us over. It's a trail crew. They've seen thru-hikers before and know we are always hungry. They give us fruit and other goodies. Shades and Pat do most of the talking, answering the usual questions.

There is a cooler of Trail Magic at Stevens Pass. I sign the register thanking them, grab a Pepsi and walk over to the pass to find a place to hitch. It's a good spot, nice and wide. Soon a car slows and stops 50 yards down the road, then backs up. He gives me a ride all the way to the Baring and drops me off at the cafe where I ask directions to the Dinsmores.

"Looks like they're coming in right now."

A motherly woman with a kind face walks in. "I'm Andrea."

"Hi, I'm Colter. Obviously I'm a PCT hiker. You should have a couple of packages for me."

"If you just cross the tracks and take a left, you'll see the sign. I'll be over in a bit and we'll find your packages."

Several hikers are eating at a cafe table, but I don't know any of them. It's funny how quickly a group identity forms. They aren't unfriendly, but I feel like an outsider. One is pontificating on every topic that comes up. I introduce myself and head across the railroad tracks.

There is a big shed set up for the hikers. There are several hikers around but I only recognize The Graduate. Soon Andrea shows up and we go to the other side of the shed with its shelves of packages. She scans the rows until she finds mine. She gives me a quick tour: the computer, the

257

lounge area, the outhouse, the washer and dryer, loaner clothes to wear while I clean up, and the showers. Last but not least, boxes of fresh Washington fruit. Nice!

Andrea takes a photo of a whiskery me for her website. Back at the bunk room I sort through all my boxes and dump out my pack to ditch trash and reorganize. There's always so much to do in town. I use the computer to update my website:

> **September 11, 2010, Day 143. Stevens Pass, Washington; Mile 2,476, 190 miles left!** *I am at the Dinsmore's, Trail Angels just west of Stevens Pass. I'm averaging nearly 25 miles a day... The trail is more rugged than Oregon and the weather much cooler. The mosquitoes are long gone now...*
>
> *I hope to finish the trail in ten days or so, on or about September 21...*

I walk over to the cafe for an excellent hot meal. It's locals in there now. Back at Dinsmore's I find an out-of-the-way piece of floor and put down one of their foam pads and roll out my sleeping pad. I meet a young couple, Happy Camper and Trash Pocket. There is a guy, Austrian I think, who says he has come over from the Continental Divide Trail.

Most of us watch a movie then we all go to sleep.

CANADA BOUND

"What lies behind us and what lies before us are tiny matters compared to what lies within us."

— Henry S. Haskins

In the morning everyone goes over to the cafe for a good breakfast, then most of us load up in Jerry Dinsmore's pickup. In Skykomish we see a couple of hikers, it's Whitebeard and 3rd Monty. We stop to ask if they need a ride, but they've got one. Their Trail Angels have a couple of wiener dogs. As I pet the dogs I realize they are the same Dachshunds, and people I saw at the Kick-Off way back in April. Small world. I miss my little wiener dog Duke, my good little friend, still enjoying the summer with his other family.

Back at the pass, I walk over to the highway to connect my steps, then thank Jerry and head down the trail. A rain shower hits. I stop beneath a sheltering tree to don rain gear and Trash Pocket and Happy Camper come by. We walk together. Trash Pocket and her sister hiked the Appalachian Trail with their aunt. She got her trail name by picking up trash she spotted and stuffing it into a designated pocket.

Happy Camper was named for his love of kicking back in camp. While it seemed that Trash Pocket really enjoyed the hiking itself, Happy Camper hiked mainly to be with her and for the reward of finally pitching camp.

That leads to a philosophical discussion of why we are out here. What is the point of thru-hiking, anyway? Occasionally I'd glance behind me and catch glimpses of Trash Pocket in her orange raincoat.

"Should we slow down and let Trash Pocket catch up?"

"Naw. When I get talking like this she just lets me hike ahead. She likes to hike more in the quiet."

Hikers have a lot in common, yet they have distinct differences in hiking styles. I find it interesting how well these two get along, yet she likes to hike quietly and he likes to talk; she likes the walking and he prefers the camping.

We reach a fork in the trail.

"I'm going to look at the guidebook," I say.

"All right."

"Left. We need to take a left here. See?" I point out where I think we are on the map. He agrees and takes his hiking pole and scratches an arrow and *C-7*.

"What's C-7?" I ask.

"It's kind of our code. If one of us gets ahead we draw an arrow and C-7 at confusing intersections." There is more to the story, I know.

We are walking in the clouds through a meadow of knee-high gold and green corn lilies. Happy Camper takes a photo of me walking through the meadow. It's so dark already at 6 PM that the photo comes out blurred, but in an artful way.

I walk on ahead. It's soggy and chilly but I find a decent tree to sit under for a snack. I hear voices and see matching orange raincoats. Their hoods are up they walk right past without spotting me in my green jacket. Later I find them sitting underneath their own tree, eating their dinner out of the same Ziploc. Happy Camper has food dripping off his beard and onto his pants, Trash Pocket cheerfully digs in. We joke about the rain as I walk past.

Campsites are hard to come by this dark evening. I see a high spot with the ground worn bare by many backpacker feet. I drop my pack. Trash Pocket and Happy Camper arrive but decide to put in some more miles. As I blow up my air mattress, White Beard and 3rd Monty appear.

"There's room here if you need a spot!" I call out.

"Thanks, we might do that." They look around but it's rather marshy and my little hill is the place to be. "Guess we'll set up here, if you don't mind."

To fit in, they have to set up maybe five feet away with our guy-lines crisscrossing. It's strange to be camping so close to other people.

During the night I hear a mouse rustling around but it's staying out of the tent. Later I have to pee. Hoping not to trip on my any tent guy-lines, I quietly crawl out.

"Hey! HEY!" Whitebeard shouts.

"It's Colter."

"Oh. Right. I was sound asleep. We usually camp by ourselves so I assumed it was a bear outside."

"No problem." One of the downsides of camping with other people. I scared the heck out of him and I prefer not having to sneak in and out when it's time to pee. Not their fault. Just the way it is.

It looks like there are patches of open sky this soggy gray dawn. The sun peaks over the horizon. The sun! Steam rises on glistening meadows. Evergreens are silhouetted black against the rising sun, sunlight streaming through the branches into the golden, swirling fog. Here is the magic. My day is already made. I'm feeling giddy with happiness in the bright sunshine. My pants and feet are soaked below the knee but not for long on a day like this. Yahoo!

A spider is spinning his web at eye level across the trail. He is nearly finished. I watch as he walks around and around the web in concentric circles, weaving the familiar pattern. I count the silken lines. He has already made 21 trips around and there are about 24 of the radiating lines upon which the net is being spun. I take several photos of the spider working in the low morning sun, and the artful workmanship of his labors. Where did this skill come from?

On a ridgetop, Whitebeard and Monty are collecting their gear. "It's a great place to dry out," Monty says.

"You're right. That's exactly what I'm going to do." I set up my tent loosely to dry in the sun. The tiny figures of Monty and Whitebeard cross a sunny slope showing the gold and red blush of fall, the snows of Glacier Peak looming above them.

I see a black bear ambling in the valley far below. I hear a rifle shot. I walk and watch and listen, and finally see two hunters on the ridge just above me, scanning with binoculars.

"Did you guys shoot?" I ask quietly.

"Yes."

"At what?"

"A bear."

"Did you get him?"

"We don't know yet. We're watching where he disappeared." They had seen a different bear from the one I'd seen. I left them as they patiently waited and watched.

Ahead, in a saddle, is a signpost:

TEMPORARY SIGN 7-18-10
PCT Detoure [sic] > Indian Cr. to White River...

Below, someone has written:

Seems to be fine. Hiked to Red Pass with no issues.

Back in 2003 a storm did severe damage to a long stretch of trail, washing out some places, knocking countless trees across the trail in others. Yogi's guide says that although the PCT isn't officially open, the trail is passable with patience, and preferred by most thru-hikers. This is another one of those decision points thru-hikers hear about for months ahead of time. I stay on the old PCT.

Near a pond, a hiker is shouldering a small pack. A thru-hiker. A hiker I haven't met before.

"Green Tortuga," he says, when I ask him his name. He talks about going to Seattle to visit his girlfriend. He was tempted to stay and not do the rest of the trail.

"She told me 'Don't quit!' She wanted me to finish, too."

At White Pass, the light and the scenery are outstanding. There is a cache of tools left by a trail crew. Tortuga decides to push on, but it looks like several miles to the next good camping.

There is a "No Camping" sign on the ridge. I walk down the ridge to a nice flat spot on the edge of the trees with a tiny brook nearby. "No Camping." A black dot moves across the sunny hillside. Through my monocular, I confirm it's a black bear. A few hundred yards below him Tortuga strides steadily along, neither aware of the other.

I am loath to hike downhill from the PCT to camp but eventually find a nice spot near a brook. The sun is disappearing behind a glaciered peak. Clouds drift down the valley, those catching the last rays of sun are a warm gold, those in the shade a cool blue. Another bear is feeding on the hillside above me as darkness falls.

It's a beautiful morning, cold and clear. The two-hundred-foot climb to White Pass warms me quickly. I take off my down jacket before I sweat. Alpine glow spreads down the peaks then fades as the sun strengthens. The trail stretches ahead of me, angling uphill through the red of huckleberry bushes.

A bear feeds steadily a comfortable distance above me. I spot another near treeline below. They are feeding enthusiastically on the berries. A third bear crosses the trail a few hundred yards ahead of me. I purposely clack my pole tips on rocks to make an unnatural noise to alert any bears I haven't seen, but otherwise I just stay alert and watchful. Yet another bear walks out of the timber and across the slope to a patch of berries where he feeds for a while before moving on.

At Red Pass, a pretty glacial valley falls away. Each rivulet of melting snow water is visible in the low sun. When I round the corner Glacier Peak looms. It's a breath-taking scene in the morning sun, a brilliant blue sky, white glaciers against the blue mountain, with the colors of early fall.

Trail leading past Glacier Peak, Glacier Peak Wilderness

For hours I round the flanks of Glacier Peak. It is so pretty that I keep pausing to just soak it all in. Especially fascinating are the glaciers themselves, real glaciers with deep, rugged blue crevasses.

The roar of a jet plane builds rapidly and a fighter appears, flying low and slow. The pilot is checking out the mountain for himself. He flips his fighter upside down, nothing between him and the mountain but plexiglass and a few thousand feet of air. He rights the plane and roars away. It's a glorious day for both of us.

The log bridge at Kennedy Creek has collapsed, its back broken midway, the middle resting on the rocky creekbed. Nonetheless, it's solid and an easy crossing. Why it didn't wash away this spring is a mystery. I see the seventh and eighth black bear of the day on the hillsides above and below the trail. Neither spots me.

The trail crosses Fire Creek Pass. I pause to absorb the beauty of the North Cascades. Along the switchbacks leading to Mica Lake marmots whistle left and right, diving for their burrows as I approach. It's getting late in the day. I vow to camp at the next decent spot. Trail crews have done an enormous amount of work in this area. Large sections of mountainside have slid. In places the original trail has been repaired, in others, new stretches of trail have been constructed. Explosives must have been necessary in places.

There's a tender spot on my left foot, on the outside of my little toe. I take off my shoe. When I first noticed it I experimented with adjusting the lacing. But it looks like a tight line of stitches may be causing the problem. My tiny knife and LED light are clipped on the back of my pack. I take the knife and cut some of the stitches whose only function is attaching a decorative strip. It feels better when I continue.

A section of abandoned trail diverges from a newly constructed switchback. I walk down the old trail and find a flat spot beneath a big tree, just wide enough to pitch my tent. I remind myself not to walk over the embankment if I get up during the night.

September 15

After crossing Milk Creek, I find trail crews haven't gotten this far. Tall, wet vegetation hangs over the trail making it hard to see. I climb more than 2,000 feet before reaching the top.

Ahead of me the trail contours the head of an open valley. A large bear is feeding 200 yards ahead. A small black ball comes bounding into view, followed by another, and yet another. A sow and three cubs! The sow stays focused while the cubs intersperse eating berries with romping around. Wrestling matches erupt then a spontaneous truce results in more berry chomping.

When they wander away uphill I proceed down the trail. When I spot them again they are far uphill. Two cubs have become distracted in a clump of trees and sprint across the slope to catch up with mom and their sibling.

I follow the trail as it sidehills around the head of the open valley. Most of these black bears are truly black, unlike California where many are the brown phase. There are three black blobs below the trail on the other side of the next ridge. Another adult with her two cubs. Now near Dolly Vista, I see another sow and cub. How many bears today? Let's see, a sow and three cubs, a sow and two cubs, and a sow with one cub. Nine bears already today, and eight yesterday!

My foot hurts a little again. I sit down in the sun and pick more stitches and remove the decorative strip completely. I discover one of my water bottles is missing out of a side pocket. Must have fallen out when I was crawling under a blowdown.

And there are numerous blowdowns across the trail. Most are pretty easy to walk around, or over, or under. Others are enormous and so long that it's a serious bushwhack to get around the ends. Usually scuff marks show where other hikers have used branches to haul themselves up and over the massive trunks.

Some logs have been sawed through. I notice the clearly visible growth rings on the end of a 4-foot-thick log. On a whim, I decide to count the rings. It should only take a few minutes to count, what, maybe 300 rings? On closer inspection, the rings are extremely close together in places.

I know I'll lose count if I don't keep a tally, so with my pen I start counting at the bark and work my way in, making a mark at every 10th ring. At every ten of these, I mark 100 years. I'm already at 200 years at only about four inches in!

It takes quite a while, but it's not raining and I can relax from time to time because of the running tally. At 400 years it gets exciting. Five hundred... 600... 658 years old! If this tree fell in 2003, that would mean the first visible rings were laid down in about 1345 AD, during the Middle Ages. Long before Columbus. Wow! That is really interesting. I'm really glad I took the time.

Results of tree ring count of a log cut to clear trail: 658 years old!

There is one especially magnificent tangle of fallen trees before things get better. A hiker is catching up to me. It's The Graduate. We talk about the trail conditions as we near the Suiattle River. We follow rock cairns upstream. He is ahead of me when we reach the river. I'm curious to see what the crossing is like. It turns out there is a gigantic cedar log across the river. The Graduate approaches it, and, without pausing, uses the log to cross the murky, roaring river. I'm of the "act in haste, repent at leisure" frame of mind in risky situations but, I admit it, I don't want to look like a weenie. I crawl up on the log and walk steadily across, focusing not on the rushing, swirling, icy glacial water, which can cause vertigo, but on the fixed objects of the log and opposite bank. It is potentially very dangerous. The Graduate has his camera out to capture the excitement. Luckily it doesn't get too exciting.

Me Crossing the Suiattle River. Photo by The Graduate

We walk back downstream a way to where the trail leaves the river. We sit down for a late lunch. I ask him a favorite "what if?" question.

"Let's say you can have one year in your life in which anything you want will happen. If you want to sleep with the most beautiful women on earth, they're yours. If you want to quarterback the winning Super Bowl team, you do. If you want to cure cancer, or rule the world, you can. But here's the catch: at the end of that year, you will lose all memory of what has happened and so will everyone else. There will be no consequences of any of it, good or bad. Would you do it?"

"Hmm. Yes. I think I'd do it. Sooner or later you won't remember anything that's happened in your life. So if you have an opportunity to live your dreams for one year, why not do it?"

"That's the way I feel. I don't remember most of the fun and laughs that I've had in my life. Does that make it meaningless? I would absolutely go for it."

I glance down at his pack. "Hey, you found my water bottle!"

He reaches back and pulls it out of his side pocket. "It was by a blowdown."

I start the long climb out of the Suiattle River valley. It begins to rain half-heartedly. When I reach Miner's Creek I decide to set up camp before darkness or a hard rain overtakes me. When it starts to rain harder I'm feeling pretty smug eating dinner in my perfectly pitched tent.

As I drift off to sleep something rouses me. It sounds like mice are scurrying around outside. I turn on my LED light and reach out and pack up my cooking gear and trash and food. The cooking gear I leave outside. The food I bring inside the tent.

I'm almost asleep when something runs across my bag. I turn on my light and see a mouse dash to the corner of my tent. I unzip the door and after several attempts manage to shoo him out. I look around and see a tiny hole where he chewed his way in. Hopefully I scared him enough so he doesn't come back. I hear footsteps coming down the trail, some hiker pushing on in the dark and rain. I can see the headlamp through the tent fabric. I hear more rustling, turn on my light and see two mice scampering about. I pick up a shoe and take a savage swing at the nearest one, barely missing him. He frantically chews another hole in the tent and escapes. The other is also gone.

In all my years of tent camping, this is the first time this has happened. I dread packing up my stuff in the dark and the rain and finding another spot, but they'll be back. I put on my wet socks, my wet shoes, my wet rain gear, and stuff my sleeping bag in its waterproof sack. Then I cram all my loose gear in my pack. Out in the rain, I break down my tent. I yank the stakes and stuff them in an outside pack pocket, then wad up the wet tent and hurry down the trail. A quarter mile away I head out into the trees in the inky darkness and make a spot roomy enough to set up in by dragging a couple of small logs out of the way. I shake most of the water off the tent then stake it down and crawl in and zip the vestibule shut. Home again. It's 11:30.

September 16, Day 149. Mile 2,553; 103 Miles to Canada

Today I'll make it to Stehekin, last town along the trail. Holy smokes I'm almost to Canada! Clouds and sun vie for supremacy with no clear victor. The map's elevation profile shows a climb of about 1,400 ft, then a smaller climb, then a long, gentle cruise to the road.

Back in the big timber, I stand gazing up at two tall, massive monarchs. Hearing the click of poles, I turn to greet a hiker.

"Hi, I'm Colter."

"I'm Neon."

"I was just looking at these two trees. They've probably been standing side by side like that for centuries." I tell her about counting the tree rings. "These are even bigger. Do you think they have any awareness of each other at some level?"

"I don't know. They sure are big, though." We hike together. Like most people at this point on the trail, she's a fast walker.

"Did you notice Hemlock Camp?"

"The place with all the rocks lining the path?"

"Yeah. Did you see the *VACANCY* sign they had hanging up?"

"I missed that." Hemlock Camp is a backcountry campsite. Somebody had a sense of humor and some time on their hands.

"Have you had lunch yet?"

"No."

"I'm going to eat lunch at Spruce Creek Camp."

The trail is in good shape and the walking is easy so we're cruising. We stop for lunch then continue, rapidly eating up trail, posing for pictures by especially-giant trees. In 2002, a Grand Fir was measured here in the Glacier Peak Wilderness that was 267 feet tall!

Neon by a forest monarch, near Stehekin

Late in the afternoon we see the High Bridge, which is on the landlocked road running to Stehekin. We walk to where the bus stops and sit down to rest our feet. Soon a car arrives. The driver rolls down his window.

"Do want a ride into town?" We happily accept. He tells us about the little town of Stehekin. We stop at the famous bakery, but it's closed. He knows the owners and taps on the window.

"Do you think these hikers could get something to eat?" he asks. "Sure. Come on in." Yes! I buy us a round of pizza. We thank the owners and head outside to eat.

Our driver drops us off in town. We head over to the office for North Cascades National Park, but it's closed for the day. I find a campsite and set up my shelter. Neon is waiting for the group she's been hiking with, planning to split a room with them. After a quick stop at the store, we head over to do laundry. A hiker is sitting at the picnic table.

"If it isn't Colter."

"Hi, Danny. Are you still going by Danny or have you got a trail name now?"

"No, still Danny."

"Have you seen Mr. T recently?"

"No, but I sure miss him. I'll never forget how worried you were about him when we left him in the snow above Idyllwild. Hey, I rented a room if you want to sleep out of the rain." I thank him, but I've already got my shelter up.

"Were you walking in the rain last night? Somebody passed my tent late," I ask.

"Yeah, that was me."

Danny and I joke around while Neon and I combine a load of laundry. I get a wonderful hot shower at the other end of the same building.

Stehekin is beautiful, with a picturesque little harbor with moored boats, and steep mountains rising from the lake shore. A bright red bus compliments the greens and blues. Float planes occasionally land and depart. Tourists wander leisurely between the businesses clustered around the harbor.

I walk to the restaurant. A group of hikers is gathered there for dinner: Danny, Max Chill, Epic, Neon, Green

Tortuga and The Graduate. I don't even recognize Green Tortuga without his hat.

September 17

It's a rainy morning. Whitebeard and 3rd Monty are in town, and tell me they'll be taking the first bus to the trail. I buy a cup of coffee and find Max Chill, Neon and Epic relaxing out in front of the restaurant.

Max Chill and I talk about growing up in Minnesota. I ask Epic if he wasn't going by Johnny or John way back at Casa de Luna.

"How astute of you," he says. We talk about all the snow in California this year. "I couldn't believe how scared of the snow you were," Epic says with a smile.

"I wasn't scared of the snow. I was concerned it was going to be a pain in the butt, and it was." Epic likes to goad people, but he's an amusing hiker to be around.

I walk down to the post office, but it hasn't opened yet. The hiker register is there, and I see many familiar names, Hiker 816, Motor, Boat, Golden Child, Wolf Taffy, Apricots and Psycho, The Walking Sisters. The first bus to the trail is supposed to leave about the same time that the PO opens, 8 AM, but I'm hoping to just grab my package and jump on the bus. The lady that runs the post office comes in 10 minutes before opening time but she's talking to somebody. She is under no obligation to open up early of course. When she finds out that I'm hoping to catch that bus she has me run out to stop it but I find out that it's just left, exactly on time.

It's probably a blessing in disguise. Now I have plenty of time to sort things out. Griff has sent me a box of good food. It's about 90 miles to Manning Park so I plan for four and a half days of food. I sort my groceries into four breakfasts and five lunches and four dinners. I'm set for breakfast today and I'll eat dinner at Manning Park!

I have an abundance of extra food which I donate to the hiker's box. Somebody's going to be happy, maybe a hiker whose own package hasn't arrived. I put together an envelope of old maps and guidebook pages and mail that home.

With time on my hands until the next bus, I walk over to the Park Service office for a visit. The ranger offers to drive me to the trailhead as he's heading out that way anyway.

"I see your cap, were you a smokejumper?" he asks.

"Yup. I just officially retired in 2008."

"There are some smokejumpers in town." He gives me some names. I know at least two of them. We check but they're not around. The ranger gets on the radio to find them. They are hiking up a trail for the workday.

"There's an old smokejumper here with me," he radios.

"Copy that... who is it?"

"Buck Nelson."

"Oh. OK." And that was it. Wow, I think, I guess they really miss me. But then someone else gets on the radio, and I know this voice.

"Who did you say it was?"

"Buck Nelson."

"OK... You might want to kick him out of your valley." They invite me to stick around for dinner and a beer. I'm tempted but I'm packed up and anxious to reach the border. I thank them for the offer and the ranger drives me to the trailhead.

On the trail I stop to photograph a cluster of crimson vine maple leaves, raindrops glistening in the sun, delicately veined with bright green and yellow. Maybe I'll try catching up with 3rd Monty and Whitebeard. They have a three-hour head start on me. I'll probably catch them tomorrow, if not today. A giant cedar stands next to the trail. It must be 8 feet or so in diameter, 25 feet in circumference! The trail crosses a stream on a nice bridge. I stop for a quart of water. The end of the bridge has been chewed by bears. On the other side, I see something gray. It's a pair of Silnylon rain pants. I look around but don't see anyone. In my mind, I can picture Whitebeard wearing similar pants and I consider picking them up. But what if they're someone else's or Whitebeard is off trail somewhere intending to come back for them? I guess it's best to leave them.

The Graduate and Green Tortuga come motoring up the trail.

Tortuga reaches for his guidebook.

"I think I left it at that picnic table," he says, annoyed. After carefully searching through his pack, he confirms it's gone but decides he'll be able to make it the rest of the way without it.

A thought strikes me. "Why don't you take photos of my guidebook maps?"

"That's a good idea, thanks."

There are only about 10 pages left so it doesn't take long.

A half hour later a khaki-clad hiker approaches, sporting a big head of hair and a short gray beard. Didn't I see this guy before, going southbound, I think, confused?

"Hi, I'm Colter. Haven't I seen you before?"

"Probably. I'm Car Hop."

"I was hoping to meet you. Are you really holding down a job and hiking the PCT at the same time?"

He explains that he has two cars, one at each end of a trail segment. Starting at the north car, he hikes south. When he reaches the south car, he drives to the north end of the next segment and repeats. He's already completed the Appalachian Trail that way and has only a few segments left to finish the PCT, also in one year. He does computer work. He works whenever he has internet access.

"I love to hike, and I like my job. It works pretty good. But do you know what the worst part is? Sleep deprivation. It's hard to find enough hours in the day to hike and work."

There are always reasons not to pursue dreams and goals. But it's truly amazing what can be done with enough dedication.

Tortuga and Graduate catch up. We talk about what we were looking for on the PCT and what we have found, the people we have met, and when we expect to finish. I ask Tortuga about the theoretical year of living your dreams, a year you'll later completely forget. He has a different take. "Why do it if you can't remember any of it?" he says.

Late in the day, they decide to camp at an established site. Telling them of my mice experience I push on to find a wilder setting. It's sprinkling rain and near dusk before I find a flat spot near a creek.

It rained last night. One hundred percent humidity, mist, and drifting fog greet me when I stick my head out of the tent. At sunrise, or what would be sunrise if I could see the sun, I'm already at Highway 20 and follow the trail across the road to the trailhead. When I emerge from a privy, two cars have pulled up. A thirty-something hiker walks up to me.

"Are you a thru-hiker?"

"Yup."

"You walked here all the way from Mexico?"

"Yeah." Anticipating his next question, I continue, "I started April twenty-first."

"You must have got an early start today. Where did you camp, anyway?"

"Down the trail a mile or so." He seems impressed by nearly everything I tell him. He wishes me luck and I look for the trail. I don't see it. I make one more careful survey of the fringes of the parking lot but I'll be darned if I can see the trail. At the risk of destroying his impression of me being a heroic mountain man, I walk back. "Where does the trail go, anyway?"

"Gee, I don't know, ask her, she hikes around here a lot."

He calls over a young woman. "This guy is a thru-hiker. Do you know where the PCT heads north?"

"Cross back over the road and take a right for another mile or two, that'll be Rainy Pass."

"Thanks!"

"You're a thru-hiker, huh? That's pretty cool. I always wanted to do that." She seems to understand my confusion, but I can't help but think that the other fellow must wonder how in the world I had made it this far without becoming hopelessly lost.

A large sign identifies North Cascades Scenic Highway Rainy Pass Picnic Area. Climbing away from the highway I hear the scolding call of a Steller's Jay. I've already climbed 2,000 vertical feet and walked seven miles. The sun appears through a gap in the clouds as I near Cutthroat Pass. I drop my pack and set up my tent in the sun. I hang my sleeping bag and socks and clothing high on branches of a dead tree. I take off my rain jacket and hang it up, inside out. Clouds sweep the ground a hundred yards away, but miraculously the sun continues to shine on me here. In thirty minutes the sun disappears, but things have dried nicely. That was time well spent. When it's rainy, dry out when you can.

The Graduate shows up on the long descent from Methow Pass. He has read a book about Teddy Roosevelt's expedition to the Amazon. Imagine a former president of the United States going on an expedition into truly uncharted and unknown country, in which several members of the party die, and he, a former president, considers killing himself so the rest can live? We discuss what made Teddy tick, to what degree he was a glory hound or a hero, and how he was a driven, self-made man.

Tonight I study my guidebook maps. My tent is in a hollow protected from the cold wind, high on a ridge. I've walked over 26 miles and climbed about 5,000 vertical feet today. It is 37 miles to Canada.

September 19

It is hard to believe that this is my last full day on the trail. It's cloudy, cool and damp again. It looks and feels like fall. The trail crosses an enormous hillside meadow, painted with the green, gold and reds of fall, and dotted with clumps of dark green evergreens. There are animals scattered, feeding. It's not elk this time, but a band of horses. As I pass they feed calmly, beautiful animals, well cared for.

They are horses from an outfitter's camp. A brown and white paint horse steps off the trail to let me pass. When I reach out my hand I can feel his warm breath.

I hike into the Pasayten Wilderness. The larch are turning golden. I can't remember seeing larch on the PCT before Stehekin. Larch are a conifer and are unusual among conifers in both turning golden each fall and losing their needles for winter.

The trail slices diagonally up a long, rocky hillside. Two hikers approach in muted colors. One has a slung rifle. It's a father and his 16-year-old daughter, returning from a bear hunt. The daughter kicks at the trail, waiting for us to stop talking. "He LOVES talking," she pipes up.

He tells me that Whitebeard and 3rd Monty (from his description) are still ahead of me. His daughter suddenly loses her balance and falls down. She's embarrassed and her father laughs. "So should we go get that milkshake?" he asks her.

"Yeah!"

It's raining again. There's a long view of the trail ahead and a wall tent on a bench in a patch of timber. I see a black bear a half mile ahead feeding on the mountainside, approaching the trail. I glance back at the tent, undoubtedly a bear hunter's camp. Although I'm a hunter I hope they don't spot the bear. When I get up to where the bear was headed I keep a sharp eye out for the bear or his tracks on the wet trail, but spot neither.

"Hi, Colter!"

I recognize that enthusiastic voice. "Golden Child! Aren't you headed the wrong way?"

"I'm headed back to Hart's Pass."

"You finished?"

"Boat and I made it to the border yesterday."

"Wow. Congratulations, that's awesome."

"Congratulations yourself. Triple Crown coming up!" We say our goodbyes and hike, Golden Child south, and I north.

It rains off and on. The sun peeks out and then hides, over and over. I take photo after photo of the glorious fall colors, patches of blue-black huckleberries, leaves red, dripping rain. A raven calls from somewhere in the clouds. From a pass I look down into the head of a valley, green spur ridges sweeping down from the left and right, bright gold and orange and red vegetation carpeting the valley floor, the arc of a rainbow above it all. It is stunningly beautiful.

I reach a ridge and see a trail zigzagging five hundred feet down the mountain, then climbing towards the next pass. There's another trail contouring from pass to pass. In Yogi's guide, Teatree is quoted as saying, *"Whatever you do, don't take this abandoned trail. I cannot stress this enough. Unless you want to DIE on your very last day of hiking, suck it up and hike your ass to the pass on the official PCT."* I follow Teatree's advice and follow the switchbacks down and back up towards Woody Pass.

I'm reveling in the bright fall colors. A patch of vegetation is perfectly composed with a wild array of colors, shapes, and textures: rough gray stones with lichens of many shades, dark green mountain heather, scarlet huckleberry bushes, fans of bright green ferns, the tapered yellow-green seed-heads of western anemone on reddish-yellow stalks. The overwhelming sense of autumn gives me a strange feeling. Fall is my favorite time of year but there is also the ache of something meaningful and precious that is so fleeting. The years are passing. Soon the bright colors and this hike will be over.

As I climb I look back and up. Long sections of the abandoned trail have slid down the mountain. The advice was sound. The trail reaches a nice flat bench, protected from wind by evergreens. It's drizzling rain and nearly 6:00. Darkness comes early this time of year, so I set up my tent and put water on to boil. There's plenty of food so I snack heartily. I blow up my air mattress and roll out my sleeping bag. After eating I secure all my gear in case the wind comes up or it snows hard enough to cover the ground. After taking a camp photo I crawl in my tent. I peel off my wet socks, shoes and rain gear, then put on my dry long underwear, socks and balaclava. It begins raining harder. It's a good feeling to be snug in the tent. As rain hammers down I pull out my camera, set it to video and film myself. "It's my last night on the trail, I did about 26 miles today I think, I'm at Woody Pass and it's raining again. The fall colors are nice, I'll finish tomorrow, it's been a wonderful adventure." When I replay it, I can barely hear myself over the drumming of rain.

September 20, 2010. Woody Pass, Pasayten Wilderness, Pacific Crest Trail

Rain patters on my tent fly. The first faint light of dawn seeps through the green fabric. I feel for my headlamp, put it on, open my food bag and look inside. A silver Pop-Tart wrapper catches my eye. I open it and munch one down, retrieving and eating fragments as they fall onto my sleeping bag and the tent floor. I eat another one and a granola bar and take a long swig of water. I have eleven miles to the border and less than 20 miles total to Manning Park. This is it, my last day on the Pacific Crest Trail.

I stuff my sleeping bag into its stuff-sack. My wet socks are in the vestibule. I reach out and wring them out one more time. I take off my long underwear bottoms and sleeping socks and put them in their silnylon stuff-sack, then put on my rain-pants and wet socks and rain-jacket. I deflate my sleeping pad and roll it up and put it in its stuff-sack. Sleeping bag, pad, and spare clothes go in the bottom of my pack inside the heavy-duty plastic trash-compactor bag. Food and remaining items go on top.

Swinging my feet outside the screen I put on my soggy shoes, and crawl out, dragging my pack behind me. I pull the tent stakes one by one and scrape the mud off them. I shake my tent hard, water flying in all directions. I stuff the still soggy tent into its stuff-sack and put it in a side-pocket of my pack. After one last drink of water, I put my water bottles in the empty side-pocket. I put on my wool gloves and my eVent mitten shells, then hurry down the trail. It must be 40 degrees. In this wet weather, I'll need to keep moving to stay warm.

Clouds sweep over Woody Pass. The trail winds through the trees and out into the open, crossing the divide several times. It is raining. Soaked bushes brush up against my legs showering my shoes and socks with icy water. My feet are getting cold. If my whole body were warmer my feet would be warmer. Normally I'd wear my poly-pro top under these circumstances, but it is the last day and I can risk getting my down jacket a little damp. I put it on, followed by my rain jacket. I wear my balaclava under my ball cap.

"Is that snow?!" I say aloud, seeing white flecks falling with the rain. I look at my rain jacket and sure enough, a few snowflakes are there on my sleeve, quickly melting.

The fall colors are better than ever, even on this dark day. Huckleberry and blueberry bushes range from yellow through orange to red. The mountain ash are similarly brilliant, some wearing their fall colors and others still dark green, providing a perfect contrast to their bright red berries. The most brilliant of all are the maples. The orange-leaved ones glow across the canyon.

My feet are aching cold. I take off my shoes and slip plastic shopping bags over my wet socks and put my shoes back on. The difference is immediately noticeable.

I pull out my GPS from inside my rain-jacket. The border is less than a mile away. As I get closer I watch for the corridor through the trees that will mark the border.

Often we don't recognize the milestones in our lives for what they are until long after the event has passed: the first chance encounter with a future spouse; the first day of a random part-time job that becomes a career. The finish of a thru-hike is different. It's an obvious, enormous milestone that you can recognize as it's happening, one you can foresee long before.

Over 2,000 miles ago in the warm dry hills of southern California, Wyoming had asked me, "What do you think it will be like making it to the Canada border?"

"I don't know," I answered. "I guess we'll have to wait and see."

Now that day is here. Ahead is a gap in the trees. An avalanche chute? No! There's Monument 78. I recognize it from countless photos of hikers posing at the border. Now it's my turn. Now it is happening to me. I made it!

The trail swings away from the border briefly then heads straight north towards the metal border monument and the wooden posts of the northern terminus of the Pacific Crest Trail. I take out my camera, set it to video and film myself taking the last few steps.

"Well this is it, September twentieth, twelve-seventeen PM, the end of the Pacific Crest Trail. This is a big deal."

I look down the foggy, dripping gap in the trees, stretching off into the distance and marking the boundary between Canada and the U.S. I set up my mini-tripod and take several shots of myself next to the wooden PCT terminus posts, arms raised in triumph.

After taking several photos I walk to the old four-foot-high metal obelisk marking the border. I try to lift the top half off. Inside, I'd been told, is the final hiker register of the trail. I can see where the monument is supposed to come apart, but the top is jammed. I give it a kick. It is stuck tight. Giving the whole thing a wiggle and I find it is loose at the bottom. And very heavy. I carefully tilt it just enough so I can grab the register, trying to avoid crushing my fingers.

It's starting to rain again. Under a tree, I open the register and read through the last few pages. So many familiar names and memories. Whitebeard and 3rd Monty were here this morning. I did 26 miles two days in a row and they still beat me. Whitebeard is 70! The Graduate was here this morning too. I read more entries...

Wow. This is done. Our feet hurt AND we're engaged!!
Cliffhanger and Milk Sheikh

Swift & Buckeye
This is what life is all about...
greater the risk, the greater the reward.
Thank you class of 2010, I loved every moment...
even the mice in some odd way.
Never felt stronger.
Best community I've ever been a part of.
Thank you, Buckeye

My hands are very cold and when they are cold they get very stiff. I'm a weenie that way. For the last couple of weeks, I've considered what I would write when I held this register. I've got a sentimental version worked out, and a funny entry to use, but they are both too long. My hands are so cold they are nearly useless. In a childlike scrawl, I manage to write:

9-20 Good luck and congrats to all. Colter

I wish I could have written what I'm feeling, but I know how this feels, and so will the other thru-hikers who read it.

I put the register and pen back in the plastic bag, tip the monument and slip the register back inside. I reach down and grab my pack-straps and swing on my pack in one smooth motion like I have hundreds of times before, except this time is different, this time is the last on the PCT.

With my hands deep in my pockets I look south toward Mexico, down the Pacific Crest Trail, my home for the last five months. It's hard to leave, to say goodbye. It's sad for the adventure to end. With a lump in my throat I turn and walk north, through the dripping trees, into Canada, towards a hot shower and hot food, still following the trail of my life.

Canada! Monument 78, US/Canada Border, Pacific Crest Trail

"Dost thou love life? Then do not squander time, for that's the stuff life is made of."

— Benjamin Franklin

EPILOGUE

After the PCT I took a bus to Vancouver, then flew to southwest Montana to fish the rivers with my buddy Griff. Griff lent me his Pathfinder for a trip back to Wyoming, where I hunted elk in the Bighorn Mountains. It was strange to be in Buffalo with Stephanie gone. I haven't seen her in years.

My little wiener dog buddy Duke passed away just a few weeks ago. He was my loyal best friend, always overjoyed at our reunions following my expeditions. I sure do miss him, but often smile when I think of his antics.

Cliffhanger and Milk Sheik are married and live happily in Brooklyn, raising their two kids.

Wyoming finished the PCT the day after I did. She continues her adventures. She has gone on to hike the Arizona Trail, the Continental Divide Trail, the Idaho Centennial Trail, the Hayduke Trail and more.

Anne successfully finished her thru-hike, and has written a very good book: *Tamed: A City Girl Walks from Mexico to Canada on the Pacific Crest Trail*.

Mr. T completed the PCT. Current whereabouts unknown.

Pat "Burglar" finished the PCT and went on to thru-hike the CDT and Appalachian Trail.

One of the "Israeli Girls" completed her thru-hike. The other, with nothing to prove, went back home to a wedding a few miles before reaching Canada.

Trail Angel Andrea Dinsmore, PCT Mom, passed away in December of 2017, a staggering blow to the PCT community. Her concern for thru-hikers in late-season snows resulted in several life-saving rescues. Thank you for everything, PCT Mom.

The Eagle Creek Trail (the Tunnel Falls trail) burned in a 50,000-acre fire started in 2017 by a teenager playing with fireworks.

In 2012, I completed the first thru-hike of the Desert Trail, from Mexico to Canada.

In 2014 I spent ten weeks on Admiralty Island in Alaska. I brought no food and lived exclusively "off the land." My adventure is documented in *Alone in the Fortress of the Bears: 70 Days Surviving Wilderness Alaska: Foraging, Hunting, Fishing*

In 2016 I hiked and paddled 3,300 miles along the Lewis and Clark Trail, from Camp Wood, Illinois, to the Pacific Ocean, including 1,500 miles of paddling upstream on the Missouri River.

In 2017 I returned to northern California, and hiked the PCT through the Marble Mountains and the Trinity Alps, where Wyoming and I were driven down by deep snow.

In 2018 I did a 1,500-mile traverse of Alaska by foot and kayak.

I still live in my little log cabin near Fairbanks, Alaska.

Additional Information

For more information on thru-hiking the PCT, please visit my website at www.bucktrack.com I've got links to a PCT gear list, a YouTube video of my thru-hike, thru-hiking advice, and much more.

Books and DVDs by Bruce "Colter" Nelson, include:

Alone Across Alaska: 1000 Miles of Wilderness (DVD)

Alone in the Fortress of the Bears: 70 Days Surviving Wilderness Alaska: Foraging, Fishing, Hunting (book)

Additional copies of this book, and my other books and films, can be ordered at bucktrack.com/Order.html

Happy trails.

If you've enjoyed this book, please consider writing a review on Amazon.com!

23038519R00163